From

Maggie

Published by Amazon: ISBN 9-798-53223-136-8

Websites: Facebook: Margaret Moxom – Author (Shop)
                   Artweb.com/Margaret Moxom
Email: maggiemoxom@aol.com

Introduction

I began this book, rather naively, thinking this would be a story of my ancestors, Mormon pioneers leaving England to set up home in Utah, after being forced out of their homes in England for their religious beliefs. They wanted what they called their 'Zion' – a place where they could settle and bring up their families and carry out their religion without molestation or prejudice.

The book is a family history, of two families, from separate parts of England, the Mumfords and the Gunns, taking their dangerous journeys by sailing ship and the ox-pulled waggon trains across the searing hot plains and freezing, treacherous mountains. There these two families would meet, develop townships and the lead characters would marry, intertwining the two families.

I have gleaned a great deal from Family Search, written by members of the Munford family. All is fairly true, except possibly the story of Eliza Rogers Gunn, for whom I could find no history and George Gunn's journey over by ship.

However, I uncovered, during my investigations, not just the prejudice against the Mormons but the prejudice against Africans and First Nations people. Buying and bartering of slaves was a way of life at the time and was carried out not just by the southern US territories but the Mormons themselves, the First Nations people, as well as Mexicans. This had to change, leading to the American Civil War.

I have not gone into great depth about this former way of life, just touched on it, as this book just set out to show the struggles of the pioneers going to Utah.

Family tree showing link from Ann Munford to myself.

	Brother of	
George Munford Birth 27 Sept 1789, Drayton, Norfolk England Death 13 Apr 1847, Drayton, Norfolk	⬅	Robert Munford Birth 26 Sept 1790 Drayton, Norfolk England Death Parowan, Iron County, Utah
Father of ⬇		⬆ Daughter of
George Munford Birth 20 Feb 1819 Drayton, Norfolk Death 12 Apr 1904 Drayton, Norfolk	George Gunn ➡ Married Ann Munford Birth 18 July 1828 Bishops Stortford, Herts, England Dired 31 May 1876 Parowan, Iron, Utah	Ann Munford Birth 24 Apr 1832 St Walstans Costessey, Norfolk, England Death 30 Apr 1922 Parowan, Iron Utah, United Stated
⬇ **Father of**		
Emma Munford Birth Apr 1844 Drayton Norfolk Death July 1909 Norwich, Norfolk		

Mother of		
George Edward Mackley Birth 1868 Norwich, Norfolk Death Jan 1958 Norwich Norfolk, England		
Father of		
Eric Gladstone Mackley ➡ Birth 28 July 1905, Tonbridge Kent, England Death 16 Mar 1992, Devon, England	Eric Mackley married: ➡ Daisy Matilda Kelley Birth 29 Nov 1904 Edmonton Middx, England Death 27 Jan 1966, Barnstable, Devon	Brother of Daisy Reginald Edward Kelley Birth 4 May 1913, London Death 16 Apr 2003, South Ockendon, Essex, England
		Father of
		Margaret Moxom (nee Kelley) Birth 8 Feb 1953, Manor Park, London E12

iv

LDS Church

Since its founding in 1830, members of the LDS Church were often harshly treated by their neighbours, partially due to their religious beliefs, sometimes as a reaction against the actions and the words of the church leaders and members. These and other reasons caused the body of the church to move from one place to another—to Ohio, Missouri, and then to Illinois, where they built the city of Nauvoo. Sidney Rigdon was the First Counsellor in the church's First Presidency, and as its spokesman, Rigdon preached several controversial sermons in Missouri, including the Salt Sermon and the July 4th Oration. These speeches have sometimes been seen as contributing to the conflict known as the 1838 Mormon War in Missouri. As a result of the conflict, the Mormons were expelled from the state by Governor Boggs, and Rigdon and Smith were arrested and imprisoned in Liberty Jail. Rigdon was released on a writ of *habeas corpus* and made his way to Illinois, where he joined the main body of Mormon refugees in 1839. In 1844, Smith, and his brother, Hyrum, were killed by a mob while in custody in the city of Carthage, Illinois. In 1846, religious tensions reached their peak, and in 1848 mobs burned the Latter-day Saint temple in Nauvoo.

According to church belief, God inspired Brigham Young (Joseph Smith's successor as church president) to call for the Saints (as church members call themselves) to organize and head West, beyond the western frontier of the United States (into what was then Mexico, though the U.S. Army had already captured Santa Fe de Nuevo México and the colonized parts of Alta California in late 1846). During the winter of 1846–47, Latter-day Saint leaders in Winter Quarters and Iowa laid plans for the migration of the large number of Saints, their equipment, and their livestock. It was here that Young first met Thomas L. Kane, a non-Mormon from Philadelphia with deep personal connections to the Polk

v

administration. Kane obtained permission for the Mormons to winter on Indian Territory, and the site was originally called Kanesville. Young continued to trust Kane throughout his own lifetime, particularly as an intermediary with the often hostile Federal government. This major undertaking was a significant test of leadership capability and the existing administrative network of the recently restructured church. For his role in the migration, Brigham Young is sometimes referred to as the "American Moses."

The experiences of returning members of the Mormon Battalion were also important in establishing new communities. On their journey west, the Mormon soldiers had identified dependable rivers and fertile river valleys in Colorado, Arizona and southern California. In addition, as the men travelled to re-join their families in the Salt Lake Valley, they moved through southern Nevada and the eastern segments of southern Utah. Jefferson Hunt, a senior Mormon officer of the Battalion, actively searched for settlement sites, minerals, and other resources. His report encouraged 1851 settlement efforts in Iron County, near present-day Cedar City. These southern explorations eventually led to Mormon settlements in St. George, Utah, Las Vegas and San Bernardino, California, as well as communities in southern Arizona.

Displacement of Native Americans
Prior to establishment of the Oregon and California trails and Mormon settlement, Indians native to the Salt Lake Valley and adjacent areas lived by hunting buffalo and other game, but also gathered grass seed from the bountiful grass of the area as well as roots such as those of the Indian Camas. By the time of settlement, indeed before 1840, the buffalo were gone from the valley, but hunting by settlers and grazing of cattle severely impacted the Indians in the area, and as settlement expanded into nearby river valleys and oases, indigenous tribes experienced

increasing difficulty in gathering sufficient food. Brigham Young's counsel was to feed the hungry tribes, and that was done, but it was often not enough. These tensions formed the background to the Bear River massacre committed by California Militia stationed in Salt Lake City during the Civil War. The site of the massacre is just inside Preston, Idaho, but was generally thought to be within Utah at the time.

Mormon arrival in Salt Lake Valley

Members of The Church of Jesus Christ of Latter-day Saints, commonly known as Mormon pioneers, first came to the Salt Lake Valley on July 24, 1847.

Upon arrival in the Salt Lake Valley, the Mormon pioneers found no permanent settlement of Indians. Other areas along the Wasatch Range were occupied at the time of settlement by the Northwestern Shoshone and adjacent areas by other bands of Shoshone such as the Gosiute. The Northwestern Shoshone lived in the valleys on the eastern shore of Great Salt Lake and in adjacent mountain valleys. Some years after arriving in the Salt Lake Valley Mormons, who went on to colonize many other areas of what is now Utah, were petitioned by Indians for recompense for land taken. The response of Heber C. Kimball, first counsellor to Brigham Young, was that the land belonged to "our Father in Heaven and we expect to plough and plant it." The land was treated by the United States as public domain; no aboriginal title by the Northwestern Shoshone was ever recognized by the United States or extinguished by treaty with the United States.

At the time, the U.S. had already captured the Mexican territories of Alta California and New Mexico in the Mexican–American War and planned to keep them, but those territories, including the future state of Utah, officially became United States territory upon the signing of the Treaty of Guadalupe Hidalgo, February 2, 1848.

The treaty was ratified by the United States Senate on March 10, 1848.

Land ownership

During the nineteenth century the federal government pursued a policy of transferring land in the public domain to private ownership as rapidly as possible. This policy was designed to encourage western expansion. Federal laws governing land distribution were already in place before Utah settlement. At settlement, Brigham Young and the territorial government established a system of land distribution, which is documented by territorial land records, but which did not comply with federal laws. For the first 22 years after settlement, land ownership was based on the Utah territorial land policies. In 1869 Congressional legislation called for the establishment of a land office in Utah and reconciliation of land titles.

All land in Utah became part of the public domain when the United States signed the Treaty of Guadalupe Hidalgo in February 1848. This land came into the possession of the United States government with a clear and undisputed title. No state contested title, and no private rights had been established previously. Therefore every original land title in Utah can be traced to a patent or other document transferring that land from the federal government. Prior to 1848, Congress had already established laws governing the transfer of land from federal to private ownership. Federal laws governed the establishment of land offices, methods of surveying, and procedures for acquiring land by purchase or pre-emption, and later by homestead.

Background

Although many European and European-American migrants to western North America had previously passed through the Great Plains on the Oregon and Santa Fe Trails, the California gold rush beginning in 1848 greatly increased traffic. The next year, both Thomas Fitzpatrick (agent of Upper Platte and Arkansas) and David D. Mitchell (superintendent at Saint Louis) recommended a council with the Indians to prevent a conflict. The United States government undertook negotiations with the Native American Plains tribes living between the Arkansas and Missouri rivers to ensure protected right-of-way for the migrants. The Congress had appropriated one hundred thousand dollars to the assembly, endorsed by Luke Lea (the Commissioner of Indian Affairs).

Because the area around Fort Laramie lacked forage for the Indians' horses, the treaty was negotiated and signed 30 miles downriver from the fort at the mouth of Horse Creek. Many Indians have referred to the treaty as the Horse Creek Treaty.

The Fort Laramie Treaty of 1851 was signed on September 17, 1851 between United States treaty commissioners and representatives of the Cheyenne, Sioux, Arapaho, Crow, Assiniboine, Mandan, Hidatsa, and Arikara Nations. The treaty was an agreement between nine more-or-less independent parties. The treaty set forth traditional territorial claims of the tribes as among themselves.

The United States acknowledged that all the land covered by the treaty was Indian territory, and did not claim any part of it. The Native Americans guaranteed safe passage for settlers on the Oregon Trail and allowed roads and forts to be built in their territories, in return for promises of an annuity in the amount of fifty thousand dollars for fifty years (adjusted to 10 years). The treaty should also "make an effective and lasting peace" among the eight tribes, each of them often at odds with a number of the others.

ix

Acceptance from all tribes, with the exception of the Crow, was procured. Several tribes never received the commodities promised as payments.

The Treaty Territory

The Lakota Sioux received exclusive treaty rights to the Black Hills (present South Dakota), to the consternation of the Cheyenne and the Arapahoe. "... the Sioux were given rights to the Black Hills and other country that the Northern Cheyennes claimed. Their home country was the Black Hills", declared a Cheyenne historian in 1967. Arapahoe chief Black Coal complained in 1875: "I have never got anything yet for my land [the Black Hills]. It is part mine, and part the Sioux... In the first place, they came from the Missouri River and reached this place, and now they have got up this far, and they claim all this land."

The Cheyenne and Arapaho, the southernmost of the treaty tribes, held an area southward of the North Platte in common (mainly in present Wyoming and Colorado).

The Crow treaty territory (in present Montana and Wyoming) included the area westward from Powder River. Little Bighorn River ran through the centre of the Crow domain.

The Lands of the 1851 Ft. Laramie Treaty

Crow Indian territory (area 517, 619 and 635) as described in Fort Laramie treaty (1851), present Montana and Wyoming. It included the western Powder River area and the Yellowstone area with tributaries as Tongue River, Rosebud River and Bighorn River.

After the Treaty

The treaty was broken almost immediately after its inception. In 1858, the failure of the United States to prevent the mass immigration of miners and settlers into Colorado during the Pike's Peak Gold Rush, also did not help matters. They took over Indian lands in order to mine them, "against the protests of the Indians," and founded towns, started farms, and improved roads. Before

xi

1861, the Cheyenne and Arapahoe "had been driven from the mountain regions down upon the waters of the Arkansas." Such emigrants competed with the tribes for game and water, straining limited resources and resulting in conflicts with the emigrants. The U.S. government did not enforce the treaty to keep out the emigrants.

The situation escalated with the Grattan affair in 1854, when a detachment of U.S. soldiers illegally entered a Sioux encampment to arrest those accused of stealing a cow, and in the process sparked a battle in which Chief Conquering Bear was killed.[1]

Though intertribal fighting had existed before the arrival of white settlers, some of the post-treaty intertribal fighting can be attributed to mass killings of bison by white settlers and government agents. The U.S. army did not enforce treaty regulations and allowed hunters onto Native land to slaughter buffalo, providing protection and sometimes ammunition. One hundred thousand buffalo were killed each year, until they were on the verge of extinction, which threatened the tribes' subsistence. These mass killings affected all tribes thus the tribes were forced onto each other's hunting grounds, where fighting broke out.

By summer 1862, all three tribes had been forced out of their shared treaty territory. "We, the Arikara, have been driven from our country on the other side of the Missouri River by the Sioux", stated chief White Shield in 1864. The elimination of buffalo also meant that the Yanktonai Sioux moved into Assiniboine hunting grounds in North Dakota and Montana, where the Assiniboine made peace with them

Before long, the Crows saw their western Powder River area flooded with trespassing Lakotas in search of bison, and "... large scale battles with invading Sioux" took place near present-day city of Wyola, Montana. The outnumbered Crows were displaced little by little. "The country from the Powder River to the Yellowstone River was their country [the Crows'], until 1859, when they were driven from it by the Sioux".

In 1864 came the Sand Creek massacre on a camp of mostly Cheyennes by Colonel John M. Chivington's army of one hundred days volunteers. It led to years of war between the Cheyennes and the United States.

Mormon Territorial Surveys

Brigham Young intended to populate the territory as rapidly as possible, and from the start declared that "no man should buy land...but every man should have his land measured off to him for city and farming purposes, what he could till." In 1847 he had a survey made of Great Salt Lake City. Plats selected for urban purposes were divided into ten-acre blocks, each containing eight lots of 1 1/4 acres. Each settler received his lot by lottery for $1.50, which was to cover the cost of surveying and recording. Settlers received separate portions outside the city for agricultural purposes. All disputes were resolved by an appeal to ecclesiastical authority. In 1850 Governor Young approved "An Ordinance Creating the Surveyor General's Office." This ordinance created the office of surveyor general and established methods of surveying. It ordered that all surveys in the territory should be made to correspond with the original survey of Great Salt Lake City. The following year the first Legislative Assembly passed "An Act to Regulate Surveyors and Surveying." This law required surveyors to provide a certificate to each person for whom a survey was made. These certificates were considered title of possession]. The law also required each county surveyor to submit true copies of the diagrams of his surveys to the surveyor general and to the county recorder.

Pre-emption

Laws for purchasing land were problematic. Many settlers did not wait for surveys to be completed so the land could become available for sale, but instead settled on any available unclaimed land. When the land was later surveyed and made available for sale, it could be purchased by anyone who had enough money to outbid the settler. Settlers could lose the land along with home and improvements. Congress addressed this issue by passing the Preemption Act in 1842. This law gave settlers first right to purchase 160 acres and allowed them up to 21 months to make payment.

The Homestead Act

The Homestead Act, which Congress passed in 1862, evolved from pre-emption. This act provided free grants of public land to any person who was a citizen of the United States and over 21 years old or the head of a household. Homesteaders were allowed 160 acres. In order to obtain a patent, homesteaders were required to improve and cultivate the land and to maintain residency on it for five years. Potential homesteaders were originally required to personally appear at the land office to file an entry, prove citizenship and other qualifications, and verify that they had personally examined the land and were satisfied with its character.

Utah Territorial Land Policies

Because of conflict between Utah Territory and the federal government, the first land office was not opened in Utah until 1869. For the first 22 years after settlement the national land system did not extend to Utah Territory, but the Utah Territorial Assembly governed land ownership in Utah. The territorial government established methods of surveying and acquiring title.

These practices and the documents they created were recognized in Utah Territory, but did not provide Utah settlers with federally recognized legal title to land. The territorial government also established county recorders as keepers of land records, and in 1888 the Territorial Assembly defined certain indexes and finding aids which county recorders were thereafter required to keep.

County Recorders

Brigham Young established a method for recording land records in "An Ordinance in Relation to County Recorders," approved 1 March 1850. A county recorder in each county was commissioned to record "all transfers or conveyances of land or tenements, and all other instruments of writing and documents suitable, necessary and proper" to such conveyances. In short, the recorder was to keep a record of every action or transaction that involved real property. Documents were to be recorded in "good and well bound books, suitable for the purpose." The books were to be indexed in alphabetical order and were to be free to examination.

The earliest Utah deeds were typically called transfers. The earliest county recorders' books contain copies of surveyors' certificates and transfers. As time passed, recorders added various types of deeds, patents, mining claims, etc., to create an ever-increasing variety of official land records. Since the law required only that these be recorded in well bound books, record types were combined or separated at the recorders' discretion. Early county recorders' books were separately indexed.

Shortly after the first company arrived in the Salt Lake Valley in 1847, the community of Bountiful was established to the north. In 1848, pioneers moved into lands purchased from trapper Miles Goodyear in present-day Ogden. In 1849, Tooele and Fort Utah in modern-day Provo were founded. The settlement of Provo was particularly troubling to the Utes, since it was at the heart of their territory. Ute chief Wakara suggested the pioneers instead move into the Sanpete Valley in central Utah, where they established the community of Manti. Tensions in Fort Utah mounted after Mormons murdered Old Bishop and Young ordered an attack on the Utes - called the Battle of Fort Utah. This was shortly followed by the Walker War.

Mormon settlers kill renegade Timpanogos at Battle Creek – *Extract from Wikipedia.*
Battle Creek massacre
Around February 1849, Dimick B. Huntington spoke with Timpanogos leader Little Chief about some of the settlers' missing cattle. Little Chief said that Roman Nose and Blue Shirt were great thieves who had decided to live off of the settlers' cattle all winter. Little Chief said that the Mormons should kill these renegades, perhaps out of fear that his tribe would be blamed and killed for the missing cattle. Captain John Scott took fifty men into Utah Valley to put a "final end" to the "depredations." On March 3, 1849, Scott's men made their way down the Provo River and asked Little Chief and his camp about where the renegades were. Little Chief's tribe was understandably worried about the fifty armed men, and Little Chief agreed to show Scott where the renegades were. Little Chief's two sons guided Scott's men to the renegade's camp near Battle Creek Canyon. Scott's men surrounded the camp, which consisted of several men and their families. The renegades refused to talk and opened fire on the company, even though they were considerably weaker. Scott's men dropped rocks on the renegades in the creek, which caused the women and children to

xvi

surrender. Pareyarts and Opecarry (aka Stick-in-the-Head), leaders of local Timpanogos tribes, watched the settlers "relentlessly shoot down" the remaining Timpanogos. This contributed to their later mistrust of the settlers during the events preceding the Battle at Fort Utah.

Initial Mormon settlement
On March 10, 1849, Brigham Young assigned 30 families to settle Utah Valley, with John S. Higbee as president and translator Dimick B. Huntington and Isaac Higbee as counsellors. They headed towards Timpanogos territory with 30 families or 150 people. It is likely that the settlers arrived on April 1 and began construction of the fort on April 3. The Timpanogos viewed this as an invasion of their territory and sacred land. As the settlers came in, they were actively blocked by a group of Timpanogos led by An-kar-tewets with warnings that trespassing would be met with death and destruction. D. Robert Carter suggests that An-kar-tewets was probably demanding a tribute for the travels of the caravan through their territory. Later, a Timpanogos chief met with Huntington, possibly Black Elk. Huntington said that the settlement would be beneficial for the Timpanogos. The chief consented to let the Mormons settle there after Huntington rose his hand and swore by the sun god that they would not try to drive the Timpanogos off their lands or take away their rights.

The settlers built a stockade called Fort Utah and armed it with a twelve-pound cannon to intimidate the Timpanogos. They also built several log houses, surrounded by a 14-foot palisade 20 by 40 rods in size (330 by 165 feet with gates in the east and west ends, and a middle deck for the cannon. The surrounding land was divided into 58, 5-acre (2 ha) lots.

Illustration of Fort Utah in 1850

Relations between the two groups started familiarly, with Mormons and Timpanogos fishing and gambling together. Brigham Young disapproved of their familiarity with one another and advised Huntington and Alexander Williams to be the sole traders. Parley P. Pratt visited and made rules against gambling with the Timpanogos and against shooting near the fort.

The fort was built on the sacred grounds for the annual fish festival and very close to the main Timpanogos village on the Provo River. The settlers fenced off pastures. Their cattle would eat and trample the seeds and berries that were an important part of the Timpanogos diet. They used gill nets to catch fish, which didn't leave any fish for the Timpanogos to eat. With the traditional sources of food gone, they soon experienced massive starvation. The settlers also brought measles, which was foreign to the Timpanogos, and they began dying in large numbers.

Old Bishop's murder

In August, a Timpanogo named Old Bishop was murdered by Rufus Stoddard, Richard Ivie, and Gerome Zabrisky over a shirt they wanted from him. Another account from Thomas Orr states that the Timpanogos agreed not to take the settlers' cattle if they would not kill their wild game. Old Bishop discovered the men hunting deer, expressed his displeasure, and the men killed him. They filled his body with rocks and threw it in the Provo River. The men went back to Fort Utah and openly bragged about the murder. The Timpanogos found the body and discovered that Richard Ivie was involved in the murder. The Timpanogos were angry, and demanded that the murderers be handed over, to which the settlers refused. The Timpanogos asked for material compensation for Old Bishop's death according to Timpanogos custom, which the settlers also refused, which enraged the Timpanogos, given how they were sharing prime pasture and fishing land. Some Timpanogos shot at cattle that were trespassing on their land or took the settlers' corn in response.

In October, apostle Charles C. Rich negotiated a peace treaty, and Brigham Young again advised Fort Utah not to hold the Timpanogos as equals, but to "have dominion" over them. Winter was especially hard and Timpanogos took 50–60 cattle for food. Travelling forty-niners traded with the Timpanogos, giving them more guns and ammunition. Williams kicked Pareyarts out of Mrs. Hunt's house after he asked for some medicine for measles, and later, three of Mrs. Hunt's cattle were missing. By January 1850, settlers of Fort Utah reported to officials in Salt Lake City that the situation was getting dangerous. They wanted a military party to attack the Timpanogos. Not knowing the story of Old Bishop's murder, Brigham Young noted that a white man wouldn't be murdered over stealing an item like a shirt or ox, and said that the Timpanogos shouldn't be killed over theft.

Drawing of Pareyarts aka Old Elk and his wife.

Mormon decision to go to war

On January 31, 1850, Isaac Higbee, who had replaced John Higbee as bishop of Fort Utah, met with Governor Brigham Young, militia leader General Daniel H. Wells and the First Presidency and the Quorum of the Twelve Apostles to petition Young for a war order. He stated that all the occupants of Fort Utah were in agreement that they should go to war. Apostles Parley P. Pratt and Willard Richards argued for the killing of the Timpanogos, since losing Fort Utah would cut off communication to the southern colonies. Brigham Young also was concerned losing Fort Utah would disrupt his plans to have a route to California and occupy every fertile valley. Brigham Young ordered an extermination campaign against the Timpanogos, with orders to kill all the Timpanogos men, but save the women and children who behaved. General Wells drafted the extermination order as Special Order No. 2 and sent them to Captain George D. Grant. In his letter, he told Grant "Take no hostile Indians as prisoners" and "let none escape but do the work up clean".

On February 1, Brigham Young met with Captain <u>Howard Stansbury</u> of the U.S. Topographical engineers who was in Utah mapping Utah Lake and the Great Salt Lake. Stansbury had also been a victim of cattle theft and supported Young's decision to go to war with supplies and the services of his physician. On February 2, Brigham Young announced his decision to the general assembly. General Wells called for volunteers. On February 4, Captain Grant headed towards Fort Utah, followed shortly by Major Andrew Lytle.

Battle

Squaw Peak was named after Big Elk's wife who died trying to escape the Mormon militia.

The Timpanogos had fortified their village with barricades made from stacked logs and fallen timber. The fortifications housed seventy warriors and their families. The Timpanogos were headed by Pareyarts, who was sick from the measles. Some Timpanogos who were friends with some of the settlers sought shelter in Fort Utah before the battle, including Antonga, whom the Mormons called "Black Hawk."

The Nauvoo Legion was sent from Salt Lake City and on February 8, they engaged the Timpanogos in battle. Their initial strategy was to encircle the Timpanogos village and kill all hostile Timpanogos. The Timpanogos fortified themselves in an abandoned cabin, and the first day ended in a stalemate. Pareyarts's braves were probably joined by warriors from villages on the Spanish Fork River and Peteetneet Creek. The next day, the soldiers mounted shields on sledges and the defending Timpanogos suffered about ten casualties and Chief Opecarry was wounded. Joseph Higbee, son of Isaac Higbee, was the only casualty of the Mormons. The Timpanogos fled during the night after the second day of fighting. They split into two groups. Pareyarts took a small group of wounded and sick and fled to Rock Canyon. Opecarry took the rest of the Timpanogos towards the Spanish Fork River. Black Hawk reported to the settlers that the village was deserted the next morning; about eight bodies were found in the camp, killed possibly by exposure to the cold or shots from Nauvoo Legion.

After having received a letter about the poor attitude of the settlers in working with Wells's troops, Brigham Young sent Wells to lead the army with the expanded mission "not to leave the valley until every Indian was out." On February 11, Wells split the army into two. One contingent, under Captain Grant's command, followed the trail of some Timpanogos who had fled up Rock Canyon; Black Hawk helped the militia to track the fleeing Timpanogos. They set

xxii

up camp at the mouth of the canyon, where they took 23 prisoners and found about a dozen dead bodies, including the body of Pareyarts. Further up the canyon, they found more tepees and killed more Timpanogos and took more prisoners. Some of the prisoners were later executed. Ope-carry, Patsowet, and their families: six women and seven children, managed to flee over the mountains using snowshoes they made in the canyon. According to Edward Tullidge, Pareyarts's young, beautiful, and intelligent wife was found dead in Rock Canyon. One account says that one of the Timpanogos women killed herself by falling from a precipice. It is possible that the woman was Pareyarts's wife, and local legends say that Squaw Peak was named for her.

The other contingent, led by Wells, divided into smaller parties and searched the southern valley for Timpanogos to kill. They first attacked a village along the Spanish Fork River, and then a village on Peteetneet Creek. On February 13, 15–20 Timpanogos families surrendered to Captain Grant in modern-day Lake Shore, Utah. Wells wrote a letter to Brigham Young asking what he should do. On February 14, Brigham Young wrote a letter instructing Wells to kill them if they did not surrender. Lieutenant Gunnison of the Stansbury Expedition reported that the Mormons promised to be friendly to the Timpanogos men. They held them prisoner overnight; but then in the morning lined up the Timpanogos men to be executed in front of their families. Some attempted to flee across the frozen lake, but the Mormons ran after them on horseback and shot them. At least eleven Timpanogos men were killed; one account reports as many as twenty. The family members were then taken captive.

Later in the day on February 14, the Nauvoo Legion spotted five more Timpanogos men on horseback, and killed three of them. On February 15, they killed three more Timpanogos men, on the Peteetneet river, - probably members of Chief Peteetneet's tribe. On February 17, they killed another Timpanogos person in Rock Canyon. In total, one militia man and an estimated 102 Timpanogos were killed.

Aftermath

A government surgeon, James Blake, went to the execution site and cut off the Timpanogos' heads for later examination. Captain Howard Stansbury wanted the heads for "future scientific study" and planned to take them to Washington. Around 50 decapitated Timpanogos heads were gathered. They were supposed to be shipped to Salt Lake, but they were held up to be displayed in front of the prisoners at Fort Utah as a warning. The prisoners, including those who sought shelter in the fort before the war, were left in the cold under the fort's canyon, some of whom were dying from exposure. William Potter, who was upset at the condition, petitioned for blankets for the prisoners, which were eventually given. More than forty prisoners, mostly women and children, were taken and placed with Mormon families "as servants" in Salt Lake City "for the purpose of weaning them from their savage pursuits, and bringing them up in the habits of civilized and Christian life". It did not go as planned, as many died and most escaped to live with other Ute bands, especially in the spring. News of the enslavement reached the US Government, and became one of the first priorities of Edward Cooper after he was appointed as Indian Agent of Utah later that year.

Chief Peteetneet, Chief Tabby-To-Kwanah and Chief Grospean discovered the decapitated bodies and asked Fort Utah about the bodies. Patsowet returned to the Salt Lake area and killed livestock belonging to Mormons in retaliation for the violence done to his tribe and threatened to kill Walkara's animals. Patsowet was then arrested and put on trial for the murder of the Mormon militiaman killed at Fort Utah. Patsowet was convicted and executed.

Fillmore, Utah, intended to be the capital of the new territory, was established in 1851. In 1855, efforts to subdue and evangelize the local Native people led to outposts in Fort Lemhi on Idaho's Salmon River, Las Vegas, Nevada and Elk Mountain in east-central of present-day Utah.

The experiences of returning members of the Mormon Battalion were also important in establishing new communities. On their journey west, the Mormon soldiers had identified dependable rivers and fertile river valleys in Colorado, Arizona and southern California. In addition, as the discharged men travelled to re-join their families in the Salt Lake Valley, they moved through southern Nevada and southern Utah. Jefferson Hunt, senior Mormon officer of the Battalion, actively searched for settlement sites, minerals and other resources. His report encouraged 1851 settlement efforts in Iron Country, near present-day Cedar City. These southern explorations eventually led to Mormon settlements in St. George, Utah, Las Vegas and San Bernardino, California, as well as communities in southern Arizona. By 1885, Mormon communities were being established in northern Mexico.

THE
GUNN
FAMILY

The Gunn Family

Father	John Gunn V
Mother	Ann Impey Brazier
	Married John Gunn V/Daniel Harris/George Holyoak
Son	William Gunn married Emma
	Children: William, Fanny, Elizabeth and Lois
Daughter	Lois (died aged 3 months)
Son	John Gunn married Caroline Barham
Son Munford	George Gunn – married Eliza Rogers/Ann
	Children with Ann: Lucy Albena, George Robert, Lydia Ann (died 5 months), John (died 7 months), Alfred James
Son	Thomas Gunn married Ann Houghton
Daughter	Mary Ann Gunn married John Adey
Daughter	Lois married Ebenezer Woodford – Lois died aged 22
Son	Alfred Gunn married Rachael Ann Fenton
Son	Benjamin Gunn married Alice G Bowdidge

THE CHIMBORAZO

CHAPTER 1

"Give me a hand with this, John, please. It is really awkward to get up the gangway of the ship."

John had been busying himself, along with the rest of the family, trying to haul their luggage up, that had to be stowed on the ship – the Chimborazo, bound for New York.

"Oh, Tom, I cannot be everywhere." John replied, brushing away water from his eyes, which was a mixture of rain and sweat. "I am trying my best with this lot. I am fair worn out."

Nevertheless, John went over to help his brother.

It was Friday 14th April 1855. It was raining – fairly heavily – and the hundreds of people milling around and trying to get their belongings stowed on board were cold and wet. The long dresses of the women (mainly dark, worsted for travel) were strewn with mud and their hats and bonnets were dripping with water. , The trouser bottoms of the men were soaked and mud-stained. People were shouting, giving orders. Children were crying – they were cold, miserable and tired – all having travelled to Liverpool, from far and wide, to start their new lives in America.

Nearly the whole family was there, having decided, soon after October last year, to make this treacherous journey together, when our mother, Ann, had been baptised into the Church of Jesus Christ of Latter-day Saints.

I, Tom, now aged 24, had travelled from London (where I had been working), with my new wife, Ann (née Houghton). Mum, (Ann Impey Harris Gunn - née Brazier), now 64 years old, would have been travelling with her new husband Daniel Harris, but unfortunately, Daniel died too, just last year – he was 67. Ann was the matriarch of the family. She was little but strong enough to keep the family together. She had a round face with grey/blue eyes and would have her greying hair tied back in a bun, as was the fashion, following the trend of Queen Victoria. Along with us were John (25) and his wife, Caroline (24); brother, Ben (14), sister Mary Ann (20), Mary Ann's husband, John Adey (23) sister Lois (19) and her husband, Alfred (17) and Benjamin (13), all of whom had travelled from the family home in Bishops Stortford, Hertfordshire.

Elderly Ann Brazier Gunn

Mary Ann had married John Adey in 1854, the year before they travelled. He was nice enough, but could be quite inept at times – all fingers and toes, so they say. So, he got ridiculed quite a bit, which caused Mary Ann to go up in a flap against the rest of us, and run to comfort John.

We have another older brother, William (aged 33) but he'd decided to stay, for the time being, with his wife, Emma, and three children. William was a big, robust, hard-working man. There was another brother, George (aged 26), working as a labourer in London. I had been working close by. George had met Eliza Rogers there and I had attended his wedding on 10 December 1853 in Stepney, Middlesex. We knew George was going to join us some time later, but no plans had been made as yet.

We had boarded the Chimborazo, a superb American three-master, which was going to take us from Liverpool to Philadelphia.

Passengers were being directed to the lower deck.

The ship was cramped with people, all with their loaded carts, being allocated to their cabins.

"It is going to be freezing – good job I have bought blankets."
This was mum speaking.

I answered, "This is the space we've been allocated. As you can see, there is no space to move – it is just crammed full with people and their luggage."

The sleeping quarters had been allocated into wards, with Mormons and guards allocated to each ward. There were bunk beds stacked high, having just narrow mattresses. The men, obviously had the higher bunks, whilst the women and children had the lower bunks.

Just as we were settling down and getting all of our belongings in order, we saw a woman, scrambling by, as quickly as she could, in what seemed to be a heavily-pregnant state. It looked like she had two small children in tow, who were crying and tumbling over people's luggage. We didn't know where she was going or if she was looking for someone, but she seemed stressed. Mum was worried that she may be in labour and followed to see if she could be of any assistance.

Just then some detective police passed by us, obviously looking for this woman. Mum came back after a little while.

"It seems she is a Mrs Sainsbury. We heard her shouting out, "I am not going back to that bastard of a husband. He has treated me so cruelly, shouting at me, punching me, robbing me of anything I possessed. I managed to save a little bit from his allowance for shopping, keeping it hidden from him, secreted it away so he could not get his greedy hands on it. So I have finally got myself a berth for me and my two children, and I am staying here. I want to get to America to be as far away as I possibly can from the brute."

We were all total shocked. A man, who we presumed was the husband was pulling at her and the children to get them off the ship, but policemen pulled him off and got him away. A policeman was posted to guard the cabin as it looked like the lady was definitely in the first stages of labour and could not be moved. A doctor was requested and we didn't hear much more until the next day, apart from the poor woman's labour screams. The next day, we heard that she had been delivered of a fine baby boy and was doing well. We saw the husband and officers pass by again and we heard that they were insisting on questioning her, even though she was still very weak. The two little children started when they saw the father. All this caused quite a commotion, with women shouting at the police "Leave her be, she is in no fit state to be moved" and other such comments. We heard the mother shouting, "If I must go, you will have to take me by force."

What happened next, was totally unexpected. The police seized hold of Elder John Williams. They wanted to arrest him on suspicion of having assisted and abetted the women in escaping with the husband's belongings. They took him off to the police station.

Of course we were all bemused and worried. There was even talk of us all being taken off the ship and that there would be untold delays before we could sail. This was a fine start to our journey and we hadn't even left port.

Fortunately, Elder John Williams was allowed to return five hours later, after severe and prolonged questioning. He hadn't been charged.

The child born yesterday was given a blessing today by Elder Joseph A Young. Mr. Sainsbury then appeared on board and, contrary to the wishes and remonstrations of his wife, forcibly carried her on shore, albeit she was still in a weak condition having been confined on Friday evening. This was under the sanctioned and protection of the law of England.

The captain of the ship introduced himself, via a loud speaker, as Captain Vesper. "Good day ladies and gentlemen. I can advise you that there are 432 souls on board today, and we are heading for the port of Philadelphia. We are due to arrive on 21st of next month. Should you need any assistance, my crew will be happy to help you. I wish you all a good crossing."

Mormons Elder, Edward Stevenson, then took a stand and, using the loud-speaker, introduced himself and other elders of the Mormon Church.

"I welcome you all, brothers and sisters, to this great voyage of discovery that we are about to undertake, to set up our new mission in Utah. I am the late president of the Gibraltar Mission, bringing with me 200 souls from the Channel Islands. On my left are Elder A L Lamoreaux, late president of the French Mission, bringing 70 souls, and Elder Thomas Jeremy, late counsellor to the presidency of the Church of Wales, bringing 200 souls; the remainder have journeyed from the London, Kent, Essex and Reading Conferences.. 200 of you brethren will be heading onto Utah, financed by the Perpetual Emigration Fund.

I have also, on my right, Elders Mills and Slack, late presidents of the Reading and Essex Conferences."

He continued, "As the evils of the world increase, the joy of the Saints increases at the event of their deliverance, which they give free vent to by their songs of gladness, although fiends in human shape sometimes strive to afflict their souls by vexatious detentions, as did Pharaoh to prevent Israel from going to serve the Lord in the wilderness.

The kindness of Captain Vesper will doubtless contribute much to the comfort of the company."

I decided to make diary notes of our journey.

Monday 16th. The ship did not clear out of port today, and the Saints by the counsel of the president and council, fastened boxes and luggage more securely, and had everything more 'ship shape.' Guards were kept today by appointment of Elders Stack and Mills and would be every night. The brethren picked to be guards felt very willing to do any duty and work deemed necessary for the comfort and safety of the passengers. A council meeting was held today comprising 1 seventy; 2 high priests; 91 elders and to 2 priests. Instructions were imparted by President Stevenson on the work to be done.

Tuesday 17th. All seemed active this morning on board as preparations were making for moving out of dock; at about a quarter to 9 o'clock, orders were given by the mate to turn off the moorings and we moved along, all being on board except three persons who were on the quay for water etc. but subsequently got easily on board. At 5 minutes to 12 o'clock the steam tug took us into tow and we pass gallantly through the gates into the river, amidst the shouts and hearty hurrahs and cheers of the Saints on board and the friends on shore.

Shortly after passing out, the passengers were all mustered on the quarter-deck to see that all agreed with the 'Passenger Book' furnished by our office to the Government Officers. These men examined all tickets - none were missing except the wife and child of a Mr Vest, who had to leave the ship in consequence of their child being ill; and, of course, Mrs. Sainsbury, who was forcibly taken away by her husband. We heard that two men had actually managed to jump on board as we passed through the last gate, but these were soon detected by the guards and kept under lock and key to be sent back with the tug. Everyone began to sing, many hymns suitable to the occasion. We were all in a light mood as we were finally off on the start of our long journey. The wind was light but favourable blowing and the sea was tranquil. We could see the Welsh Mountains in the distance. It gave me a strange mixture of feelings seeing those mountains – yes, we were off to a new world and a new life with hope for the future, but also a sense of nostalgia that I would never again see my homeland.

We saw other vessels departing on the same tide, dressed up in their best, with sails fully raised, billowing out in the breeze. Prayers were said for a fair wind and favourable weather with thanks to our captain and crew.

Three marriages actually took place today, on board – those of John Pickett and Rosetta Stringer, David Rees and Martha Eyon, followed by the marriage of David Williams and Ann Walters, which was conducted by President Thomas Jeremy in the Welsh language.

I got talking to one of the Welsh singers, Joseph Thomas Perkins. Fortunately, he could speak English. He told me his journey to Liverpool. "I came from my valley in Dowlais, Glamorganshire. My father-in-law gave me £33 for me and my family to emigrate to Salt Lake Valley. I have a little lad, Tommy, who was born 9th June last year. Thankfully, my father-in-law gave me other money besides this to help us to Liverpool, otherwise we just wouldn't have been able to get there."

He continued, "We travelled by stage coach to Abergavenny and then by train, staying at a house for a week, waiting to get on board." We talked about seeing the Welsh hills in the distance as we left port and he seemed quite overcome. "Yes, I will never see them again, but we had to go, there was nothing more for us in the valleys, they just did not pay us enough to live and wanted us to work even longer hours for less money. I could not afford to feed my family."

We cleared the port of Liverpool on 17th April 1855.

There was not much room to move around, with the lower deck, being filled to capacity. The top deck had to be kept free for the crew to manoeuvre the sails. We had to sleep and eat, basically, where we were, with the necessary use of the chamber pots in a sectioned off area.

The ship was in full sail and, as we left the port, the breeze got up and we started to shiver. Mum got out blankets for us to wrap around ourselves and we were soon warm, in fact it got hot and stifling, with the smell of damp woollen clothes and unwashed bodies pervading. We could hear the waves lapping at the sides, throwing up spumes of sea water and the ship was rocking and rolling, making it very difficult to stand upright without swaying and having to hold onto something –

ropes or bannisters. Some people were already feeling seasick and making a rush up top to the sides of the ship, or to the buckets. We had to amuse ourselves, playing games, card games, telling stories and other such pursuits.

Once the children in the other parties had stopped running around and exploring, and had settled for the first night, the crew lit paraffin lamps, hung from hooks and closed the hatch door. We didn't know whether or not to feel grateful for that, as the wind chill had increased as darkness fell, but then the air around us became still and musty. Some were finding it difficult to breathe and began coughing.

I began to think back how we had set out on this expedition. I was cuddled up to my wife, Ann. We'd got married on 26 February this year. I was 26 and Ann was 23. While there, he went with some friends to a meeting of the "Mormon Church" at the Finsbury Branch. One had been favourably impressed and was baptized on 4 June 1854. We had all been brought up as Catholics, in our family home in Bishops Stortford, Hertfordshire but we became dissatisfied with the teachings and joined a group of 'Protestant Dissenters'. Dad had been a cooper and owned Wick Brewery and Distillery in Pulteney Town, but he had died, very unexpectedly, at the age of 41, from what the coroner said was an infection of the brain. I was just 12 years old. This left mum to look after seven children, although my brother William was 18, so well able to look after himself. What made matters worse was that mum was pregnant when dad died, with my little brother, Benjamin, who was born 3 months and 10 days after dad passed away.

Mum couldn't manage on her own. She was doing her best, taking in washing and boarding lodgers to help earn a living.

We did all we could to help her with us boys finding work and Lois, as a teenager, found work as a nurse's maid.

Then mum met and later married Daniel Harris, on 4th April 1852 at St Mary Newington, in Surrey. It was strange having a step-father and we never really warmed to him. I didn't know if mum really loved him, but he offered to marry her and she accepted, as she desperately needed a partner and the extra money that Daniel could provide. I suppose he must be a good man, though, taking on so many children belonging to another man. Off course, then Daniel died.

I think that is when mum decided there was nothing left in England for her and hearing of the Mormon's wishing to set up a new home, away from the persecution they were experiencing – to find a place they could live and preach safely - we all decided to pack up and go with her. Many people did not understand, or want to understand, our beliefs. We were seen as misfits, outcasts. We were even having stones thrown at our windows, with paint smeared across our doors, telling us to take our ungodly, blasphemous and immoral beliefs elsewhere. We still believed in God the father, Jesus the son, and the Holy Ghost, the same as any other Christian. Also, they taught that, in Mormonism, the central part of God's plan is the atonement of Jesus Christ. The one purpose of earthly life is to learn to choose good over evil. People inevitably make mistakes, becoming unworthy to return to the presence of God but Mormons believe that Jesus paid for the sins of the world and that all people can be saved through his atonement. Mormons accept Christ's atonement through faith, repentance, formal covenants or ordinances such as baptism, and consistently trying to live a Christ-like life. This is something we were brought up with, so none of us understood this hatred towards us – we weren't harming anyone and we all believed that the Mormon faith was the correct faith. It was time to go.

Where we differ in faith from the Protestants and Catholics is that we believe there are three distinct beings and that the Father and Jesus had perfect human bodies – they had been human at one time, while the Holy Ghost is a spirit without a physical body. We also believe that there are other gods and goddesses outside the Godhead, such as a Heavenly Mother – who is the wife of God the father – and that faithful Latter-day Saints may attain godhood in the afterlife. What others find difficult to believe is that Joseph Smith taught that God was once a man on another planet before being exalted to Godhood. In the Book of Ezekiel, Ezekiel had a vision where he sees an immense cloud that contains fire and emits lightning and brilliant light. The centre of the fire looked like glaring metal and, in the fire, what looked like four living creatures, winged but humanoid. There were also four shiny object each appearing like a wheel intersecting a wheel. These objects could fly and they moved with the creatures. There were other instances of this in the Bible, plus the missionaries taught us that, in Hindu mythology, the gods and their avatars travel from place to place in flying vehicles called Viman. There were many other citings in ancient mythologies, based on the idea that ancient creation myths of gods who descend from the heavens to Earth to create or instruct humanity. These contacts brought advanced technologies to Earth. I was quite opposed to this teaching at first but the missionaries cited numerous instances, in various religions all over the world, which seemed to corroborate these teachings. They believe that other religions have a portion of the truth but that the Mormon Church is the only true and living church. I had to admit that these stories opened up a new world for me, a new way of thinking, and I was intrigued. So I joined the sect.

14

"You were the first to be baptised, Tom, were you not?" This was John.

"Yes, and I managed to convert mum soon after. She was baptised on 20 October 1854, fourteen years after dad passed away. William was not over keen, no matter how much we tried."

"Yes," this was mum, "John you remember, you made a determined effort to teach him about the gospel when he was ill with typhoid fever. "

"Ah but, he was still having nothing of it." John replied. "In fact, he got most resentful at my trying to influence his religious beliefs. He got quite angry, so I backed away – let him be. He did not like the fact that the missionaries were going door to door and canvassing people to accept the faith. He thought it was an encroachment on people's lives, and they were irritating – in fact, if they came knocking, he would either not open the door or give them a piece of his mind. It was not until dad passed, which really shook him, when he seemed to come round to our way of thinking. He had taken dad's death hard, wondering why his prayers for dad had not been answered, and started to investigate the Mormon gospel. He was finally baptised on 22 February 1853 and confirmed a member."

"That is right, John," mum continued, "and we were so pleased that he finally understood the cause."

The next morning saw the sun rising and it looked like it was going to be a good day. The rain had subsided.

The ship's crew came round with ship's biscuits - hard, brittle and tasteless they were but we were hungry. We were also advised there was porridge in the galley, so we went up with bowls, that mum carefully released from where they had been stored. There were long queues, waiting for people to be served and more porridge to be made to feed the hundreds on board. We didn't actually get served until nearly lunch time. This was a daily event.

There was also something they called 'Scouse', a sort of stew. Luckily, mum had made loads of pies for the journey, which we could have cold, followed by fruit, for our evening meals. There was also a back-up of tinned produce. Mum had made bread too, all of which had to be rationed out in mean slices to last at least some of the journey, until it was only fit for the birds that circled overhead. There was hot water on the go in the galley, for making tea, but nothing else was provided by the crew, so anyone who hadn't brought enough food with them would have to last on porridge, a small plate of Scouse and the morning ship's biscuit. We were watched, eagerly - the eyes of these hungry passengers, watching us eat the small portions we had. Our food larder had to be guarded and, later on in the journey, when food was getting scarce, we found ourselves stood over by hungry children, begging, waiting to pounce on any little crumb we dropped. We didn't feel Christian refusing them but we had a large family to feed and, what little we had, had to be eked out. When nothing was forthcoming they would go and play on the ropes, climbing where they could.

A few of us were allowed at a time to go on the top deck and I escorted mum up the wooden ladder.

"Look at those children, what are they up to?" this was mum, "Well, you know what young'uns are like, they get themselves into all sorts of mischief." I answered.

"Well, their parents should keep them in control."

"Oh, let them be, they are enjoying themselves and there is nothing much else to do."

Of course, the captain was notified, and he had strong words to say about safety on board and reprimands to parents to keep their children in order.

When I had a bit of free time, I found myself lolling over the quarter-railing or attempting to climb to the main top on a calm day and muse on the tranquil sea, to gaze upon the piles of golden clouds, just peeping above the horizon. It was good to get away from the hubbub below and put my thoughts in order. I would fancy these gold clouds as some fairy realms and would people them with a creation of my own; then watch the gentle, undulating billows rolling their silver volumes as if to die away on those happy shores. There was a delicious sensation of mingled security and awe with which I looked down from my giddy heights at the monster of the deep at their frolicking capers.

Other times, I would walk around, talking to people I met. I got to know a historian while on board. His name was Mr W G Mills. I used to see him scribbling away in his notepad and was intrigued. I introduced myself.

"Oh, Tom. What I am doing is just a daily event on the occurrences on board ship, the weather mostly and how the ship is behaving."

I told him I was writing a few notes too. I took a look at his note for Wednesday 18th. 'A dead calm this morning, not a breath seemed to disturb the waters. The sea was smooth as oil. The usual business attended to. At 12 o'clock the wind blew at north, northwest. A small fishing boat came alongside and, by persuasion of the captain, sold several passengers some fresh fish.'

"Very interesting, Mr Mills. It is good to keep a diary. Much more interesting than my notes."

"Yes, not belittling your own notes, but I have been published and may well publish my report, when I get settled."

"I do not know how they are going to cook those fish though – there is hardly room to get in the galley."

"Do not worry, the ship's cook with see to them. The crew seem most gracious in helping us."

I looked in on him the next day and read his transcript.

'Thursday, 19th. All bustle this morning as usual in cleaning and cooking but all very orderly. Came in sight of Ireland today. This afternoon the wind turned round to East, a very fair wind, and with the light wind filling the canvas, our gallant ship moved on majestically at about 8 knots an hour. The fair wind, and ample breeze seemed to cheer everyone. Canvas was crowded on by our captain, who seemed anxious to catch every blast to drive us along. Several spankers were put up or out today – these are gaff rigged fore-and-aft sails - and our vessel seemed like a huge bird on the waters without spread wings, gaily floating along.'

It was well written, informative and interesting to read. He had a way with words that brought a sense of poetry into the journey, something I hadn't thought about on this sometimes mundane journey – just comparing the vessel to a 'huge bird on the waters without spread wings, gaily floating along' gave my spirit a sense of uplifting and I thanked him for that.

Later on, it was Friday 20th, about quarter to 2. We were up top with a few other families. There were a few children playing and I saw a young infant toddling around, unsteadily. "Hello, little girl" I beckoned to her. "What's your name?" I didn't think she really understood me – she was only about 23 months old but she smiled and patted my outstretched hand in only a way a toddler would do, as I knelt down towards her. She toddled off with her brother, and I turned back toward my family, smiling at her antics. It was only by chance that I turned around to look at her again that I saw her brother carrying her up the ladder, they must have gone below. She was much too heavy for him, as he was only a couple of years older, and he was struggling. I didn't know where their mother was, but obviously she hadn't noticed. I made a run towards the hatchway to help him, as, although there were people nearby, they were either sleeping or looking elsewhere.

"Get that child," I screamed, and made a running leap but, just at that moment, the ship lurched again and I fell short, just out of reach, only to see the boy drop the toddler down the ladder.

19

I hoisted myself up quickly, and scampered down the ladder. The mother followed me to pick up the child, which was now screaming, and I passed the child into her open arms. The mother was stricken with grief that she might have lost her little girl, and hugged her close, even though the baby's face was covered in blood.

"Oh, thank you, sir, thank you God, for saving my little one." She managed to get out through her tears. Yes, she was alive, but in a sore way with a head injury and a broken arm. Elder Lamoreaux, acting as surgeon, came promptly and energetically attended to the case.

She was bleeding profusely from nose and mouth and seemed to be choking up blood. The skull over her right eye was very much swollen and her little eye closed up. He stripped the child and washed the blood off. He applied a solution of camphor and bandaged the head, then laid her in a blanket. "Is there anyone here who has nursing experience?" He called out to the onlookers. Mum was there, "I am not a nurse but have had experience of wounds and sickness tending for my large brood." Mum was taken on to help Elder Lamoreaux.

They did what they could, rendering much sympathy towards the child's parents. Elders Stevenson, Jeremy and Mills administered in the ordinance of the hostel for the restoration of the child, Mills anointing and Jeremy sealing it. Elder Lamoreaux paid every possible attention to his little patient, which seemed to revive wonderfully, praising Jehovah that the child had not died.

We didn't hear any more until Sunday when mum returned to give us the sad news that the child, Mary Price, had, unfortunately, died at 2 o'clock that morning. That was so sad and I felt somewhat to blame that I couldn't get to her in time. Her parents were Mr and Mrs Jeremiah Price. They had come from East Glamorganshire in Wales.

There were no further incidents like this, although there were two births. Why they wanted to travel on such a dangerous voyage, I said to myself, when they were so near giving birth, beggars belief.

The ship with a good steady wind, scudding along well at about 12 knots an hour. However, the coughing was getting worse and people were getting sick. People were trying desperately to keep themselves to themselves, hiding in their cabins and bunks, or going out onto the top deck, hoping the sea breeze would blow the sickness away. People were advising various remedies, some even comical. "Old Neptune seems to be letting us know we have trespassed upon his territory and is inflicting a penalty for doing so." – this came from an old sea salt of a man.

Women and children were at night lashed to their berths, for in no other way could they keep in. Furniture rolled back and forth endangering limb and life. The waves swept the deck and even reached the staterooms... Children's voices were crying in the darkness, mother's voices soothing or scolding, men's voices rising above the others, all mingled with the distressing groans and cries of the sick for help, and, above all, the roaring of the wind and howling of the tempest made a scene and feeling indescribable.

A meeting was held today on deck when all that could possibly leave their berths were there to hear on how best to keep save and medicate themselves. At the same time the body of the poor child was brought forward, sewed decently up in clean cloth, with a bag of stones attached to it. The body was laid on a frame. After singing and prayer with lectures on the subjects of resurrection, parents and children, led by the President and Elders Jeremy Lamoreaux and Mills, the hymn "Now she's gone we'd not recall her" was sung, and she was cast into the watery element.

The captain and the brothers were kept busy, apart from the normal running of the ship and prayer services, as three marriages were solemnised and four baptisms took place on board. We heard that four more had applied for baptism on the arrival at Philadelphia.

We were left to the mercies of wind and waves, both of which, thankfully, were mild and gentle for four days, when we took fair wind as we were leaving soundings, having the blue sky and rolling billows to gaze upon -a new but majestic scene as, coming from Hertfordshire, I had not visited the coast before, let alone been on the sea. The cheerful countenances of everyone on board, told in their faces that their earnest desires and prayers had been answered. The predictions of the prophets, who foresaw the sons of Jacob gathering from every nation, kindred, tongue and people, to the inheritance promised him and his descendants, told the joy of the hundreds on board, who had for many years earnestly desired and prayed for deliverance.

The Mormon brothers conducted regular singing sessions and we joined in, singing songs of Zion. As there were emigrants from France, Wales as well as England, it was amusing to hear these different sections take up the songs in their own languages, especially the deep-throated Welsh tenors, who came through loud and clear, and harmonising superbly, as if they had all been singing together for years, even though they probably came from diverse areas of Wales.

Each Sunday presented a different spectacle, no less curious, on the upper deck. The main capstan was transformed into a sacred pulpit from which our choicest orators preached under open skies to all passengers and crewmen.

On Saturday 21st, the wind was blowing a good breeze at east by south. The ship was rocking more than yesterday and quite a number of the passengers were sick this morning, not able to stomach any food. The cooking galley was nearly deserted this morning, the old saying verified there "the first come, the first served" without waiting for sections to be called in rotation. The ship sailing about 10 knots an hour.

Elder W. [William] G. Mills composed a hymn of praise to God for the present circumstances and occasion as follows:

When on our Mother Earth we trod
And oft admired her gorgeous robe;
When wandering thru life's varied scene
At will upon the solid globe;
The goodness of our God we knew

And felt the power of His command;
We praised and loved His holy name
And owned this providential hand.
Thus now when on the watery sphere
When every wave is crowned with foam;

The Chimborazo's "wooden walls"
Our temporary floating home;
With horizon of sky and sea
That circumscribes us like a ring.
We see the kindness of our God,

We feel the power of ocean's king.
Then let our numerous voices blend
In songs of deepest gratitude
To him, whose hand controls the sea,
And guides us over the briny flood,

He claims our praise, so let us be
Humbly obedient to his word,
Be faithful now and evermore
To gain all blessings from our Lord.
May we still feel his favouring hand

While traveling over the trackless deep;
The winds in storms and gushing sound
or calmly over nature sleep
God bless our worthy president
The council, president & Saints,

The noble captain, mates and crew
And may we have no just complaints
Oh! May we live as Saints should live
our walk & conversation good;
As living testimonies to

The gospel covenant received
Be cheerful Saints all will be well
Angels watch over our gallant ship;
And for the power that brings us thru
Let it be heard from every lip.

By Monday 23rd, there hadn't been much in the way of recovery of those on board, but some felt well enough to go up on deck to take the air. Mum and my wife had been sick and were feeling washed out and awful, so stayed below. The rest of the family were fairly OK. Mum and Ann were feeling very weak, and their faces wore a green tinge. We managed to get some bowls for them to retch into. "Here, come on mum…, let's see if we can get you sat up. We have some weak tea. Try to sip it." This was Lois. Mum just gave a weak groan. She wasn't well at all. Mary Ann was looking after my wife, who was fairing a bit better than mum.

Alfred and Ben, being youngsters, seemed to thrive, larking about, running from side to side to amuse themselves. The captain kindly supplied the sick with gruel, which they relished and said they felt a little better afterwards.

Tuesday 24th. Most of the passengers were now sick, including John, Mary and myself. The vessel had rolled last night for a short time sending unfastened packages scooting from one side to the other. We had all been alarmed at this, hearing screams from some women and children crying. We didn't know what was happening and thought this would be the last of us, fearing we were going to capsize. The boards of the ship were creaking and groaning, which naturally added to the tension. The crew had been busy again, lashing anything they could to posts and pillars and anyone not sick, was asked to help. Ben and Alfred had busied themselves helping to tie ropes round boxes.

"Please try to keep calm, all of you." This came from crewmen, patrolling the lower deck. "Please be advised this there has been a change of wind to the north and the sails had to be altered accordingly."..... But our fear was not controlled until the wind died down. Luckily this event did not last long.

The crew were kept busy dispensing sand over the pungent heaps and sweeping these up, then swilling buckets of water over the deck and through the wards below. The buckets had to be emptied regularly, lowering them down on ropes to be washed out by the raging waters. Any able men were also put to the task of cleaning up. The captain advised us all that we had sailed a distance of 1,143 miles from Liverpool. He was a good man, trying his best to calm everyone down and ordered medicine to be distributed to the sick. He even supplied soup from his own table for the comfort of the delicate on board. The next night, the vessel was rolling again, considerably, and I could hear people praying.

By Wednesday 25th, the sickness had not eased. Bedding had to be washed and was placed on deck at the front to air...I heard that a boy, by the name of Prior, who had been misbehaving in the galley today was being questioned about is behaviour. He was requested to apologize to the council and captain, but refused to do so. We were all aghast at this. This was not how we expected our children to behave, although I imagine he had been bored. I remember doing something similar myself when I was a lad. I'd got into a temper and smashed a few plates. Mum was fuming and sent me out to chop wood – a hard task for a young lad and my hands were so sore afterwards, with blisters developing. I believe Prior was put in the brig for 24 hours, with no-one to talk to and just gruel to sustain him.

A smart breeze broke up on us today, a kind of storm. Bands of lightning flashed across the sky, lighting up the horizon. The waves were high and coming down in loud crashes onto the deck The crew were made busier than ever, with the dangerous task of climbing the masts, which were slippery and soaked, clinging on for life, in order to take down sails. There were no fatalities though and we gave them all a round of applause. Ben was enthralled with it all, "I would love to be able to do that." "Well, you are not, young man." Ann (our mum) replied. Ben was only 13 and I suppose, as boys do at that age, thought he was capable of anything and wouldn't get injured.

Thursday 26th. People were still sick but nothing of a serious nature – save for a young man, named Joseph Elliott, son of Priest James Elliott, who have a fever. He was attended to by Elder Lamoreaux, who had him removed from his berth to that of his father's in order that he was closer, so that they could look after him. On the whole everyone appeared better but the wind was still unfavourable with the ship still being tossed around in a heavy rolling sea.

Suddenly, and to the astonishment of everyone one board, the wind seemed to cease, as if by magic. This caused the vessel to lurch and roll desperately. Even the captain was baffled. He had not experienced such a phenomenon in all his days of sailing. Everyone fell silent too as if we were expecting the silence to end with a deafening crash, to awaken us out of this coma of silence. Something awful was expected and awaited. We all stood in our tracks, stopped what we were doing and waited.

To our relief, the wind started to blow again and nothing unforeseen occurred. We could all breathe again – breathe a sigh of relief. Someone, who seemed to be in the know, stated that, if this event had happened during the night, we would have been sure to have lost one of the masts. This got passed around the ship, creating another spasm of praying and thanking Jehovah. On hearing the commotion the captain appeared with a beaming smile and kindly expression to cheer us all up.

The next day showed not much change. The wind was light and unfavourable. We all carried on with our set tasks.

The wind died down again on Saturday 28th so we couldn't make much progress, however, the calmness of the water did much to aid the recovery of the sick and many were able to go up on deck again.

We took fair wind until the 29th and we advanced prosperously. We were then becalmed for four days, and were drifting back by the tide. The captain was worried as, if we could not progress, the food rations would be depleted sooner than expected. We were all given less to eat and to some, this really meant hunger. This day being Sabbath, the captain allowed two meetings on deck. In fact, the President Stevenson instructed the Mormons on board of the necessity of fasting and prayer, for the continued mercies of God that we should be favoured with a fair wind It was agreed that all of us should fast and pray on Tuesday next, the first day of May.

I heard many people actually grumbling at this as we were all on tight rations anyway and people were suffering without having to fast on top of that. I heard one of the crew say, "What's the good of fasting – that'll do no-one any good.

Haven't we seen that many have been sea sick and haven't been able to hold down what little sustenance they receive, but this has to be replaced, which won't be done by fasting!" I had to agree but didn't say anything. After the prayer meeting, the captain requested more sail and a fair wind continued for five successive days and nights, and which brought us safely over the banks of Newfoundland. We passed one ship dis-masted. The wind had stirred up the sea, now, which was lashing the deck, sending loose boxes and tin-ware floating from one side to the other, while the crew desperately tried to restrain them, yet again.

Several large fish were seen rolling in the sea. "What are they", Ben asked.

"I think they may be porpoises or dolphin." Replied John. "Can you see their long, rounded beaks?"

"Beaks?"

"Yes, I do not know how else to describe them. I believe they are mammals and give birth to live young."

Everyone was fascinated and went to the sides to view them.

On Monday 30th, the wind was blowing splendidly, with the sails filled out, and no sign of rain. President Stevenson issued 494 yards of nankeen – a sort of yellow cotton cloth. These were to be sewn up into waggon and tent covers. The poop deck was covered with men and women engaged cheerfully in sewing them up. It appeared quite a place of industry. The females in my family, who were well enough, were doing their bit with this nankeen.

However, the next day, May 1st, a heavy breeze was blowing and the sky became heavy and dark. The ship was rolling quite a lot, which brought on bouts of sickness again. The cooking galley was virtually empty as most of the Mormons were fasting.

We then we had a few days of disagreeable cold weather, attended with snow and rain, and winds fluctuating, which is quite common at the mouth of the St. Lawrence River, where the ice of the Lakes Erie and Ontario flow down.

I heard officers and crew saying, "The Mormons had better fast and pray again." This was said in somewhat good heart as it seems our prayers had been answered for a fair wind.

I got speaking to a lady called Mary Ann Ford Simmons. She was not having a great time, having been sick and was feeling very much under the weather. She'd also run out of the food that she had brought for the journey and, even though sick, was lacking in energy and was desperate to get on solid ground again. I gave her one of our remaining apples, which she devoured gratefully. She told me her story, "We left Brighton for Liverpool, leaving all of our furniture and carpets. All we could take were clothes and bedding and said goodbye to dear old England. We came on this old tub as storage - we had no money to pay the cost of a cabin. Oh, Tom, when are we going to get there – first we have too much wind, then none at all, and now it's turned freezing. I've had a miserable time from day one. As soon as we land at Philadelphia, I am gonna get me a good supper and breakfast. I can just see that bacon and eggs, looking up at me."

"I think I'll join you – a plate of bacon and eggs would suit me fine."

Wednesday, 2nd May. The sky still looked gloomy with several showers of rain falling in squalls. At 8am Caradoe Palmer Beynon, aged 11 months, died of inflammation of the chest. She'd had trouble breathing. Steam inhalations were given with Friar's Balsam, but she couldn't be saved. Her parents were from Methyr Tydfyl in Wales. The child was consigned to the liquid tomb, after singing & prayer by Elder Thomas Jeremy about half past two o'clock. It was such a shame.

A case was reported today of two sisters being mesmerized. Elder Stevenson was up in arms about this and forbade this practice.

We had a favourable wind for the following day, Thursday May 3rd and people were beginning to feel a bit better. . There was good news as we had arrived at the soundings of Newfoundland.

Everyone was bemused to see whales, blowing streams of water from their blow holes. We all looked on in awe to see such huge creatures, jumping high out of the sea in an arc before diving down again. The sound emanating from them was an eerie wail.

The weather turned cold on Sunday May 6th. There were meetings – the English on the poop deck, addressed by the president and Elders Sutherland and Slack, whereas the Welsh met on the forward deck and were addressed in their own language by Elder Thomas Jeremy and others. Everything seemed to be in order and all were well.

Yesterday's cold weather turned into rain with biting wind for the next couple of days. Mum got the blankets to wrap around us. What made it worse was the stores were out of drinking water. Buckets were put on deck to catch the rain. People were beginning to get dehydrated, their skin pinched and suffering terrific headaches. There was sea water, naturally, but that had to be boiled and strained and the steam captured, so the salt could be syphoned off, before using it for cooking.

"Well, we've passed the sounds of Newfoundland," this was John, "We should be sighting land pretty soon."

"I hope so" mum answered, "I really want to get my feet on stable ground. I still feel queasy." I opened our last tin of potatoes in sugared water, and gave her a sip, then passed it round to everyone else in the family. The potatoes would be our lunch – one half of a potato for each of us.

We finally got close to mum's wish the next day, Wednesday 9th,.when the call went up, "Land ahoy." The wind had dropped too, so people were a lot more cheerful. It had been a long, eventful journey, but we had survived, and there was a great feeling of relief. People started sewing the nankeens again.

The next day there was even a bigger turnout of sewers on deck. Land was in sight and the next stage of the journey had to be prepared for, so there was quite a hive of industry taking place. A great many were speaking and singing as they worked. Of course my sisters, the wives and mum were all there working industriously and even us men took thread and needle, under their instruction. The boys were keeping us all supplied with tea. "Hey, where's the sugar, there's no sugar in mine." John moaned. "Aw, there's none to be had. They've rationed it. You'll have to lump it." replied Alfred.

On Monday 14th, the sun had come out as our ship was greeted by several pilots from New York. We really felt that this was a home-coming and all thoughts of the lands we had left were far distant. Everyone thought that we would soon be docking, what with the pilots coming out, but it took another two days of wind and rain, when we couldn't work on the nankeens. Our exuberance was turning a bit sad with this delay plus quite a few were getting sick again.

More and more people were calling for a bit of sugar, to put on their porridge. No more water was available to make tea. "Come on Captain, have a heart, we're all working hard here, and I am running out of steam. Just a bit of sugar will keep us going." and similar requests were being shouted out. A little while later, portions of sugar were made available. Our president came to tell us that, as a lighthouse had been seen in the distance, "I, therefore, felt it prudent to release the ration on the sugar." A loud applause was given with shouts of approval and grateful thanks.

The next day a pilot from Philadelphia came on board to a round of cheers. We make Cape May, and the breakwater and lighthouse. We passed beautifully up the river Delaware, seeing land on both sides.

Saturday 19th. About one o'clock this morning the wind being ahead we anchored about halfway up the river. The Saints were sewing again today. A small party, as we lay idly in the river, went ashore, under the direction of the president, and enjoyed themselves on terra firma for a short season, and visited two farmhouses. They brought with them a few fowl & eggs & milk, and the much-needed water, which were quite a treat to a few of the passengers.

It was Sunday 20th. A meeting was convened on the deck at 3pm. The steam tug came alongside and moored waiting for the morning to tow us up the river. Meetings were held in the various sections, when the Lord's Supper was administered. They were visited by the president and council and everyone was in good spirits.

Monday 21st. The steam tug took us in tow this morning about 9 o'clock, in connection with the "Parthenia" another emigrant ship. The scenery was delightful to view with flat green meadows. We weren't out of the wood yet though as there was a great mishap when the hawser from the tug to the Parthenia broke and the Parthenia was heading ashore. We had been close on her stern and, to the astonishment of everyone we looked like we were going to crash into her. There were shouts hollered out for "Hold on tight." With extreme good fortune and the quick-thinking of the captain and pilot, our ship just clipped her starboard stern, with no bad damage. We were then towed further up to Wilmington Creek where we were put to anchor all night.

At 6 o'clock on the morning of Tuesday 22nd we dropped anchor again, having been towed that little way further. Cries of "Philadelphia, Philadelphia" resounded around the ship. We all got our final orders and instructions. At about 9am a doctor came on board to check over each of the passengers. Luckily, everyone passed his inspection.

We had arrived, we were safe. We'd got through this first part of our journey. Maybe I could get that bacon and eggs at last with Mary Ann Ford Simmons!

PHILADELPHIA

CHAPTER 2

We were all going our separate ways. Between two and three hundred of the emigrants were going to continue the journey to St Louis by way of Pittsburgh, while the remainder, including my family, were to try to find temporary employment in and around Philadelphia. The ones going to Pittsburgh were going by rail, then steamboat down the Ohio River and up the Mississippi and Missouri Rivers to Atchison, heading for Mormon Grove. This was to be the starting point for the plains. We heard that this group were overtaken in Pittsburgh by the emigrants who crossed in the Samuel Curling, and the excellent and commodious steamboat, 'Amazon', under the presidency of Elder Edward Stevenson. Both of these companies combined now numbered nearly six hundred. They were due to arrive at St Louis on Saturday, June 2nd. The plan then was about one hundred and forty passengers would start out two days later, sailing for Atchison on board the Amazon. About three hundred others, who had been with us on the Chimborazo, were to remain in St Louis, for a couple of weeks, awaiting orders from the Perpetual Emigration Fund company agents in regard to their further progress. They were to camp out a little way from the city in fine, open country in a healthy location. It hadn't been decided at the time whether they would be sent through to the Valley that season or not, but news came back that they were finally to embark on board the steamer Ben Bolt, which sailed from St Louis for Atchison on the 19th June.

We, as a family, did not have enough money to pay for the onward journey to Pittsburgh. We just had enough to get us on board the Chimborazo. Also, we didn't know when William and his family would be joining us, and had arranged to meet them in Philadelphia, whenever that would be. So, we made our way there, arriving on 27 May 1855. We were still waiting for George too. He'd joined the Finsbury Branch of the church and was baptised just as we left on our journey, on 15 April 1855. Once we had found accommodation in Philadelphia, we wrote to him. It took a while before received any letter back, as it seemed he had moved, having joined the Walworth branch for a while, then moved to the Lambeth branch.

We found what work we could, with the women working as maids and child-minders. Ben and Alfred found work down by the docks, loading and unloading. I found work in a brush factory. John found work in a brewery. He had experience in our father's brewery back home – the Wick Brewery and Distillery.

There was one happy event while we were there. Lois, our sister, had met Ebenezer Woodford. He was a salesman and came from Chichester. All the family and friends that we had made there came to the wedding which was on 4 January 1856. It was a bitterly cold day and we were all wrapped up in coats, scarves and gloves.

They were very happy, although Ebenezer could be a bit overbearing at times. I suppose that came with the territory of him being a salesman.

THE GEORGE WASHINGTON

CHAPTER 3

We heard, eventually, that our brother, William, had secured passage on the "George Washington" leaving Liverpool, headed for Boston, Massachusetts. He would be bringing the whole family, - his wife, Emma (Baxter) and his children William (just coming up for 13), Fannie (11), Elizabeth (6) and Lois (4). They had got talking to someone called, Elizabeth Judd, aged 27, while waiting to board. Elizabeth had joined the Mormon Church, and also wanted to leave England for a better place. She offered to help out with the children. Elizabeth was pretty, in her own way, but, unfortunately, this was marred by a weak left eye. No-one was put off by this, as her kindness and personality shone through.

The family were struggling with their boxes and packages but had managed to get hold of a trolley cart. "Is that the ship we are going on, dad." That was William.

"Yes, that is the ship, the SS George Washington – is she not grand?"

"Why do you call her 'she'? She's not male or female, it is a ship?"

"Oh, William. That is just a term – all ships are referred to as 'she'."

"Come on everyone."

William was 35, and Emma 36. William was a square-jawed, well-built, muscular man with dark brown hair. He was intelligent-looking but always with a worried look on his face – probably caused by having a young family of four to look after. Emma was slight, with a chiselled face with her dark hair drawn back into a bun, covered with a bonnet. She looked very pale and quite pained at times, giving her a bit of a stuck-up look, but she was anything but, and very kindly.

The ship was due to set off on 27 March 1857 from Waterloo Dock in Liverpool, going to Boston. She was a 1534 ton, 198ft x 41ft x 29ft ship built in 1851 by John A Taylor at Chelsea, Massachusetts. She was a square rigger with 3 decks, square stern, and a billethead. The entire ship had been chartered by the Mormon Church.

I, William, continued speaking to the family, saying, "I have heard that a Mr George Q Cannon, one of the missionaries here, has predicted that this ship will make a quicker crossing than any previous vessel has before. He reckons the voyage will be completed in six weeks – which will be a record time."

Once we had all be settled into our allocated cabins and berths, the captain introduced himself, via a loud-speaker apparatus that allowed his voice to be heard on all decks. "Where is the captain, I cannot see him, dad, where is he speaking from?" This was Fanny.

"He will be in the wheel house up top... shush... so we can listen to what he has to say."

"I am your captain speaking, Mr Josiah S Cummings. I welcome you all on board. There are, in total 827 Mormons travelling today. Your presidents have asked you to assemble on the top deck at 3pm for introductions and instructions. I wish you a care-free journey to Boston."

So, at 3pm we all began to gather on the top deck. We were packed like sardines.

President Benson introduced himself and 14 returning missionaries.

After singing one of the soul stirring songs of Zion, prayer was offered up by President J. A. Ray for the blessings of the God of Israel to attend the Saints while journeying to Zion, and for Heaven's blessings to rest upon all Israel, in their various conditions in life, etc., to which a hearty amen resounded from the bosom of every Saint on board.

President Benson then proposed Elder James P. Park to be their president, and Elders J. B. Martin and C. R. Dana to be his counsellors, which was unanimously agreed to. The vessel was divided into five wards, and the following elders were selected to be their respective presidents: -- Israel Evans, B. Ashby, J. Carrigan, D. B. Dille, and J. C. Hall. Each ward is divided into districts and a teacher appointed over each district to see that the public and private prayer is attended to and that wards are kept clean and pure by frequent ventilation, sweeping & washing. A. [Amos M.] Musser was appointed secretary for the ship. All these officers were sustained by unanimous vote.

We were advised that every passenger has 10 cubic feet allotted him for the luggage and a berth sufficient for his person, according to law. All adult passengers have had to pay £4 and 5 shillings for their passage; under eight, and over, £3 5s, infants one shilling. "Each adult will be allocated provisions of 132 [-] of water, 3gms of bread or biscuit of flour, 1 gm of oatmeal, 1 gm of rice, 1 gm of peas, 1 gm of beef, 1 m pork, 2gms potatoes, 2 ounces of tea, 1 gm sugar, and of mustard, a 1/4 ounce of ground pepper, 2 ounces of salt, & 1 gill of vinegar. The water is to be issued daily."

During the meeting several hymns suitable to the occasion were sung by the brethren and sisters in a spirited manner, one of which was -- 'Ye elders of Israel come join now with me,' etc., with the chorus 'O Babylon, O Babylon, we bid thee farewell,

About 6 o'clock President Benson departed, bidding us all farewell Three cheers were given making the air ring with – "Huzza ! huzza! huzza!" -- Handkerchiefs and hats were waved by the crowd standing on the dock, until we were out of sight.

Finally sitting down and able to relax, I began to think back to the start of our journey. On Monday 23 March I had got everyone up at 3am, and we had breakfast. Checking that we had everything we needed loaded up on the cart, we made our way to the station, taking one last long look back at the house that had been our home for the last few years and where the youngest two children, Elizabeth and Lois, had been born. The train left for Liverpool at 5am. It had been a long, tiresome ride of two hundred and sixteen miles. I left the family at the station while I hunted around for accommodation for all of us. I managed to find lodgings at Mr Jones', Number Eleven, Hunters Street. It was not much but it would do, for the short times we would be there. I then fell into a deep, much-needed sleep.

We had stayed in Liverpool all the next day and took the children to have a look at the fine ship, the George Washington, which we would be sailing on....... Now we were aboard that fine ship and were leaving the docks.

We found ourselves in the morning at anchor in the Mersey. Government officers came on board and discharged their duties. On Saturday 28th some of us rose early to watch as a steam tug came and towed the ship out into the Irish Channel.

As I saw the blue line of my native land fade away like a cloud on the horizon, it seemed I had closed one volume of the world and its concerns, and had time for meditation before opening another. That land too – what changes would I see? What could I expect? Would I ever revisit England and the scenes of my childhood?

In a few fleeting hours we were out of sight of land. A dense fog assisted amazingly in obscuring it. Quite a few people had collected into groups throughout the vessel and were singing quite appropriate hymns such as, "Yes, my native land I love thee", and "On the gallant ship we ride", "The gallant ship is underway".

We left the tug with a fair wind. Guards have also been appointed to see that a watch is stationed at every hatchway, every night to prevent anyone trying to board the ship and also to stop people wandering around after a certain hour at night. There were rumours going around that we might try to be boarded by others, not of the faith, trying to travel with us, as they believed our Mormon ships never sank and never ran into trouble. They were willing to pay over the odds, but the Captain was quite adamant that the ship should not be boarded by non-Mormons. We have on board English, Welsh, Scotch, Irish, Swiss, and Yankees, a medley of people and languages. The captain appears kind, obliging, and affable with all. The chief mate, although quite repulsive in appearance and somewhat rude and condescending in his manner, is nevertheless obliging when approached.

On Sunday 29th, the sea was quite rough with the wind swirling around in gusts. Some of the passengers were beginning to get quite seasick, becoming quite pale in appearance. Emma, my wife, and the children were fine for now, although I admit I was feeling a bit groggy myself. The children were busying themselves helping to keep the ward in order, which the children loved, especially little Elizabeth, who was showing herself quite adept with a broom, even though only six years old. "Look daddy, aren't I clever, I've swept the dirt into a pile, just like mummy". "Yes, you're doing a good job there, little'un." Little Lois, though didn't like the dirt and was making "uhh, dirty" comments at Elizabeth's sweepings..

I was busying myself, along with many others, looking after the sick passengers who had no-one else to look after them, providing them with tea and water, and any food they could possibly keep down and providing and cleaning sick bowls. It was a dirty job, but I took it in my stride with a smile and a comforting word to them.

Things got worse though as, by Tuesday 31st, the weather turned stormy with the sea rising in great waves. I took to my bed too, this time, along with nearly everyone on board. I just lay there and groaned, with a bowl at my side. It was like being in a floating hospital.

During all of this, with the doctor being run off his feet, Mrs Mary Anne, wife of Thomas Jenkins was delivered of a fine daughter.

The wind didn't let up until Friday 3rd when the passengers started feeling a bit better and some went on deck. I was better myself and could play with the children, relieving Emma for a while. I got the story books out to read to them as a group.

The next day I was acting as steward, helping with the issue of rations. There were about ten of us, but it still took about five hours to issue provisions for one week for the whole company.

The day after, it was decided that the whole ship needed to be fumigated. I was not sure what I was meant to be doing but followed orders. This involved getting everyone on deck and then burning tar between the decks. This steam actually helped a few people who had breathing issues, and created a healthy atmosphere. This was carried out a few times during the journey.

I got talking to a Mrs Jarvis. She seemed to be sitting on her own and looking a bit crestfallen. "My husband just brought one suit of clothes, so nothing for our use with us. He wouldn't let us bring anything. I had a nice furnished house too, but we left everything – we even had good new carpets on the floors.

I suppose, in hindsight, we are young and foolish, but my husband wants new things.

"Where is your husband now?"

"Well, that is a story, to be sure. I do not know if you know, but the cook, taken on to prepare food for everyone on board, was taken sick – seasick! So, a cook had to be got quickly. They found out my husband was a seafaring man and asked if he was up for the job. He agreed, and I haven't seen hide nor hair of him since. I thought I should be having quite a pleasure trip with my husband but I do not think I have exchanged a dozen words with him. He has been cooking for all the eight hundred on board, just with one assistant, a Mr William Hutchings. He is at his post for 12 hours on the trot, non-stop. I am glad I have got you to talk to as I was getting so bored. I mean, he just goes to bed as soon as his work is done, as he's so worn out by then, then has to start up again at six in the morning.

"Well, you can always join us. I have four young children that need to be kept amused, and they can be quite a handful, although we have been very lucky to have met up with someone I can now call a friend, Elizabeth Judd, who has been helping with the children, where necessary."

"Thank you. Yes, I love little children and can tell them a few stories, play a few games" So, Mrs Jarvis came to amuse herself with the children and to get to know my family while I was kept busy with chores and looking after the sick.

Quite a few passengers had been sea sick, and some actually confined to their beds.

We'd heard that there was another man who was having trouble breathing. There was a doctor on board and he was called to administer what he could to aid his breathing. This was a man called John Shuttleworth, aged about 60 years. It seems everything was done to help him but he had an asthmatic attack, made worse by sea-sickness. It seems he had been taken unwell in Liverpool, having been suffering on and off for the past four months, but his son and friends, who accompanied him, were of the opinion that the sea-air would benefit him. He died about 12 o'clock last night. At 8 this morning, his body, after a few minutes of exhibition for his friends and son to say their final goodbyes, was sewn up into a sheet, a bag of sand fastened to his feet, and lowered over the bulwarks into the watery grave. May he rest in peace.

There was another death on Sunday 12th. Sarah Ann, daughter of Sarah Ann Coggle of Southampton, died of fever. She was only 11 months old. The poor child had been adopted by George and Mary Hatt, so she hadn't had a good start in life, only for her life to be taken so quickly. We didn't find out what happened to the child's real mother, but I imagine something tragic had happened. Prayers were said again, as the poor child's body was lowered to the waves.

I returned, with my wife, Emma, to Mrs Jarvis again, who was playing cards with my children. I told her, "I was asked to go to the hospital to help two sick ladies, a Frances Puddiford, who fortunately got better, and another Mrs Jenkins. This Mrs Jenkins was in labour and having trouble. When I got there she was delirious. I told her I would go to get my wife and that, although she's not a nurse, she has had four children. Unfortunately, my Emma could not help her and even though there were numerous people looking after her, taking turns, she died."

"Oh, I am sorry to hear that."

"She was only 25 years old and came from Herefordshire. The baby survived, but the mother died - leaving a poor grieving husband with three other children to care for as well as the baby."

Mrs Jarvis continued. "I dread living in Boston. I've heard it is an evil city. I hope we get out of there soon. I would rather be where I was – I was happy there."

I commiserated with her and said, "I am sure everything will work out. None of us know what to expect but at least your husband would be free, once we land, to sort out work and a place to live."

After a brief prayer offered by Amos Milton, the body of Mrs Jenkins was, like her two predecessors, consigned to the watery deep as the only resting place suitable for her body.

This Amos Milton was the one that seemed to be organising the rations as well as everything else – doctoring and services over the dead, as well as supervising the tarring of the deck.

I got to know him as I was doing my bit, issuing rations and the deck tarring, although he couldn't sit down and have a conversation, as I could see he was overwhelmed. He managed to say, "Oh, I've been so fully occupied, and still am, taking care of the sick and helpless, that the time passes away without my noticing it and, to me this sea journey thus far has been extremely brief. The opposite of a kettle watched, and all that, applies – I have no time to sit and watch a kettle boiling."

Several children on board now have the measles. I am keeping my children away from the others, where possible, although some say that it's good for children to catch the measles early, but still, I didn't want to see my children ill. As it is they are all now suffering with diarrhoea. Poor little Lois is crying and Elizabeth and Fanny are quite fatigued and listless. William is bemoaning the fact that he has constipation. Emma and Elizabeth have given them all Kaolin and Morphine and Gripe Water to William.

After raining virtually non-stop, the wind calmed by Friday 17th. The wind was blowing from the south and we were making good headway, but then it changed to the west. The seas were running high and the ship was rolling from side to side causing many of us to get nauseous. It was about 4pm when, all of a sudden a cry went up of 'Fire, Fire'. I looked around in the direction the cries were coming from and ran to see the most awful sight I had ever seen. The cooking galley was all in a flame, the blaze issuing out of each door with a sizzling fury. The blaze was also coming out of the stove pipe to the height of several feet above. I ran to offer my assistance, along with most people there – getting buckets of water raised from the sea and being passed in a long line, arm over arm, to try to quash the blaze. Smoke was billowing out, making it difficult to breathe. Someone shouted out, "The flames are licking up above to the main sail." Someone else shouted out, "If that goes, the fire will spread to the other sails and there'll be no way of stopping it apart from chopping down the mast, and then we'll be stranded." So, the buckets of water were directed to the sails and stove pipe.

I could see Mr Jarvis, Mrs Jarvis's husband, endeavouring to unfasten the door to the galley to get out, but could not, something must have fallen down in front of it. He was shouting and kicking at the door. Luckily, he managed to make his escape through the flames out of the back door of the galley, unhurt, but Mr Hutchings (who, though suffering with sea-sickness, had heard the shouts and came running to see what he could do) and two others, one a Mormon and one a sailor were in the midst of the flames. They realised the main door was blocked and they too had to take their lives in their hands and throw themselves through the flames, which were now burning fiercely, to get to the back door to get out.

Luckily they managed to escape. Also, as luck would have it, it had been raining and the sails and rigging were wet and the flames just sizzled and did not burn. Also, there was a barrel of water close by, which was lifted and poured over the flames, extinguishing them. The three people, who had been trapped in the galley sustained severe burns, the worst being Mr William Lawrence Hutchings, cook with Mr Jarvis. His face and arms were burnt, his left arm more so. The elders did what they could at the time, applying oil to his burns. I could see that his left arm was burnt from the fingers to the elbow and the skin coming up in great blisters. The elders then wrapped his wounds and put him to bed.

The fire originated from a barrel of grease, which stood between the stoves and, what with the rocking of the ship, it emptied a part of its contents on the red hot stove and, of course, instantly burst into flames.

I happened to see Mrs Jarvis run into the arms of her husband, thanking God that he was uninjured.

"I do not know what I would do without you. I would be lost in a wilderness of strangers."

"I am OK, woman. The fire is all out now. Mind you, there is a real mess to clean up."

"But it is dangerous. It is not your job. Can they not get anyone else to help you apart from a young lad? In fact, can they not get anyone else at all – give you a rest? You are worn out. Someone needs to speak to the captain."

"Ok, woman, I will speak to him."

A meeting was called. Obviously Mr Hutchings could no longer work. At last, after much discussion, and prompting, a man stepped forward to share the load – so six hours toil, each person. The barrel of grease was moved somewhere safer and a lid fastened to it.

On the evening of Friday 19th a cry went up. "Cape Cod lighthouse". This meant we were forty miles from the city of Boston.

The next morning we could all see the lights on shore as we were just within a few miles of Boston. A pilot soon came on board and we were safely anchored in the bay of Boston. The voyage had taken only twenty three days – a new record.

Everyone on board was in a joyous mood, thinking we would soon be on dry land and heading off to our various destinations. However, by the evening, the wind had increased to a regular storm, with snowfall, the ship rocking and rolling, and then we found ourselves drifting.... The anchors were not holding us. Such a panic ensued on board. We were totally helpless, and at the mercy of the storm. Many were down on their knees praying. The sails had been taken down, but there was nothing to be done. The ship was dragging its anchors for about a mile and we were heading for certain destruction on the shore, to be smashed against the sea wall.

We spent a very restless, sleepless night wondering if we would survive, if the life boats would have to be lowered or if, indeed, we would have to swim to the shore, with all our belongings on board, sunk to the bottom, along with the ship. Women and children would be in the lifeboats but the men would have to try to swim to the shore.

I suppose all those prayers saved us as the morning found us still intact. A tug came and towed the ship to the docks. Elder John Taylor soon came on board. He was offering passage through the states by railroad to Iowa City for ten dollars and fifty cents each adult, five dollars 25 centre for under 16s and under children under six to go free. He said the fares had been much reduced

I looked at Emma and she at me. "Oh, Emma, we just have not got enough to pay the tickets for the whole family to go onto Philadelphia by train, even though the tickets have been reduced. We just cannot go further. I will have to find work here, if I can, and put us up in lodgings."

"Dear William, if that is the only way, then what must be, must be. We will survive, somehow. I am sure you will do your best to find us all accommodation and work.

The captain got on the megaphone. After announcing that, unfortunately, there had been four deaths on board and one child was born, he continued to say "I am free to acknowledge that on no previous voyage have my passengers conducted

51

themselves so orderly and peaceably as yourselves; cleanliness, morality, sobriety, reciprocation eminently conspicuous in your conduct and character. I wish you all a good journey and safe conduct to your various destinations."

Our first impressions of Boston was that it was a very large and beautiful city. The country a little from there is very hilly and almost covered with rock. Streams of water come out of the rocks both sides of the road from the mountains.

Mr Amos Milton was there, on the dock, busy with his lists of passengers, marking off, who was going where and who had paid what. He was also changing up English and French coin into American, giving change, and approximating the cost of extra luggage. I went to change what little money I had, with him.

We had enough for accommodation for the week and found lodging for us, albeit rather seedy and cramped. Emma was not happy and I could see a train of tears on her cheek, but there was not a word of complaint that issued from her. The children were all quiet. I could see they were tired and depressed to be thrown into this hovel. I am sure they were remembering the lovely house we had left in England, and were totally bewildered as to what was going to happen to them.

"Do not fret, my dears, this is only temporary," I said, trying to keep their spirits up.

Our luggage safety deposited, I then went out to find some kind of work, whatever I could. I was hungry, and I am sure my poor family were too. I had to bring them back something to eat, with the few pennies that I had left.

I started asking around at the docks and, luckily, was given a job unloading ships. It was hard work and what little energy I had was running low. Someone, seeing how I was struggling, offered me a piece of dry bread with an apple. That was enough to keep me going and I was paid that same day, so was able to get something for us all to eat, sinking back into the less than clean mattress and going into a deep sleep immediately. I knew I would have to be up at the crack of dawn to queue up for jobs being offered for the next day.

My experiences of Boston turned out not to be the beautiful city we had first arrived in. I had be very careful, moving around Boston, especially around the dock area, as there were notorious characters roaming around, looking for anything they could take and weren't above coshing you over the head, to get what they wanted.

So, time passed, with me taking any job that was going, back-breaking work some of it, but I was getting paid and we were saving as much of it as we could.

I got to hear that there was another Mormon ship coming in, due in on 3rd September, the Wyoming, having left Liverpool on July 18th. We would just about have enough money for the train to Philadelphia by then, so aimed to meet up with other Mormons and travel on with them, at least part of the way.

I left Emma, the children and Elizabeth Judd at Boston station, with our luggage, while I went to the docks to get instructions about the onward journey of the Mormons.

Brother Taylor was leaving Boston, accompanying those going on to New York and Philadelphia.

Brother Taylor warned all, waiting on the platform, travelling with him, to beware of pickpockets. "One of the passengers, Melissa Rice, has had her purse stolen, containing $40 and some promissory notes from her pocket." This was quite a loss and presumably gone for good to the rogue, who was just thinking of his own comforts and belly.

We left Boston at half past three going south to Philadelphia.

On taking a walk through the cars to stretch my legs, I recognised Mr Milton again, who had travelled with us on the journey over. I managed to have a quick word with him. He was polite, although he looked extremely busy making various lists of the passengers' names against the number of their tickets, together with their ages. He was also making reports for the "Mormon" and "Millenial Star" office concerning the emigrants' business and so forth. He was travelling with us as far as New York but, from there, would be taking a much convoluted route, which he seemed interested in telling me. "From New York I am going to take a sailing boat for Albany, going along the Hudson River – a journey of about 144 miles, from there, the train to Buffalo. If you ever get to go in that direction, young man, the Hudson River is beautiful and the scenery delightful. The Catskill Mountains are clearly visible from Albany. I plan to leave Albany, by train, at 12 noon, reaching Utica at 6pm, Rochester at 9pm, then Buffalo at 11pm. However, the train from there can be quite demanding. The rails have been unevenly laid, which causes much jolting of the cars, and I admit lead to a disturbed night's sleep. However, the first class cars alone in this country are to be preferred to those in England."

"Oh, I doubt if we will be travelling first class, sir."

"Quite, young sir, but as this is my regular passage, and taking into account my age, I try to obtain the best journey as I can, for my own comfort. I am undertaking an extremely long journey and do not want to be exhausted beyond repair upon my arrival."

"I understand, sir."

"From there I travel by road, which is extremely dusty. Yes indeed. I will put up at Chicago at the City Hotel. The next morning I head onto Rock Island and should arrive by 5pm. We cross the Mississippi River to Davenport, arriving in Iowa City about 9pm. The wide prairies look natural and the numerous prairie hens seen along the line bring to mind pleasant reminisces." At this point Mr Milton gave a cynical smile, changing the subject somewhat. "Yes, you and your family will have to be wary on your travels. You won't be safe until you get to Utah. I've heard there was a man up ahead and he ran against another man, shoving him off the track. I believe this was totally by accident and, fortunately, no serious injury occurred, however, I did hear a snippet of a conversation between two parties upon the merits and demerits of "Mormonism". One said that a party of 1,500 passed Cleveland a few days since, for the west. He said he did not wish them any particular harm, but would have been gratified to see them all go over a bridge and break their necks. Very liberal!"

"No, sir. That cannot be. We have come to America for the freedom to carry on our religion, unheeded, without the opposition and derangement brought upon us in England."

"Quite so, sir, and should you ever get to Salt Lake City, you will find the comfort you have been seeking. My aim is to get to Salt Lake City between 4th and 24th September, although the last part of my journey will be by waggon. Brother James Little at the camp a couple of miles from Iowa, has bought cattle and waggons but the waggon train will not be able to set out for some time yet, for there is not grass sufficient to sustain the cattle....But now, young man, I must continue with my work."

I thanked Mr Milton and left him to his transcriptions.

WILLIAM AND EMMA GUNN

CHAPTER 4

"Oh my. It's William and Emma and the family." This was Ann, our mother, as we entered the door of the house they had rented in Philadelphia. She flung her arms around us all one by one.

"We knew you were on your way, but did not know exactly when you would be arriving. It is so lovely to see you all again."

Then everyone else came up to shake my hand or give hugs of welcome. I introduced Elizabeth Judd, as a friend we had met at the docks, in Liverpool, who also wanted to emigrate and had been a great help to Emma with the children.

It was a small house and crammed to the rafters with people and their belongings.

"Oh, mum, do you have space for us all?"

"Well, we will make space. Do not worry! I will get the boys to move everything around and create sleeping areas. We will need more mattresses, and that is a fact. Thomas, John, take the trailer and go to the market, see what you can find."

Mum had a beef stew on the fire, "I am sure you're all really hungry so, even if it's not great, I am sure it will suffice." So we sat down to what for us, after the scrimping and scraping, was a hearty meal, with the addition of succulent bread and butter with mugs of tea.

There was someone I didn't recognise. Seeing me look at the stranger, mum commented. "Oh, of course, you would not know this gentleman. This is Ebenezer Woodford, Lois' husband. They got married in January last year, remember, I wrote to you about him." We shook hands heartily. "There's another addition to the family too," Ebenezer said, smiling. Then Lois brought forward a little baby girl, in her arms. "Let me introduce you to Tacy Ann Woodford, born 2nd June just passed. Try not to wake her, she's sleeping."

"Oh, she's beautiful, Lois.

Oh, it's so good, to be here at last, mum." We've had quite a horrendous few months, what with the voyage over, then having to find work in Boston."

We, over the course of the next few days, told everyone all that had befallen on our journeys, both ours, and mum's and the rest of the family's when they came over in 1855.

The little house had to be re-arranged to accommodate us all, with my girls top to tail in a double bed, that is, Fannie, Elizabeth and Lois. The boys shared another mattress, on the floor, my William and my brother, Benjamin. In another room, it was decided to put all the women together, mum (Ann), my wife (Emma), sister Mary Ann, sister Lois, John's wife Caroline and Elizabeth Judd, while we men had mattresses in the living room, that could be stood up and stored in the corner when not in use. So, the men together were me (William), my brother Thomas, brother John, brother Alfred, Ebenezer (Lois' husband), and John Adey (Mary's Ann's husband), not able to move with fear of waking the others. Of course, little Tacy Ann had a cot to herself in the women's room. I can tell you one thing, every morning the windows of the living room had to be opened wide, no matter the weather, with all these men sleeping so close together, in the same room. "John Adey, you son of a b..." was the normal morning carousal, as he tried to get up, stepping over and, more often, on the men beside him. It was more like a barracks than a living room.

We were all waiting for the day when we could start out on the next stage of our journey to Salt Lake City, but we had to wait for George to arrive from England, with his wife, though where they would sleep was no man's business. Of course, we wouldn't all be in the house all the time, as there was work to be done. I got work with a brush family first of all, but then found work with the Baldwin Locomotive Works.

LOIS GUNN/WOODFORD

CHAPTER 5

We all seemed to be getting on with our lives, saving as much as we could for the long journey onwards to Utah when, out of the blue, tragedy struck. Lois became very sick. She was sweating profusely, with her pulse racing, then suddenly collapsed in a heap. Mum and Ebenezer helped her into her bed, and applied cold compresses but she lapsed into a coma. A doctor was called when there was no sign of a recovery. Unfortunately, he could not do anything to revive her and he pronounced her dead. The whole family was called to attend at the end of the day's work and got busy making a funeral shroud for her. The women, especially, were bemoaning her death, which seemed to come on so unexpectedly. The doctor said it could have been a brain haemorrhage. All of a sudden, Ann screamed, "I just saw her breathe, she gave a sigh." The doctor was adamant that this did occur and that he had seen it with past patients. "It is just an escape of air in the lungs – it occurs quite frequently – but I assure you she has passed."

To everyone's astonishment, Lois opened her eyes. The women assembled almost fainted with shock. Then she spoke, "Come closer please, I cannot see you, you are just shadows in my vision."

We all stepped forward to hear what she had to say. "I have been to the spirit world and what a beautiful place it is. I have been talking to dad, and my little sister, Lois, who passed away, and after whom I was named, and other friends that I have lost. Little Lois was so cute and it was so good to see dad again and speak with him. Dad told me that I am going to die at 12 o'clock this night."

The family were saying things like, "No, no, Lois, you're on the road to recovery now. You're not going to die. You will pull through."

Lois continued, "I am concerned about our brother, John. He has broken away from the true church and gone over to the Godbeite Movement and renounced our beliefs. Please try to bring him back to the fold." John was there, and was looking on in utter amazement. Yes, it was true he had broken away, but had not told his family. He was keeping this a secret until what he thought was the right time. We all looked at him, and he nodded his agreement, hanging his head.

Before we could say anything further, Lois started speaking again, "I know my brother, Ben, will remain true to the faith and will see that mother gets to Zion."

We heard nothing more from Lois as she collapsed back into her coma. She died on the stroke of 12 midnight. on 10 March 1858. She was just 22 years old.

She left a loving family, her husband and her small daughter, Tacy Ann.

John never did return to the Mormon faith.

GEORGE AND ELIZA GUNN

CHAPTER 6

I had found it difficult to save enough – times were hard, but we needed to join mum and the rest of the family in Philadelphia. They were waiting for us before they could continue their journey to Utah.

My wife, Eliza (née Rogers) and I had got married on 10 December 1853, at Saint Dunstan and All Saints Church, in Stepney, Middlesex. My brother, Thomas, had been there as best man. Why we chose December, I've no idea, because it was bitterly cold, but I suppose, love is what it is and we wanted to be together. Eliza had been working as a maid for a family in Kensington, but had to leave once we got married, so it had been very difficult to save, just with one wage coming in.

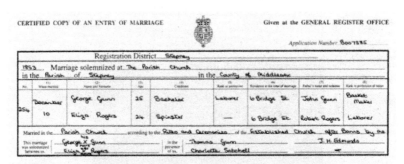

Marriage of George Gunn and Eliza Rogers

Anyway, we decided it was now or never. The family wanted to move on as it was just too crowded with everyone there, especially since William and his family had arrived. They didn't want to get a bigger place, or even two, as that would take so much from their savings.

I had made investigations as to when the next ship would be leaving England and aimed for the Underwriter, which would be sailing on 30 March 1860. I got the price of the tickets and had been in contact with mum's brother William Brazier and his wife, Caroline, that is to say, my aunt and uncle, who would be travelling with us along with their 17-year-old son, Charles. Uncle William had been the only other member of mum's family to join the church. The ship was due to arrive in New York on 1 May 1860.

What with Eliza not working, it had been difficult to save. Going through our finances, I realised we didn't have enough.

"Eliza, dear, taking all into account, train, ship, food, accommodation in Liverpool, train the other end, I can pay for you to go, but I won't have enough for the journey myself. Uncle William wants financial assistance too, as he's got three people to pay for, and I've offered to help him out. The cost of a passage is about £6 and 10s per head and I have been advised that a clear sum of £5 should be set aside to furnish each family when they land at New York. I've only been earning 12s a week, and most of that has goes on rent and food and what other things you have felt the necessity to buy."

"Oh, George, what are you saying? Do you mean to send me over to a strange country, on such a long journey, without you by my side? Surely you cannot mean that? Ooh, you can be a right one George. I'd like to batter you black and blue." And she made a step towards him with her arm in the air. George ducked, but knew she wouldn't hit him. Instead, he grabbed hold of her and kissed her gently.

When they had parted from each other's arms, George tried to explain. "Well, no... and then again, yes."

"Come on, George, tell me.... will I be travelling without you?"

"Well, I've been thinking it over and the only conclusion I can come to is that you travel on the ship with Uncle William and his family, whilst I try to work my passage on board another ship."

"But you've got no knowledge of seamanship! Have you ever been to sea? I'll answer that for you...No! So, who is going to take you on? I am angry George, and none of your kisses will put that right. You can be a real so-and-so at times, you."

"I will find something, do not fear. I may even get there before you. They are always crying out for people to man the boats, fishing boats, whaling boats, whatever."

Eliza then started to cry. George tried to put his arm around her, only for it to be flung back.

"I will find something, you see, Eliza... and you'll be safe with Uncle William and Aunt Caroline, and you will have my cousin, William, there too. He's big and strong enough to help you with your luggage."

"Oh, just get out of my sight, George. You've upset me enough. This is something we have planned so long for, to do together and, what happens, you go your way and I go mine. Fine marriage this is!"

"Oh, surely you see there is no other way, Eliza?"

Eliza was still crying. "Just go", she managed to say through her tears.

Nothing could appease her, so I went out and walked around for a bit.

Nothing had changed when I returned and I made matters worse. "You're a beautiful lady, Eliza, and I love you but, if you had not spent money on getting yourself new dresses and shoes and getting your hair done, I would have had enough money to come with you. As it happens, I have now got to work my passage."

Eliza threw a book at me, something she had been reading. I ducked and it hit the wall behind me.

"So, you want me to be a plain old Jane, like your sisters, with hair scuffed back in a bun? Well, that is not me – I like to look nice for you."

"For yourself, you mean!"

"Fine, have it your own way, but I have scrimped and scraped for the past six years since our marriage, and not a sign of a child from you..... maybe you're not the man you think you are!"

65

Well, that was enough for me, as I stood there in total shock. I finally managed to say, "Did you want to have young babies dragging at your skirts on the voyage, frightened they'd fall overboard? No, I dare say you didn't – that is why you have kept yourself away from me these past years. Anyway, that is the way it's going to be. Here is your ticket for the ship," which I placed on the table. "Uncle William will be in contact to tell you where to meet him. There's enough money too, for your railway fares and even accommodation, as required. I will see you in Philadelphia and here is the address where my family is staying." I slammed that down on the table too.

"I am going to pack and I will make my way, as best I can to Liverpool and on to Philadelphia. I hope to see you there."

GEORGE GUNN ARRIVES

CHAPTER 7

RMS Persia

"George, how lovely to see you at last." This was basically echoed throughout the room as I stepped over the threshold. All stepped up to hug me or shake my hand. George was handsome, with a moustache that really suited him.

The main living room had been turned back into a proper living room with no sign of the mattresses.

"How was your journey?" "Where is Eliza?" "Where are Uncle William and his wife and son?" "Are you here on your own?"

All these questions being fired at me and given no chance to answer.

"I will answer your questions when I have had a time to take my coat off, sit down, and have some of mum's wonderful stew, that I can smell wafting through."

While eating the stew, mum started talking, "Oh, you should have seen us a couple of years ago, before William arrived. We just didn't have place to move, with mattresses down here, where the men slept. We were right higgledy-piggledy. But, since William's arrival, and him getting a job, meant that we could afford to rent the top floor as well, so another two rooms, and another kitchen. We are still all bunked down together, but at least we have a bit more space now. Anyway, tell us about your journey and why you seem to be here on your own, not that we're that pleased to see you, but just..... come on, what has happened?" This was echoed by the children, "Uncle George, Uncle George tell us your story."

I put down my spoon finally, and had the last bite of the bread, then started my story.

"OK, if you are all sitting comfortably, I will begin...".

I didn't want to tell them about the row with Eliza, just said that the others would be following on later and that they should be on board ship now, making the crossing.

"Well, I had not managed to save enough to take the passage, so I thought the best thing was to work my way over. I got on board one of the Cunard Line Royal Mail packet ships going from Liverpool to Boston. I boarded the Persia, an express passenger liner. It won the Blue Riband in 1856 for the fastest westbound transatlantic voyage. She is the largest ship in the world – an iron hulled paddle wheel steamship, with two sails.

She even survived hitting an iceberg in 1856, because of her iron hull. Her fastest eastbound voyage has been recorded as just 9 days, 10 hours and 22 minutes and a westbound voyage of 9 days, 16 hours, 16 minutes – a real fine ship.

"My, that is incredible, George." This was Thomas, "our journey took six long weeks."

"Well, I wagged my way on board, telling them all the experience I had had – as you know, I've never been at sea before, but I had to get a working passage.

I was put on sorting the post for America, into cities, towns and area, then I was put on stoking the boiler. Really hard, back-breaking work, a real dirty, sweaty job. You know there were two men on board, real crooks. They stole a calendar......they both got six months each!" I said, while laughing.

Everyone joined in. "Oh George, we have so missed you and your antics so much." This was mum.

"Anyway, I am here now, so as soon as the others arrive we can continue onto Utah."

Mum introduced me to Ebenezer Woodford, and little Tacy Ann, who was now walking and babbling. It all seemed nonsense to me but the others seemed to understand that she was saying she was pleased to meet me. So, I picked her up and swung her round, which produced a fit of baby giggles.

I then picked up little Tacy Ann's rattle. "Two men are hiking through the woods, when one of them cries out, 'Snake! Run!'.

His companion laughs at him and say, 'Oh relax, it's only a baby.... Did you not hear the rattle?" I said, shaking the rattle. Everyone laughed.

"Ok, George, it is lovely to see you, but settle down now." this was John.

Everyone told me their individual journey experiences, the gales, the sickness, the deaths, even the marriages. By this time I was exhausted.

The next morning, I questioned everyone about the area. What the neighbours were like, what the work was like.

William was most forthcoming.

"I do not suppose you've had much chance to have a look around at the area""

"Not really, I came straight from the railway station, down by the docks, and this place is just around the corner. It all looks a bit rough, to tell you the truth."

"It is the cheapest place mum could get when they first arrived, not having any money to spare and waiting for the men to get jobs, but we stayed here, waiting for everyone to arrive. Yes, it is a bit rough – all dockland areas are rough, but there is more to it than that. Philadelphia is a hubbub of all nationalities coming from all over the world, and all religions. There is a huge black community – not slaves, they are free men, but these free men are aiding fugitive slaves escaping from the south. They have their own African Methodist Episcopal

Church. What is strange is that quite a few of the southern plantation owners, and slave-owners to boot, have second properties here. It causes a lot of ruckus between the free blacks and these cotton plantation owners. The raw cotton is brought here to be manufactured, made up into textiles then, in turn, some of these clothes are sold back down south, for the slaves to wear!"

William continued, "Apart from the blacks, there are people immigrating from Ireland, Southern Europe, Eastern Europe and Asia, as well as Puerto Ricans from the Caribbean. You wil find there is a community of Germans too, all looking for industrial jobs, many working on the Pennsylvania Railroad, which has hired 10,000 workers from the south; others working in the US Navy Yard or the well-educated in finance, publishing and major universities."

William carried on while I listened intently. "The number of immigrants coming in was the reason we were able to get this house. The rich moved west of 7th Street, renting out their homes, converting them into tenements and boarding houses.

Small rowhouses and tenement housing have been constructed south of South Street to house the great flood of immigrants, but that is not enough and people are sleeping rough, wherever they can find shelter. The place has now become a literal pigsty with people keeping animals in pens in the narrow streets."

"I had noticed."

"Well, where there is animal muck, and human muck, there's illness and cholera and smallpox is rife. That is why we are so pleased you have finally got here and, as soon Eliza, William and his family arrive, we can get out."

John added to the conversation, "As William said, there is out and out war sometimes. The native Philadelphians are up in arms against the number of immigrants coming in, and I do not see as I blame them. If I were in their shoes, I would feel the same. There is competition for jobs and the Philadelphians resent newcomers and their various religions and ethnicity. We've even been pelted with rubbish in the streets, and sworn at. We've seen anti-Catholic, anti-Irish demonstrations and violence towards them as well as violence directed towards the black communities. I've even heard of the burning down of their churches in the past. In fact, from what I hear, the Quakers and other abolitionists are offering safe houses associated with what they call the 'Underground Railroad' and several anti-slavery societies have been formed to try to counteract the working class and ethnic whites."

"Yes," cut in Thomas, "I think we are not far from an all-out war. It is stalemate at the moment, following the 1854 Act of Consolidation, that brought more control over the whole state of Pennsylvania, but something is going to happen soon, I can feel it – it is like an electric charge in the air. There had even been gangs, in the past, so I have been told, calling themselves the likes of the 'Moyamensing Killers' and the 'Blood Tubs', who controlled various neighbourhoods."

"Well, it's a good job I turned up when I did, and the more reason to be on our way, and quickly." I replied.

THE UNDERWRITER

CHAPTER 8

The Underwriter was captained by Captain Roberts, a very fine gentleman. There were five hundred and ninety four Mormons on board. We were in a second class cabin. We went on board. It was a drizzly day. We are William Brazier, brother to Ann Brazier Gunn, his wife, Caroline, their 21-year-old son, William and myself, George Gunn's wife, Eliza Rogers Gunn. George's Uncle William was 54 and had been a carpenter, which I supposed this would come in handy in our new homestead. He was a kindly-looking guy, with an unkempt, sandy beard. His wife, Caroline was 49, and it was beginning to show, but she looked after herself well. Her hair was still blonde, set into drooping curls, showing at the front of her bonnet, as was the fashion about ten years ago. Their son, William, although 21, was, I suppose, to be kind, young for his age. He still acted as though he were about 14. I was 31, with dark, curly hair. I thought myself quite good looking and considered myself fashionable, although, of course, George hadn't let me buy anything nice in a while. Well, I knew we had to save for this trip, but I didn't like to look dowdy. It just was not me!

Anyway, here we were, finally on the ship, although George, the blighter, had left me to travel with his aunt and uncle and, of all the things, blaming me for spending too much – I was only trying to look nice for him. It was so boring being with them and I would wander off here and there, talking to other people.

I remember, on 27th there was a man fell overboard, before we had set sail, but he was not drowned although he had hurt himself a little in the fall.

After starting out fine, by 6th May we had a rough cold day and rough night. One of the main sails blew to pieces. I could scarcely walk about as the ship rocked so very much. People were falling down and spilling their soup and potatoes and cakes and pies and the tin bottles and boxes were rolling about. It was mayhem with men and women sliding under the berths and crushing into the berths and boxes and hurting themselves.

There was the usual sea-sickness that was to be expected. I was feeling sick and went to bed and did not get up 'til the next morning. Then things picked up and the weather turned out fine until 17th – that was that day a child died. She was only about 4 months old and got thrown overboard at 7pm. A Swiss woman died the next night. She was thrown overboard too. She must have been in her mid-50s.

Food had been enough until we were about a week away from landing. Then it was rationed. Now we were just a day or two from New York and I was beginning to feel the pangs of hunger. All our extra rations we had brought with us were now used up.

I was listening to Uncle William and Aunt Caroline chattering. I did not know where young William was, probably amusing himself somewhere.

Well, I am glad we are nearly there." This was Uncle William, "Yes, I am feeling quite hungry. There does not seem to be much on board. People are queuing up for any scraps they can get." This was Aunt Caroline

"It will be good to have my feet on solid ground again." Uncle William said.

"Oh, it was not as bad as I expected. I have heard so many stories of people being ill, and dying, that I was prepared for the worst. At least we have made it, all in one piece." This was his wife, Aunt Caroline.

"It was a strange feeling passing Ireland, and out to the vast ocean." Uncle William added, "Quite frightening really, knowing that there were so many fathoms of water beneath us and just our little ship bobbing up and down in the waves, like a leaf in a vast lake. Then we saw an island, near Belfast. There were loads of little birds floating on the water – I did not know what they were but they resembled Bore hens."

"Funny enough, have you heard the accents of people around here? They nearly all seem to be Irish." This was Caroline.

"Quite, there has been a multitude of Irish emigrating, the most actually staying in New York."

Young William returned and continued his father's recollections of the voyage, "Yes, apart from Ireland, we could see the hills of Scotland, the very high ones anyway, covered with snow. Of course, then we had the gales, and had to go down below, as we were getting soaked."

"Quite a few people were seasick, but then the sun came out." This was Caroline.

"Yes, I had a fall in the night," the father said, "and bruised my nose and forehead. It still aches a bit."

"I know, poor thing, but you'll be as right as rain soon." Caroline said, giving William a quick peck on the nose, to soothe him.

"Then I had another fall, and bruised my knee."

Young William then piped up, "I would like to bet you do not get a kiss on your knee, father!"

"That is enough of your cheek, young sir, but yes, most definitely you would win that bet, William." Was the father's reply.

"It was a bit choppy though, father, the wind was so strong it tore the sails to rags and overturned everything in the cooking galley while you were there."

"Yes my lad, but I did manage to save our dinner of rice, but was obliged to hold onto the post of the door while I ate mine."

"I wish we had that dinner now." Caroline said.

"What about that day when I had been asked to help you serve out stores and provisions for everyone. The sea came up rough in the night and everything got swamped with water?" Young William commented.

"Yes, son, I do not really care to remember that, I had a job to keep my hat on but went down to our berth and found our cans untied, bobbing up and down in water. I got crushed in the berth, trying to pick the cans up, then the luggage fell down on me, right on top of my head."

"Oh, you have been in the wars, this journey, dear."

"Does father get a kiss on his head now, haha?"

"He has already had one, and less of your impudence, young man."

I was bored of this conversation and wandered away. I could still hear them speaking though, "Now, where is that Eliza going to again, she is always wandering off?"

"Oh, let her be, she obviously does not want to be stuck with us old fuddy-duddies, and young William."

I returned after a while. I was looking around to see if anyone had any spare food and had got talking to a nice young man and his family, who I had befriended on the journey, but they were out of food too. "Where did you get to, Eliza?" Caroline interjected

"Oh, nowhere much. Just talking to someone I met on the ship. He's going to Philadelphia too, so I thought we could all meet up and exchange experiences aboard the ship."

"Does he know where we will be staying?" this was the father.

"No, but he has told me where he will be staying."

"Well, it would be nice to exchange stories. Is he here with his family?"

"Oh, I believe he has come over with his brothers and sisters. I have met some of them, people around my age and we have lots in common."

I started walking around again and was approached by the Chief Officer, looking very handsome and smart in his uniform. He introduced himself, and I to him.

"Excuse me for asking, sir, but do you know where I can possibly get anything to eat? I have not had a bite to eat since yesterday, not even a scrap, and my stomach is growling and I am beginning to feel a bit faint."

"I do happen to have a meat pie in my cabin, which you could share with me, Eliza, if you so wish."

"That would be wonderful, sir. You are my saviour."

"Then follow me." He led me to his cabin and indeed he had a meat pie with gravy, which I relished, and he poured me a glass of red wine.

"Now Eliza, will you give me for kiss as a favour for your meal?"

"Oh, sir, I could not. I am married and could not deceive my husband. I thank you for the meal, but I cannot agree."

"Just a kiss, Eliza. Your husband cannot object to that, surely? Where is your husband anyway? I did not see you with anyone."

"I am planning to meet him in Philadelphia. He went on ahead."

"And leaving his lovely young wife unattended. Shame on him."

"I must go now, sir, and thank you again for the meal." I said and got up to go.

Just then the Chief Officer jumped up and barred my way to the door. He grabbed me and kissed me.

"There, you've had your kiss, sir, now please let me go."

"Let a beauty like you escape. No dear, you are going nowhere, yet."

He was pushing me against the wall of the cabin. I let out a scream. He put his hand over my mouth and with his other hand deftly undid his buttons to expose himself at high mast.

Then he pushed me towards his narrow bed, skilfully kicked my feet from under me whilst pushing my shoulders so I fell flat on the bed. He then raised my skirts to reveal my naked body, fell on top of me while, like a man expert at this task, parting my legs with his knees. I started to scream again, that is when he grabbed a glove that was to hand, and stuffed it in my mouth. I began pounding with my fists against his head and body, but he slapped me violently around my face, then pinned my arms down with his elbows. He then penetrated me, and commenced systematically to course in and out of me, until, with a sigh, he was sated.

He dressed himself again. "Right, you can go now. If you are feeling hungry for any more of the same, you know where you can find me." and gave me a shove towards the door.

I ran, as fast as I could, through the crowd of people on deck, not seeing properly through my tears, and eventually found the rest of the family.

"My dear Eliza, what has happened to you? Your dress is torn and your hair is out of your bonnet."

"I …..have been r..raped - taken bodily." I managed to utter through my tears."

"My dear, come and sit down. Who was it, I'll have his guts for garters." Uncle William pronounced, waving his hands like fists in the air."

"The.. Chief ..Officer." I stammered.

Uncle William ran to his office and confronted the man.

"Yes, Mrs Gunn was here, we had a nice lunch together. I was feeling sorry for her, but I did not molest her, as you say. I did not even touch her and we left on pleasant terms."

"You rogue. I'll see the Captain and see what he has to say." And Uncle William stormed off. He knew he would not stand a chance in a fight against a fit, young sailor, not at his age.

"I will certainly look into this, Mr Gunn." was the Captain's response. "This is indeed a very damning report on a member of my crew. Leave it with me and I will investigate your claim."

Uncle William came back to the family. "I do not think we are going to get anywhere. I cannot see the Captain reporting on his Chief Officer. They will close ranks."

Aunt Caroline had adjusted my attire but I was still shaking uncontrollably. I had bruises developing, my arms and legs hurt, and my face had a nasty-looking red weal. "D..o no t tell George what happened, Aunt Caroline. I could not possibly bear him knowing my shame."

"But he should know, what if you are found to be in the family way, what then?"

"I suppose he will have to know then. Oh George, you bugger. This is all your fault." I said under my breath. "If you had not left me to do this journey without you, this would not have happened." and I burst into tears again.

....

81

We arrived at New York on the first day of May. When we reached New York we landed at the old Castle Garden of lower Manhattan. This was the receiving station to accommodate mass immigration. Alien women married to US citizens became US citizens by law. We then went to the harbour master and reported the incident.

"We have received frequent complaints made by female emigrants arriving in New York of ill-treatment and abuse from the captains and other officers, the New York Commissioners of Emigration are in the process of carrying out an investigation into the treatment of passengers on board ships bringing immigrants from Europe to the United States. We regret to say that, after reaching the high seas, the captain, or a high-ranking member of his crew, frequently selects some unprotected female from among the passengers, induces her to visit his cabin, and when there, abusing his authority as commander, partly by threats, and partly by promises of marriage, accomplishes her ruin, and retains her in his quarters for the rest of the voyage, for the indulgence of his vicious passions and the purposes of prostitution; other officers of the ship often imitate the example of their superior, and when the poor friendless woman, thus seduced, arrives at this port, they are thrust upon shore and abandoned to their fate. You are lucky, Mrs Gunn, that you had your family with you."

We gave him our address in Philadelphia, where he said he would contact us if there was any resolve to our complaint. We had to leave it at that.

Then the train arrived and we loaded our baggage on board. The train's whistle blew and we were soon all steaming off for Philadelphia, with the smoke from the funnel trailing alongside, necessitating us having to close the window. We had the option of two lines running between Philadelphia and New York – the New Jersey Rail Road & Transportation Company and the Camden & Amboy Railroad. We were on the former.

On arriving at Philadelphia station, we were greeted by a commotion of people moving luggage, shouts and hollers.

There was a man hauling a large trolley of cases and luggage. "I will ask this porter for directions." And Uncle William stepped forward to get his attention.

"Alright, he was quite helpful and gave me directions but he said, he would come back for us and our luggage and would take us there, as it is not far, for payment, naturally."

"Yes, I suppose we need assistance, we cannot lug all this ourselves." Caroline said. "I have really had enough, and I am tired and dirty. I want to get away from this filthy place, and the atrocious smells."

She was right, the smell was quite horrendous, a rotting cabbage smell mingled with fish and something else quite obnoxious.

We didn't have to go far, just off the first row of tall, narrow terraced houses. These were mainly shops with awnings, displaying wares for sale. The road was a dirt road, with horses and carts traversing hither and thither.

Behind this row of shops we eventually came to where the family were staying. The porter told us that these were called rowhouses, typical of Philadelphia. They were brick houses, narrow in structure, having anything from two to four storeys, being attached on both sides to neighbouring homes, all set out in blocks.

"They remind me of the terraced houses back home," young William commented, " but narrower and taller, with wider front doors and steps up to them – and Georgian windows, with little squares of glass panes, all symmetrical with the next building."

"Oh, they may look fine, William," I commented, "but this street is as narrow as the houses and have you seen we've been passing little alleyways that seem to be dumping area for garbage. The smell coming from them is horrific, something like a farm. I am beginning to get nauseous. It's worse than at the station. Look, there is a pig sticking it's snout out of a cage of sorts. What have we come to, some sort of zoo? This is atrocious – how can the family live next to such squalor?"

84

I obviously was not in a good mood when we stepped over the threshold and basically accepted pecks on the cheek from the family, but didn't return the compliment.

George greeted me with a hug, "I am glad you finally made it Eliza, so good to see you again, safe and sound. I trust your journey went as well as could be expected, although the stories I have been hearing from the others, would make your toes curl."

"They haven't stopped curling, George, ever since I started this detestable journey."

"But, darling, you are safe now. Here, sit down. Mum will make you all some tea and something to eat, then I am sure you will feel better."

"I feel dirty, George. I am dirty and stained, and am so travel-weary that I could lie down and not wake up again, and I have a terrific headache."

"You will feel better after a good night's rest, my love. We've all had to undertake this horrendous journey, at some point, starting with most of my family coming over in 1855.

After a good wash, in a tin bath in the downstairs kitchen, and a few hours' sleep, I was feeling a bit more like myself. I had sunk down on the mattress offered and gone into a fitful sleep. In my mind I was still on the ship, with people crowding in on me, no privacy, with the ship tossing and turning - people being sick around me, and the gross smells pervading the ship. This plus the awful rape, the horror of which I could not shake off. What if I were pregnant? This was mixed in with the awful pandemonium and stink of Philadelphia station and the alleyways nearby filled with putrefying garbage and animal excrement. I woke up crying. I found George lying next to me and woke him.

"Oh, George, I am not cut out for this. It's more than a person can take." Looking round and standing up, I let out a stifled scream, "George, is there no privacy here either..... there are others sleeping in the same room. We are crowded in with people, it is like being back on the ship again. Where is our lovely house we had? No, I cannot live here, George. I have to get out." and I ran downstairs. George got up and followed me.

"Eliza, there's nowhere else to go and we are leaving here imminently, on our way to Utah, where I promise you will have a lovely home again."

Everyone else downstairs was looking on, astonished, at me, and my distressed state. I could see them thinking that I'd lost my mind. They couldn't understand.

"You and your promises, George, they are not worth a fig." I looked round at the boxes piled high and the mattresses. "You are all like those pigs, living in a pigsty, nose to nose, snuffling around for food with the other swine."

That was enough for Ann, "Now you listen, girl, we will have none of that talk. We are good, honest people, going about our lives in the best way we can, and if you do not like it, then you can find somewhere else."

"Mum, you cannot tell Eliza to leave." George begged, "She is just upset. She will calm down and apologise, will you not Eliza?" directing his gaze me.

"Oh..., can you not see that I am frightened, George. I have this horrible premonition, that I will not survive the journey to Utah. I have heard all these horrible stories of people dying of thirst and starvation, and having to walk a lot of the way. I am not up to it George. I am sorry – I have thought it through. I have got friends I made on the ship and I am going to stay with them. I am going to pack my things up. I beg you not to follow me...... I will apply for a divorce." I said, through her tears, "I may go back to England – I am missing my friends and home.... and I still have a headache." I sat down, heavily, with my head in my hands.

"I am sorry, mum, Eliza has always been highly strung, but she has never been like this. I should never have made her come – and she is right, the journey would probably kill her..... I will let her go to these new-found friends. It seems to be what she wants. Maybe these so-called friends can persuade her to travel on, or help her out with her ticket back."

"Oh, I do not know George," Ann intervened, "I can see that Eliza is not well. No-one's at their best when they are not well. I will make her a Camomile tea - that should help her headache."

Mum prepared the tea. "Eliza dear, drink this, it should help. We will talk about how you feel and see if we can calm your fears. We can all see you are very distressed. We want you to come with us, and we will keep you safe. We can all make good homes when we get there and you can have nice things around you once more. Once you have rested a bit more, and the headache has gone, you will feel more yourself and we can tell you the plans for our onward travel to Utah."

"Yes, love, it is no good staying here, "George said, "As you said, it is not a nice place to live, but there is nothing back home for you and I doubt if your friends here will pay for your ticket back, so cheer up, we'll soon be out of here, and I want you by my side. We are going to make a good place, and a new life, you and me, together."

I gave a weak smile as drank the tea. They could, obviously, see I was not happy and my brain was twirling with all sorts of thoughts. I said nothing, for the moment.

JOHN SMITH COMPANY (1860)

CHAPTER 9

Getting all our things together in carts, we travelled, as a family, from Philadelphia to start our journey west. We travelled as far as the Missouri River, where we joined the Captain John Smith Company at Florence, Nebraska. Here we remained for five weeks getting waggons and supplies ready for the journey across the plains. We were staying in tents and mud huts.

Brigham Young

There was a mill, that Brigham Young had supervised the construction of, as this was needed to grind corn, wheat and rye to create cornmeal and flour products. Cabins had also been built, known as Kimball Row. These consisted of thirteen adjacent cabins, for the homes of the church leaders Heber C Kimball and Newel K Whitney at either end. Trade was conducted with the American Indians at trading settlements in northern Missouri and Iowa, exchanging household goods and small amounts of cash for foodstuffs, such as hogs, grain and vegetables, and supplies for the emigration effort. Young people were also producing handcrafted items such as willow baskets and washboards for sale, which our family participated in. Even with this trade, the diet in the camp was mainly corn bread, salt bacon and a little milk, with occasional fresh game or domestic meat.

I, Emma Baker Gunn, the wife of William, (George's older brother) had helped, along with everyone else to make preparations for the journey, including making waggon coverings. The men all helped getting the supplies on the waggons and water barrels, as well as our few belongings.

4 TH WAGON TRAIN RECORD
IMMIGRATION OF 1860

J H 31 December 1860 Supplement Film #1,259,746

Emigration of 1860 (4th Wagon Train)						pg. .41,42
Names	Age	Wagons	Yokes of Oxen	Bread Stuffs	Cows	
George Gunn	31	1	2	700	1	
Elisa "	29					
William Brazier	52					
Caroline Brazier	49					
Charles "	17					
Mary Ann Adey	27					
Ann Gunn	64					
Benjamin Gunn	19					
John "	34	1	1 1/2	550	1	
Caroline "	27					
John W. "	4					
Louisa B. "	2					
Priscilla "	1/4					
Thomas "	29					
Anne "	27					
Frederic "	4					
Emilie "	2					
Amelia Jane "	1 mo.					
William Gunn	38	1	1/2	385	1	
Emma "	40					
William "	17					
Louisa "	15					
Fanny "	10					
Betsy "	8					
Betsy Judd	30					

91

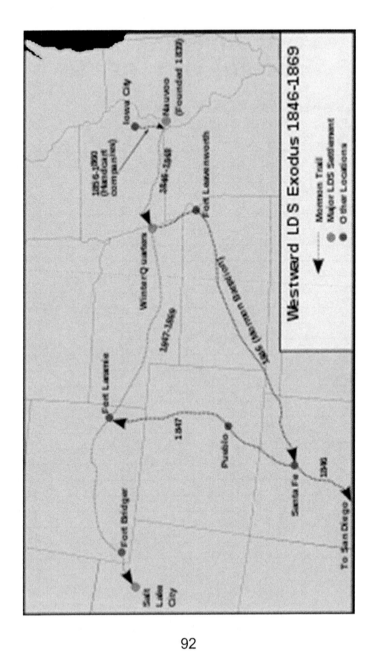

We met a trapper who told us that, in the area of Utah Lake, there was fishing, wild fruit, timber and good grazing. The local Indians raised good crops, including corn and pumpkins, but that there was ever-present danger of frost. So, we were mostly pleased about that, although the idea of frost meant the possibility of our future crops rotting, so we'd have to think over what crops we could possibly grow. Still, that was way ahead. We had to get there first.

George had one waggon, 2 yokes of oxen, 700 bread stuffs and one cow. His brother John, had one waggon, 1 ½ yokes of oxen, 550 bread stuffs and one cow. William (George's older brother) had one waggon, ½ yoke of oxen 385 bread stuffs and one cow. In those three waggons, twenty four of the family left Florence on 15 June 1860 in the fourth waggon train of the year, led by the presiding Patriarch of the Church, Captain John Smith, headed towards Salt Lake City. There were a total of 39 waggons and 359 people in the waggon train.

Carried in other waggons were arms and ammunition, 15lb of iron, pulleys and ropes, fishing gear, farming and mechanical equipment, cooking equipment and at least 1000lb of flour plus assorted other foodstuffs.

Captain Smith and his crew were inspecting the waggons to make sure they weren't overweight. He told us a story of one group of pioneers he had coming across, "This particular waggon train had overestimated the number of goods they could haul on a long journey. As the oxen weakened under the strain, the waggons had to be lightened by discarding prized possessions, including, would you believe, book collections, family china and furniture. Just east of the Rocky Mountains, I believe the family name was Kimball – yes that was right – well, they dug a large hole, wrapped their piano –

yes, they had actually bought a piano, of all things, well they wrapped it in buffalo skins and carefully buried it. An ox team retrieved the instrument the following spring and transported it to Salt Lake City."

We all stood, mouths agape at this – "Of all the silly sausages" William stammered out, "Did they have no sense?"

"And the poor oxen." My daughter Fanny (15) commented.

Most of the travellers were walking, as the waggons were loaded up plus there were many just pulling their belongings in hand carts, as they had not been able to afford a waggon. So, it looked like we would be walking all the way to Utah, through the prairies and over the mountains. I really didn't see us all making it, I mean, the most any of us had ever walked was into the nearest town and back again – possibly 6 miles there and 6 miles back.

"Oh, William, how are we going to survive, walking this great distance – and the children? I never, in my wildest dreams, thought we would all be walking. I thought we would be in the waggon – that is what we paid all that money for. They expect us to walk 10 to 14 miles a day. Yes, I could do one day, but the next day I would have to rest up as my legs would have turned to jelly."

"I do not know, Emma, but there is no room in the waggon. You will have to come up here with me on the bench, or take turns with the children when they get tired."

I was feeling miserable but the others in the team – 39 waggons and the hundreds of walkers, were keeping their spirits up, singing, mainly hymns, to help them on their march, so I walked with the children beside our waggon – trying to keep them occupied with 'I spy' games and telling stories as we went.

At the close of the day, we would join in song and prayer for the goodness of the Lord unto us.

Several times we travelled with or near Captain Patterson's Company and Captain Sharp's train. On 5th August, the English and Scandinavians from Captain Sharp's train enjoyed dancing.

On 10th August, we stopped for a heavy rain storm, with lightening, that struck the ground near some of the waggons. It hit so close it shook the people and the animals.

Eliza was acting strangely during this storm. She had been complaining of her headaches throughout the journey. With the lightening coming down she suddenly started screaming a barrage of swear words, some of which I had only heard mention of spoken by the roughest of vagrants. We thought she had gone mad and people were looking on, watching her in amazement and mothers were taking their children as far away as possible. George tried to comfort her but she was having nothing of it and he ended up having to shake her physically, telling her to pull herself together.

"What's got into her?" I said.

"No idea, Emma. She's had these headaches for a while now, all I can think is that the noise of the thunder and lightning is making them worse."

"But, I have never heard language like it in all my days."

"True, and I am not sure what to do about her. Nothing we have given her for headaches seems to work. It's as though she is possessed."

We had travelled quite a distance when William suddenly gave a loud holler and the waggon stopped. I had been walking a bit to the rear of our waggon and went up to investigate. . "One of our oxen has died, Emma". William shouted out, looking quite perplexed and worried. "What are we going to do, we cannot possibly continue just with one ox?"

"I will ask around, William, if anyone can spare an ox." We were all crestfallen – stopped in our tracks before we had gone any great distance.

Then little Lois (aged 7) had the bright idea of putting our milk cow in the yoke to help pull the cart from then on. Well, we all thought that this would be too much for the little cow and it would not be able to take the strain, but as no-one was coming forward with a spare ox, so the little cow was put in the yoke. As it happens, the little cow did her part and managed to pull the load the whole journey through.

At night we had to sleep under the waggons or wherever we could find a place. The lucky ones grabbed a place by the log fires that had been lit in the evening. I was really tired now. I'd had my second rush of energy and this had depleted, so as soon as I lay my head down, I was asleep.

The walk continued and it was getting hotter each day. I had been sweating and my eyes and mouth were dry. I woke up one morning, and I just couldn't stand. My legs felt numb and swollen. I tried to get to my knees but could not get any further, even with the children trying to pull me up. My legs hurt and seemed to weigh heavy. William began rubbing my legs with liniment, which helped a bit, as I could feel the heat.

"Your eyes are swollen too, Emma and it looks like you have some sort of rash, a sort of butterfly shape over your nose and cheeks."

"Oh, lovely, I must be a sight! Come to think of it," running my tongue around my mouth, "the inside of my mouth has really sore lumps too and my glands are swollen. Oh William, what have I got? Is it catching?"

William asked around the camp for anyone with doctoring skills, but no-one had seen anything like it and were a bit scared to come too close. Some offered pain-killing drinks and I was advised just to rest and stay out of the sun, if possible.

So, William got busy re-arranging the waggon to find a space where I could sit. I managed to stumble to the waggon, and William lifted me in and wrapped a blanket around me.

We stopped at a few forts, Guittard's Station Swales and Fort Kearney, where we could rest up and buy goods we needed – those that had money to pay for them! Guittard's Station had just been opened as a Pony Express station and was a 12-room, two-storey lodge to accommodate people passing through – basically a clump of board houses on the far side of a shady, well-wooded creek – the Vermillion, a tributary of the Big Blue River. It had two stables with over 20 horses where riders could exchange their horses for fresh mounts. We heard that Fort Kearney had been purchased from the Pawnee Indians for $2000 in goods.

We came to a swampy place in the road and other waggons had made deep ruts in the trail. Benjamin realised that the oxen pulling their waggon were small and it was late in the day. He asked another waggon driver if he would help them get out of the rut, but, so much for brotherly love, the man refused. So Benjamin unhitched the oxen and let them feed on the grass while he dug in front of the waggon wheels. After they had rested and fed for a while he hitched them up and managed, thankfully, to get the waggon out of the swamp.

They had not travelled very far when they came to the other waggon that had passed them. This waggon was caught in the swamp as they had been. Benjamin said, "Brother, I will pull across and bring my team to give you a lift out." The other man had tears in his eyes, having refused help to Benjamin before. Benjamin hitched his team in front of the other man's and they were soon out of the mud. From that time on, they were the best of pals, looking out for each other, making sure they were safe.

The company was unmolested for several days until one dark, cold night when the tired, weary travellers were preparing to camp. Our Captain rode ahead but soon returned giving the startling command for us to yoke our oxen immediately and move on as there were Indians not far away. The damp, cold air was piercing to our half-protected bodies. William wrapped Lois and her sister Elizabeth in blankets as the damp, cold air was piercing their little frocks. They plodded along beside the wheel of the waggon in which I was propped up against the luggage. I was too weak to walk and there was no room in the waggon for the children so, they had to walk. In the bustle and confusion of moving camp, somehow or other the oxen became frightened of something and, suddenly, I found myself lurching forward as all the oxen, with waggons in tail, started stampeding. I heard a scream – it sounded like Lois. I was shouting out to William but he was desperately trying to bring the oxen to a halt. When everyone finally got their oxen under control, William jumped off and ran back. He found Lois lying on the ground, holding her arm and screaming. "I was knocked down, dad." She managed to splutter out through her sobs. "The wheel of the waggon caught me and I was knocked down. It hurts dad, just here." And she pointed with her other arm to her collar bone.

"Looks like your collar bone is broken, lovely. Hold on and I'll get someone to help." William managed to get a kind lady from the company, who was very efficient as a nurse. She set the broken bone as best she could and then our band of enduring folk moved onward again. William took little Lois up in the driving seat with him but the rocking of the waggon jolted her arm, as it rolled over the uneven ground, so my brave Lois said she'd prefer to walk.

We suffered many hardships and heartaches. Sometimes the children and the older people were given rides on the waggons for a short time, but no-one complained, even though their feet were blistered and their bodies wracked with pain. They all kept in good spirits. The general feeling was that it was like an adventure and they were going to their promised land.

Passing through the Great Plains, a wide open area, with not a tree in sight for hundreds of miles, we could see a party approaching us, slowly and tentatively. "We've got company - Indians", people were whispering, frightened to call out but not knowing what to do and if we were in danger. We were all on tenterhooks as to what to expect. Were they going to attack us? But, as they came closer, they seemed a woe-begotten group with one horse between them and the others, mainly women and children, on foot. One approached and went down on his knees, holding out his hands, as if begging.

"They want food", George shouted out to the others, "Give them something. They are not going to attack us." At this, some of the women started going through their provisions, to see what they thought they could spare and a few went forward and placed these items on the ground before them. They stepped back and the items were snatched up and handed to the rest of the group, who began to eat, as if they were starving. We waited a while. They didn't go, but then the leader approached. He seemed friendly, smiling. He sat down in the earth and beckoned people from the train to sit down with him. We and the others all watched, bewildered as Captain Scott and a few of his crew sat down with them.

Anyway, after that, we had got new friends, and we learnt a few things from them, such as what began to be known as "Buffalo chips". The Indians had learned to make the best of what resources they had, including using these buffalo chips to make a slow smouldering fire, as there were no trees for firewood. This fire was well suited for baking bread in skillets. We had travelled some hundreds of miles without scarcely seeing such a thing as a tree or a stick of wood, so it had been difficult to get fuel to make fires for cooking and we had been using what bits of brush we could find. These buffalo chips were just the job and we'd never thought of using them to make a fire. We had seen buffalo on the plains and we had been following their tracks as a guide on our trek – along with the tracks of previous waggon trains.

The funny thing was, and I don't know if you have guessed, but these buffalo chips were the droppings from the buffalo, that had hardened in the sun. Some of the boys called them 'chewed grass', but you've got to be very careful in examining the under parts or there might find them not as hard as you would wish.

Elizabeth (now 9), was helping me one evening, as I really was not up to doing much, and she decided to gather some of these chips, even though she knew what they were and was rather loathsome of doing the task. She was not very far from camp, and had turned to look back at the camp to see if anyone was looking in her direction.   If they had seen what had happened. She started shaking her hands. We all had the horrible thought that she had been bitten by a rattle snake.   As it turned out, she had turned over a very large chip and had found it soft on the reverse and had got some of this muck on her fingers. She started shaking her hands to get it off, but it wouldn't budge. Of course, we all had a laugh about that but poor Elizabeth was not amused and stomped off to find a stream to wash her hands. She didn't forgive us for a long time for laughing at her. Oh well, at least she would know what to expect next time.

So, it was not all trudge and drudge on the trial. Apart from the singing and merriment when we camped every evening, there was one bit of mischief, on a Saturday in August. As people woke up in the morning, a lot of hilarity broke out as people looked at each other. It seemed a couple of the lads from another camp had paid us a visit and besmeared some of our faces with tar and waggon grease. "Oh well", I said, "it might improve their complexions!" and laughed.

Some of the men had brought rifles with them, thinking them useful if they saw any game that could be cooked, although none of them knew how to fire them, not having used them back in Great Britain. So, a few of them would practice, setting up tin cans on rocks.

One of the men, Henry Howell, one night, being on guard and it being nearly morning, saw something dodging around the waggons. Another man, on guard with him, Charles Lamb, thought it was a woodcock. Henry was going to shoot it but Charles said, "Don't you will alarm the camp. Don't shoot." So, taking heed, Henry picked up something to club it with and chased it a considerable distance from the camp where he killed it. Charles went running up, calling out, "'Tis a skunk!" but it was too late. The mischief was done and Henry was smothered with this awful stench. In chasing it Henry said later that he had noticed a smoky smell and thought it was some ember from a camp fire. He'd not come across a skunk before.

"Oh, phew, what a stink!" Charles said, smartly back-stepping from Henry. Poor Henry had to change all of his clothes – and even had to throw his shoes away as he'd kicked the skunk before despatching it. "I cannot afford to throw my clothes away" he moaned, so bundled them up and washed them in the river. The fact of the matter was that, even changing his clothes and washing, the smell still lingered. His wife told him not to come anywhere near her and he had to eat his breakfast at some distance from the camp. What was worse was that the stink was making poor Henry feel quite nauseous, but a whiskey from his wife helped a little.

When we were getting ready to start out again, Henry took the clothes that had been steeping in the river and tied them under the waggon. When we had travelled a couple of miles, the sun became warm and the bundle started to steam and the putrid skunk odour started wafting around again, to everyone's disgust. It took some nights of taking the bundle and rinsing it

102

off in the river, along with himself, before he and the clothes got a semblance of normality again.

Talking of guns, something else tragic was to befall our family. John Adey, Mary Ann's husband, who was known to be a bit clumsy, accidentally shot himself in the right arm. We were about 60 miles east of Ash Hollow, south of McConaughy Lake. He was drawing his loaded gun from the waggon, when something caught the trigger and the full shot entered his right arm above the elbow. Of course, Mum, Ann, and Caroline rushed to his assistance bathing and bandaging his arm. It was in a right state as the bullet went in at such close range, but had passed through the arm, leaving a gaping hole at the back. They were calling out for Mary Ann, John's wife, as she was nowhere to be seen. It seems she had fallen back with the waggons to the rear of the train. She knew nothing of the accident until she read a message, that had been written on buffalo bones by the roadside, then came running. John said he was alright and everyone thought he would recover in time, but he then started to get a fever. Room was made in their waggon, having to throw a few things out and just leave them on the trail. Mary Ann and Caroline and mum took it in turns to sit with him, trying to keep his fever down with cold water compresses, but there was nothing else we could do for him and, unfortunately, eight days after the accident, he expired. Mary Ann was naturally bereft and we all did what we could to comfort her. Prayers were said over John's body, and a grave was dug where we were. We didn't even have wood to make a wooden cross, so make a pile of stones over the grave. We'd seen such piles of stones on our journey, realising that other people on this same trek, in previous years, had also died.

Eliza was playing up again. She'd made some cakes with the brown wheat flour and they'd turned out as hard as iron.

"I feel absolutely useless," she complained. "I cannot even cook here properly, and my cakes are normally so good. You have had them yourself, George, many a time, but these are just fit for the oxen to eat." At that, she got the cakes and started throwing them.

"Look, they are not even breaking when they land!" Then a tirade of swear words followed. "They are not fit for xxxxx" and so on.

"Eliza, stop that," George shouted. "You are causing a commotion, everyone is looking at you."

"I will not xxxx stop, you xxxx xxxx. Bring me out here in the waste of a land, would you. You're just a good for nothing, waste of space. What have you ever been xxxx good at, apart from making my life a xxxx misery?"

She was obviously hysterical so George slapped her a couple of times around the face.

All the family had gathered round. "I do not know what to do with her." George bleated. "She's out of control. Why does she hate me so much, I mean, everyone's in the same boat here, having the same hardships?"

Aunt Caroline opened her mouth as if she were going to say something, but then changed her mind. Obviously, it had been some time now and Eliza was not pregnant by the cad on board the ship. She had promised Eliza not to tell George what had happened.

"I think she needs a doctor," Aunt Caroline finally whispered.

104

Eliza by now had calmed down and was acting as if nothing had happened, ignoring the whispered remarks.

"You children," this was mum, Ann, "If I hear any of you repeating any of these bad words your Aunt Eliza has uttered, you'll get a good hiding – do you understand? I am not joking, and there is nothing to laugh about" this was said after the little ones started sniggering. "Your aunt Eliza is not well and she does not know what she is saying. You would not want anyone laughing at you if you were ill, now would you? I am not too old to give you all a good tanning. So, be good children and mind your Ps and Qs, otherwise you'll feel my hand, now run along."

Little Elizabeth, Lois and Fanny looked close to tears now. They had never been told off by their grandmother, who had always been so nice to them. Ann looked at them standing there, sort of rocking from side to side, with their thumbs in their mouths, not knowing whether to run or stay. "Oh little'uns," Ann said, as she'd calmed down seeing their little sad faces, "Just be good and do what I said and you'll come to no harm. Now run along."

"When we get to Utah, get a doctor to have a look at her." Uncle William commented to George.

"I will, Uncle William, but that is a long way away."

"We'll just have to keep an eye on her."

We had crossed the south branch of the River Platte and heading towards the North Platt at Ash Hollow. After many miles following above the flat river bottom, we met our first big

105

trail, getting down from the table land into the river bottom. The trail wound around the top of the bluff out to the point of the hill. We'd had a hard time getting down Windlass Hill at a 25 degree angle, going down about 300 feet. Ropes had to be tied to the waggons and the wheels were making ruts in the hillside. Naturally, anyone in the waggons had to be taken off, including myself and Eliza. As William got me out of the waggon, I winced, trying not to cry out. William kissed me softly and lay his cheek against mine as he tenderly carried me to be looked after by the women in the family. It was thought better to tie Eliza to a tree out of harm's way. I hadn't made any improvement since riding in the waggon - in fact I felt drastically worse. I thought at first it was just the jolting of the waggon and being cramped up in the back, but I was really beginning to feel like an old woman with rheumatism – all my joints were swollen and my fingers becoming gnarled. I was in great pain. My fingers and toes had turned purple in colour and I had problems focussing. I didn't want to tell anyone, as they had enough worries, and what could they do anyway? I just had to bear with it and hope a doctor would be able to cure me when we got to Salt Lake City.

Anyway, I watched as the wheels of each waggon were locked to help slow the descent and ropes tied between the waggons and trees to create makeshift winches. The men were putting all their strength in to maintain a strain on the ropes as the waggons descended. There was a lot of hollering out of orders and the men were trying desperately to prevent waggons from actually toppling over. It was quite frightening to watch.

We finally made it and we overnighted in Ash Hollow which seemed to be a beautiful area with a fresh water spring, abundant with wood and grazing. It was like a fairyland with blooming wild roses and verdant vales. It was all such a relief to have come down that hill, safe and sound and breathe in the pleasant aroma of this land of Eden.

However, our happiness was soon marred by Captain Smith telling us this was the site where General William S Harney's troops had won a battle over the Sioux in September 1855 – the Battle of Ash Hollow. He added that it was also the burial ground of many who died of cholera during the gold rush years from 1849. So, so much for being a beautiful site – it was a site of warfare, and illness - much loss of life.

There had been three deaths in the company before arriving at Laramie. William Glover, aged 80, died on the 1st, John [Cartwright] Cherrington the 10th, and Emma Blackner on the 15th of July. The last two were children not a year old.

•

Chimney Rock, Western Nebraska© Weldon Schloneger/Shutterstock.com

The roads had become heavy and sandy and the poor oxen and our little cow found it hard going, having to rest them often. We were now about half way to the Salt Lake Valley. Along the North Platte River we came across a sight to behold. Captain Smith told us all that this was Chimney Rock. Yes, we could quite belief the reason for its name as a huge chimney like protuberance exited from the top of what seemed to us to be a mountain. It really looked like it had chimney stacks on top, made out of rock.

Travelling on, we came to what was known as Scott's Bluff.

"Scott's Bluff that we passed along the way – that huge white escarpment - was originally well-known to the native Americans who lived and hunted nearby. This included the Plains Indians and several other tribes. They called Scott's Bluff 'Me-a-pa-te,' the hill that is hard to go around." Captain Smith told us this story on our next stop, whilst seated around the glowing fire, against the night sky, giving an eerie, ghost-like impression to his story. "It has a strange story attached to it. Hiram Scott, a fur trader, was going east accompanied by two companions. Anyway, most likely, Scott contracted a severe illness and he was transported in a bull boat on the North Platte River in hopes of reconnecting with a larger trading party. Along the way, their vessel overturned; the group's rifles and food supplies were lost. Well, it seems that his companions abandoned Scott on the north bank of the river, leaving him to die. The following year, a party went back to bury his bones, but his bones weren't found where they'd left him. On searching far and wide, his remains were actually discovered on the opposite side of the North Platte, near the bluffs which now bear his name. So, it appeared that Scott managed to make the crossing before his death. Well, there are various recountings of this story. Some say his companions deserted him and he crossed miles of frontier before dying. Others theorise this was an act of self-sacrifice on Scott's part, where Scott insisted that his companions leave him behind, as he was dying and he would only slow them down. Others suspect foul play may have been involved. Well, we'll never know, folks."

Scott's Bluff

The first segment of the journey to Fort Laramie took six weeks, with the company arriving at the fort on 1st August. The company halted for repairs and to re-shoe the draft animals. At this point, the company took the established Oregon Trail toward the trading post at Fort Bridger.

I was not the only one having physical problems. As we travelled, more and more people were succumbing to something. We were travelling parallel with the Little Blue River now. Captain Smith was advising people to be careful where they got their drinking water from, and to wade further into the rivers for fresher water. "You will see there is human and animal waste and garbage at the water edge – steer clear of this." In fact, the family had reported back to me that they had also seen the carcasses of dead animals. A lot of people in the train had taken of this water, before hearing Captain Smith's warnings plus the only places to bathe and launder were in the rivers. There were now cases of cholera and dysentery, and also diphtheria in the children.

The Little Blue River died out but a few miles further on, we came to the Platte River. This is a meeting of the North and South Platte Rivers. Over most of its length it is a sandy, broad, shallow, braided river with many shallow channels and islands and ever-changing sandbars, on which were settled, and swooping over, swans, geese, ducks and other birds of various sizes. Some of the men would go out with their guns, as was necessary as our stocks of food were depleting. It was lovely to see them swooping by, but we needed them for food, and most people saw them as God-given.

We stopped at Fort Laramie, in Wyoming, so we could rest and re-stock our provisions

We had to cross the River Platte again, at Fort Casper. Here, luckily a bridge had been constructed, for which we had to pay a toll. Captain Smith told us that there used to be a ferry here up until 1853, which was discontinued after the competing toll bridge was constructed. He told us the story of the Martin Handcart Company that forded the river on 19th October 1856. "The river had been freezing, leading to exposure that would prove fatal to many members of the company. After camping near Red Butte heavy snow started to fall and continued falling for three days. The company came to a halt as people were dying. For nine days the company remained there, during which time 56 persons died from cold or disease. On October 28th, an advance team of three men from the Utah rescue party reached them, stating that help was on its way and urged the company to start moving on."

At Willow Springs, we had to dig holes for the animals to have water.

At a difficult crossing of the Platte, just before encountering the Sweetwater River the company were able to cross with comparative ease as previous companies had constructed a ferry at that location, and there was a manned post to help waggon trains with this crossing. A toll was required of about $1.50 per waggon, or more, depending on the size of the waggon, to help them cross.

The discomfort from the heat was heightened by the ever-present dust on the trail through Wyoming. The heavy traffic ground the earth into a fine powder that crept into every crevice and shrouded the waggons, people, and animals. Needless to say, this proved gruelling, along with everything else we had to endure, with people coughing and retching. We had scarfs covering our faces to try to prevent the dust getting down our throats but meant we were even hotter still.

The trail headed directly south west from this River Platte crossing. Before we hit the Sweetwater River, we were amazed to see this huge mountain of a rock looming up in front of us, about 130ft higher than the surrounding area. "Yes, this rock is made of granite and came into existence when God created the world. It is more than a mile in circumference. It is called Independence Rock - basically, it is a time guide for everyone on these trails. If we have not reached this rock by Independence Day we are lagging behind and are in danger from getting bad weather in the mountains ahead." Captain Smith advised us. "So, as we are now into August, we have missed that deadline. We'll just have to see what the weather has in stock for us. So, I am sorry but, we cannot spend more than a day here, then we will have to be on our way again."

Camp was made by the Sweetwater River, where we could take on fresh water. There were large grazing areas so people busied themselves letting their oxen and cows graze in the fields, while tackling their laundry or resting their poor limbs, bones and feet before beginning anew the rigours of the western trail through the mountains. A lot of people went to take a stroll to the foot of this mountain.

I, Caroline Brazier, was busying myself with the laundry whilst my boy William (21) went to investigate the rock. He returned about an hour later. "I've carved my name in the rock, mum, and the date. Others were doing it too."

"That is nice William, so your name will be there for all eternity."

After a day's rest, the waggon train started off again. We were getting into more difficult terrain now, wading the waggons across the Sweetwater River numerous times, but Captain Smith advised it was the only way through. This required the waggons to be caulked, to make them watertight, so they could be floated across. Where the crossings were shallow, waggon boxes could be raised by putting blocks on the axles. In deeper water, eight or more teams were hitched to one waggon, which allowed one of the teams to always be on solid ground and have some degree of control over those that were swimming. During that crossing, a rope was often carried along, fastened on each side of the river, and then used as a guide for the swimming animals.

The company now faced a more rugged and hazardous journey, and were concerned about negotiating the passes of the rugged Rocky Mountains. We were met by a trapper, Miles Goodyear, who owned a trading post at the mouth of the

Weber River. He enthusiastically, told us about the agricultural potential of the large Weber Valley.

We came across a narrow gorge cut through the rocks by the Sweetwater River. This was known as 'Devil's Gate'. There was a small fort there. Captain Smith told us that this was actually where the Martin Handcart Company was rescued. Two or three people thought they would get a closer look. It had been rough going but it was a beautiful site. They said the mountain appeared to have been split open and was made of red granite with a stream of water running through it and around it, with large rough boulders lying in the bottom. One side of the gorge looked as if it had been broken from the other.

We then faced a gruelling 18-hour trek up Rocky Ridge to camp at the crossing of Rock Creek. There were moans and groans from everyone looking up at where they had to climb with all the waggons and handcarts – having to haul the waggons on ropes. We were all exhausted with cries of "I cannot do it." "I cannot go on, I've no more energy."

We noticed, as we climbed higher, it was getting cold with a biting wind. "It feels more like winter here, mum." This was Mary Ann (daughter to Ann Brazier Gunn). "Yes, we should all wrap up a bit to keep the cold out, especially the children."

Some didn't survive – it was just too much for those already weakened by the stress and strain of the whole journey, lack of food and illness.

The next day, those remaining entered the South Pass, a 20-mile wide pass at an elevation of 7,550 feet above sea level. "This was one of the most important landmarks." so Captain

Smith told us, "Near here is Pacific Springs, so called because the waters run down to the Pacific Ocean."

We were all so pleased to hear this – to think that we were the other side of this mountain range, the 'Continental Divide', and it would be downhill now. We'd be able to get out of this biting wind. There was even snow on the ground as we trudged by and we noticed that the ponds we passed were frozen over. A couple of the men busied themselves chopping through the ice to fill their water containers.

The company pushed on through South Pass. We had another ferry to cross – over the Green River. Thank goodness this ferry was here, so we didn't have to unload everything and wade through the river. The word had been that we would have had to swim our animals across. We'd heard so many stories of people trying to cross this river. One story told was of the animals baulking at the height of the river, emphatically denying to cross. The waggons had to be caulked and swum across the stream, which was extremely difficult and required considerable time.

As it was, the ferry over was still perilous. A cable had been stretched across the river and fastened to large cottonwood trees on either side. A raft or boat had been fastened to the cable with ropes and pulleys and once loaded with a waggon, the raft was hauled over. Everyone had to get out of the waggons and the oxen were unhitched from the waggons. It was a bitter cold day and everyone had on overcoats and boots. The first load that was put on the boat were four of the largest animals, then four others, the waggon party, besides two men, who ran the boat. The rest of us were watching on

115

the bank. When they got to the centre of the river, the water started coming into the boat, which frightened the animals and they began stomping around. This started off a lot of screaming and shouting of orders, and panic was setting in as it looked like the boat was going to capsize. It looked like everyone, animals and all was about to be tossed into the waters and drown.

Luckily the boat load was saved. Anyway, the men had learnt a lesson from this first boat load and orders were given not to overload the next boat loads.

The rest of us could do nothing to help, just watch and pray with each raft load that went over. John's wife, Caroline, who was just 24, was looking rather stressed as their waggon contents were being loaded onto a raft. "If the raft up-ends, we'll lose everything we have, that is all our food and belongings from home. We won't be able to survive the journey. We just cannot lose everything we have." And she began to cry. We all tried to comfort her. Ann commented, "The men are doing what they could to stabilise the loads and, basically, if the worst came to the worst, everyone will help us out."

"But, the others have only got provisions for themselves, they won't be able to. We'll starve. Plus all my precious things from home. I'll never be able to replace them."

It was the turn of Caroline and John's waggon contents to be loaded onto a raft. It was rocking precariously with the tide. The next minute, Caroline screamed, then we saw her run to the water's edge and it looked like she was going to throw herself onto the raft. "I am not going to lose anything." Men were wading in the water beside the rafts and, hearing the cries, waded over to stop her getting onto the raft. "You will get killed if the raft overturns – get off."

"I will die anyway, if we do not save our provisions." They managed to get her off, kicking and screaming, and over to the other shore.

So the raft was pulled over and their belongings arrived safely on the other side. Caroline was soaked from the swell of the river. We could all hear Tom over the other side of the river, giving Caroline a right telling off but all she said was, "Well, the raft was rocking so much, and I had to try something." Tom let it be, at least she was safe and got a blanket for her to wrap herself in as she was shivering quite dramatically.

I, Emma, had looked on at all these events unfolding. Unfortunately, though, I had started getting very unwell and I was not well enough to even stand. I did not know what was wrong with me, but kept coming out in hot sweats and shivering at the same time. When it was our turn to load our animals and waggon, William was so tender, lovely man that he is, and, with George's assistance, they managed to place me on the back of our ox, and stayed by my side to keep me from falling off.

Green River

It was a slow process, and took us all day, but we all made it, eventually. That night we camped on the bank of the overflow stream. A report was passed round from Captain Scott that we'd had a narrow escape as he'd heard that another team, about 25 miles further up the river, had had a boat capsize on them and oxen and men went into the river. Men had been clinging to the yokes on the oxen but three or four men had drowned.

Also, thankfully, the ferry was operated by Mormons and, being Mormons, we were ferried over for free. The controllers of the ferry earned money instead from other emigrants travelling to Oregon and California. "Thank goodness" – this was Uncle William, "We have no more money. It's all gone on tolls and buying provisions. I hope we get through soon as we're all so hungry, just eking out what little we have."

"We're all in the same boat, Uncle William." George replied. We were all looking at our family, all gathered round and shaking our heads. We had all lost loads of weight, with our clothes hanging off us. I had actually lost my appetite, possibly because of my illness, and was very weak.

As we struggled on a young man by the name of Hyrum Walker accidentally shot himself. He was obviously tired, exhausted and not thinking straight. Our Captain, John Smith, immediately put another man in charge of the company and with a mule team he took the injured man to Salt Lake to the doctor.

Eliza started playing up again. She'd been reasonably quiet for some time now, sunk into her own thoughts, not really talking to anyone, just walking. George and the rest of us had done what we could to cheer her up but were getting no response. It was as though she had cut herself off from everyone and was not aware of even where she was, just plodding on. One day, however, she appeared, without her usual bonnet on and started parading around. It's then we noticed that she had cut her normally dark, curly hair – not just cut it, but had hacked at it, cutting out great lumps, leaving bald patches near her scalp. "Do you think I look nice, George?" She asked quite calmly. "I could not wash my hair on this xxxx horrid journey, so I thought I might as well cut it short. Do you think it suits me?"

The next minute that smile changed to a grimace and she ran forward towards George with the scissors in her hand, aimed like a dagger. George, thinking on his feet, managed to grab hold of the arm wielding the scissors and twist her arm around her back, and held her in a tight grip. She dropped the scissors, with a yelp of pain, and uttered "I want to kill you, George. You're the devil in disguise."

"Get some rope." George yelled out. George then tied her arms around her back.

Of course we were all astonished. "She has finally lost her mind, George" Uncle William stated. "Do you think we should contact one of the Brothers so he can pray for her?"

So, George went to one of the Brothers, who came to see Eliza. Eliza at that time was sitting on the ground murmuring quietly to herself. She didn't seem to be aware of who was around her. The Brother interviewed her at length and came back to say, "Apostle Parley Pratt states that it was not the spirits who had followed Lucifer to earth who possessed humans, but rather it was the spirits of the departed, who are unhappy, and who linger in lonely wretchedness about the earth. The more wicked of these are the kind spoken of in Scripture, as *'foul spirits', 'unclean spirits'* spirits who sometimes enter human bodies, and will distract them, throw them into fits, cast them into the water, into the fire, and such like. They will trouble them with dreams, nightmares, hysterics, fever, and the like. They will also deform them in body and in features, by convulsions, cramps, contortions, and so on, and will sometimes compel them to utter blasphemies, horrible curses, and even words of other languages.

What I have seen in your wife are the blasphemies, and horrible curses, bad dreams, nightmares and hysterics. I do not think she has a demon that had got into her, as I have tried various languages and she was not speaking in tongues. However, she could have a malevolent minor spirit. I will get the other Brothers together to try to exorcise it."

As they performed their exorcism, sprinkling holy water and laying on of hands, followed by a blessing and denunciating the evil spirit, over and over, requesting it to leave the body of their sister Eliza in the name of Jesus Christ, poor Eliza got even more agitated, standing up and fighting physically with the Brothers, spitting at them, swearing, "Tell your God and his followers to go to hell, and to leave me be." There was no expected foaming at the mouth or demonic apparitions or speaking in tongues. A second anointing was performed with raising her hand and commanding the spirit away in the name of Jesus Christ and with the power or authority of the Melchizedek priesthood.

She was left crying in a heap on the floor. There was nothing else could be done for her. She was considered violent to herself and others and tied to the back of our waggon to keep her out of harm's way. So, this is the way we progressed, with Eliza following on behind the waggon, like a prisoner, mumbling quietly to herself.

....

We finally reached Fort Bridger, which provided an opportunity to restock much-needed supplied. Local Native Americans had offered things like fur, fresh meat and moccasins, but the fort had now been purchased by the Mormons, who stocked things like clothing, grains, dried fruit, salted port and ammunition as well as providing blacksmithing services.

We looked at what was on offer, but we had no more money. Poor little Elizabeth was crying because she was so tired and hungry. The other children just looked sad and exhausted. They had no energy to play and were just slumped down, or even lying on the ground. Several members of the party were suffering flu-like symptoms, fever and severe headaches from "mountain fever". Someone said this was probably Colorado tick fever, which is carried by the Rocky Mountain wood tick. They also had a rash – small spots of bleedings, starting in the wrists and ankles. Others had muscle pains and vomiting.

Captain Smith saw the plight of everyone there. People were starving, exhausted and sick. Some had even lost their waggons and belongings along the way. All they had left was what they were wearing, which were now complete rags. Of course, everyone helped those in need, where possible, but we were all in the same boat and feeling desperate.

Captain Smith addressed the bedraggled group. "I have sent one of my men on by horse, to ask for a relief expedition to come to our aid. They know we are here and I expect charitable help any day now."

There was obviously great relief and murmurs of thanks went out to Captain Smith, but that didn't help the here and now, with crying, starving children and adults, none of whom had the energy to carry on. Many of the hundreds that had originally set out on this trail, had already died and been buried along the way.

It was common for established Oregon residents to mount relief expeditions to aid those just arriving. Pack trains organised by charitable settlers regularly met the new arrivals at The Dales to help them along the final leg of the journey.

Captain Smith addressed all the remaining members of the party. "As you know, I have sent for reinforcements, food and medical supplies. However, it is still a trek and it may be days before we see any sign of anyone coming to rescue us." There were moans from the pioneers and disgruntled whispers. Captain Smith continued, "What I suggest is that we unload anything we do not need from the waggons and leave them here. Your belongings will be safe as I will set a guard on them. The weaker ones of you, the sick and elderly and children, can then ride in the waggons to meet the rescue team. Once rested, and taken on food and medication, the rescue team will guide you all safely to Salt Lake City. Once you are settled there, I will arrange for waggons to be sent out to retrieve your goods. One of each party here can return with these waggons to lay claim to your belongings."

This seemed like a good idea and everyone was in agreement. So the waggons were unloaded, the pioneers seated in the waggons and the train set off again.

We passed by some prominent rock formations near the Utah-Wyoming border. Word got around that this rock formation, with towering pinnacles, was called The Needles. It was near here that Brigham Young became ill with the same Rocky Mountain spotted fever that a lot of our party had become ill with. He had been so ill, he thought he was going to die and would have to be buried there. I didn't have to imagine his torment as I could see the suffering of the sick all around me plus I was so sick myself. Brigham Young had to progress onto Salt Lake Valley in a bed in the back of Wilford Woodruff's waggon.

We then passed through Echo Canyon. A deep and narrow canyon, well-named as it was a veritable echo chamber. Quite eerie, in fact, and any of the children, who were not too ill, enjoyed themselves shouting out, and hearing their own voices echoing back to them. Buffalo, Native Americans and explorers used this natural pathway between the lush grass of Wyoming and the salt deserts to the west. We were told that, just two years ago, there had been a Mormon rebellion against the USA, who wanted to prohibit the Mormons of Utah from practising polygamy. The US army was sent but a Mormon militia dammed the creek with a rock wall at the Narrows, and built other fortification to deter the soldiers. Luckily they were never needed, but the stone relics can still be seen.

We were seeing now, the first signs of an established home-steading – set up by a James Bromley. In July 1846 the Harlan-Young party drove their waggons past this site and down the nearly impassable lower Weber River. They found a rocky canyon with a raging river at the bottom. This was impassable, so they came up with the idea of blazing a new trail to the west. It took 21 days to travel the 36 miles to the Great Salt Lake, which proved fatal for them in the Sierra Nevada later that autumn. Brigham Young found a way though, through this new trail, in 1847, bringing 80,000 Mormon immigrants in their waggons, handcarts and on foot.

It was here that the relief party met up with us, providing fresh food and medication. It was such a joy to see them, coming up the path towards us. Some even ran up to them, to hug them. It was a party atmosphere, those who were up to it, singing their praises, while devouring the food and fresh water on offer - although most of us came to regret it afterwards, having been starved for so long. Still, we were now ready to trudge on further, to our new home.

We passed by what was called Big Mountain. It was actually dwarfed by the surrounding Wasatch mountain peaks but we were now at the highest elevation in all of our trail – 8,400 feet. This was an awesome place at the mountain top. It was so windy, that they people walking had to hold on to each other to save themselves being blown over the cliff top. The waggon cover was blowing back and forth, making a cracking sound. We hoped to God it would not split, otherwise we would be open to the elements. The views were beautiful though, of the valleys on both sides, and so peaceful, with such vibrant colours that I (Emma) even began to get a feeling of well-being. Of course, this did not last.

We actually, now started to come across made roads, the Golden Pass Road and a road hacked through Emigration Canyon to the bench overlooking the Great Salt Lake basin. It was here that Brigham Young and the first wave of Mormon pioneers, after months of extremely rugged travel, arrived in the Salt Lake Valley. Brigham Young stood on a high vista and told his followers, "This is the place".

Salt Lake Valley

125

We entered the Salt Lake Valley, through Parley's Canyon, on 1 September 1860. I was so pleased when William shouted out that we had finally arrived, because I had been very poorly most of the journey, sickly and very weak. I didn't even have the energy to sit up in the waggon and William had somehow made room for me in the back of the waggon, curled up with a blanket around me. It was an awful journey, even though I was sitting in the waggon, as ever stone or rock the waggon went over, sent a judder through my body. He had to lift me bodily off the waggon as I was feeling so dizzy and could feel myself falling if I tried to stand – I was shaking and my legs wouldn't support me, then I would start coughing violently with the effort.

I heard refrains of joy being shouted out as we entered our destination in Salt Lake Valley. We could see fields of potatoes and turnips and Brigham Young had established a town for us and was building the Salt Lake Temple. There were houses and buildings and encampments set out for some couple of thousands of pilgrims. All seemed to be a hive of activity.

Captain [Franklin] Brown's company separated on the Weber, some of the immigrants going down that stream to Ogden, others taking the road to Provo and the balance came on to this city, arriving on Tuesday evening or Wednesday morning.

We understand that there was but one death during the journey.

At about noon on Thursday, Capt. [Jesse] Murphy's company arrived at the Public Square, Eighth Ward. There were two births in this company after leaving Florence and no deaths, and their cattle were in good condition on their arrival.

126

Capt. [John] Smith, after arriving on Saturday, the 25th ult., with his sister and her son, went back to meet his company on the Monday following, and came in with it the following Saturday, arriving about the middle of the day. Some of those in his train had taken other routes before reaching the city, and there were only about twenty waggons in the company when it reached the camping ground.

On Sunday morning, Elder Wilford Woodruff, George A. Smith, Lorenzo Snow and F. D. Richards went out to visit Elder James D. Ross' company in Emigration Canyon. They held a meeting at 1 o'clock p.m., at which Elder G. A. Smith preached an excellent discourse, directed more particularly to the Swiss Saints, Elder Daniel Bonelli interpreting the address. Elder Smith gave the Saints good counsel relative to the various duties devolving upon them, told them to live their religion and be faithful in all things. Elders Woodruff and Richards followed with some spirited and appropriate remarks.

Capt. [James D.] Ross and company arrived in the city between eleven and twelve o'clock on Monday—all in good health and spirits. They have had but little sickness on the journey, and only one death, and that is reported to have occurred in consequence of eating unwholesome meat, in disobedience to counsel.

Each of these companies, on their arrival, were soon dispersed-some going to one place and some to another—most of the immigrants having friends and acquaintances, who had preceded them to these valleys, ready to receive them and bid them welcome to their "Mountain Home."

Elders Woodruff and Richards followed with some spirited and appropriate remarks.

"So far as we have seen and heard, the Saints that have crossed the plains this summer were in good health and spirits on their arrival here; and if they continue to keep the commandments of God and heed the teachings of those having the right to counsel them in things pertaining to their salvation, they will never have occasion to be sorrowful under any circumstances that may arise; otherwise, they may wish to return to Babylon after a while."

William, I and our children, as well as Elizabeth Judd located to, the Jordan area near the Jordan River, where we were due to spend the winter. Conditions were poor and food and necessities were scarce. The home was basically a dug-out, with no windows or floor and with only a quilt or robe for protection at the door. Elizabeth looked after the children and cooked, with my daughter, Fannie, who being the oldest girl had to shoulder most of the responsibility of caring for me and the younger children. The food consisted mostly of coarse brown bread and molasses. From what I remember, William was so tender and caring, and got the help of neighbours to tend to me, while making up fires from what he could find, mainly sage brush, but I was in and out of consciousness most of the time – and in such pain – every part of my body ached. The disease, whatever it was had reached my lungs and I was finding it difficult to breathe. My chest ached and my hair was falling out. I also had shingles- red blotches on the right side of my body, which had turned into itchy blisters that had affected my eyesight even more, with my eyes red and sore, so even my skin was painful and I seemed to have a palsy on one side of my face.

I softly whispered "Elizabeth", I didn't have the strength to call. She came and sat by my side. I beckoned her closer and whispered hoarsely to her. "Elizabeth, please call William over.... I have something to say to you both." William came close, kneeling beside me.

"Yes, my love. I am here."

"I haven't got long to live.... I feel my life ebbing away and I will be grateful when it is all over .....and I am free of this ghastly pain." Both gently took hold of my hands.

"You have loved me William, with all your heart..... but you need someone to love you back and care for you..... and you, Elizabeth, have been such a good friend. You need someone to love you and care for you too. .... When I am gone, and it won't be long now.... I wish you both to marry... and soon, do not delay. You will be good for each other. ... I give you my blessing....."

I then closed my eyes.

....

Emma's health was very poor and continued to fail and she passed away on 23 January 1861. She was buried in the Salt Lake Cemetery. This left William with four children.

In the summer months, Indians were frequent visitors. Sometimes they came in great numbers, hunting in the mountains east of the settlement. Times were hard. Food and clothing was scarce, only finding wheat and oats to boil up. The winter was severe and the snow was deep. At one time it snowed almost constantly for six week until they were almost buried.

This wasn't any way of survival and William looked for work elsewhere.

BUILDING A LIFE IN UTAH

CHAPTER 10

William and Elizabeth Judd were married by Brigham Young on 26 February 1861. Shortly after their marriage they moved to the old fourth ward in Salt Lake City. Here their first child, Susan, was born.

The family went their separate way. The Gunn family matriarch, Ann Brazier Gunn and her son Thomas, daughter Mary Ann and son George went to southern Utah and located in Parowan, Iron country in the spring of 1861. Thomas then went on to make his home in Adamsville, near Beaver. Benjamin was with them for a short time, then he returned to Salt Lake, where is made his home. The other sons and daughters remained in Salt Lake City.

From Jordan, William and his new wife, Elizabeth and the children relocated to live in the 4th ward in Salt Lake City – a new brick home. Their first baby was called, Susan.

While living here his work kept him away from his family for he was helping to building the first road through Parley's and Silver Creek Canyons. As payment, he received food and supplies from the church tithing office.

He was a big, robust, hard-working man – a fine specimen of manhood with a splendid physique, and kindly blue eyes. The spirit of colonisation, so strong among the early settlers in Utah, led him to a little settlement (to be known as Hoytsville) about 35 miles east of Salt Lake City, located on the Weber

River, about eight miles south of the mouth of Echo Canyon. This settlement was only four years old. He bought some land from Andrew Johnson and a Mr White, who possessed squatters' rights. When this land came onto the market, it was surveyed and each owner received their deeds of title. He built a log cabin, consisting of two rooms, a kitchen and bedroom. However, their only source of water in the summer was the irrigation ditch. In the winters they had to haul water in barrels from the Weber River. The family turned 80 acres of sagebrush into fields of grain and green, inviting, meadowlands, where their cattle could grow.

....

George's wife, Eliza, was taken to a place where she would be looked after. Brigham Young arranged this. There were no hospitals or infirmaries or even sanatoriums. There were no trained nurses, just women acting as midwifes, as was usual at the time, but she couldn't stay with George. She had become a danger to herself and others. Brigham Young, as church leader, divorced George and Eliza – there was no going back. George heard, soon after, the Eliza had actually died. They never found out what the reason was, not being able to do autopsies, just mention of an illness that had affected her brain and which had led to her death.

People who knew George said he was a good natured, jovial man, who loved to tease the girls. I suppose, being free of Eliza now, his own personality could come to the fore. He felt released and became more outgoing.

Soon after he came to Parowan he acquired land in the valley and planted crops.

He set up the first tannery with William Holyoak and John Brown close by to the abattoir, so he could buy the hides. They eventually were able to obtain machinery and set up a harness shop in connection with the tannery, using their own leather to make and repair harnesses, bridles and other leather goods. It was a good business and had a lot of custom.

William Holyoak had a brother, George. Mum (Ann Brazier Gunn), would come into the tannery every so often, to catch up on news and to buy anything she needed. They had cotton threads there, that she needed for her sewing. One particular day, William Holyoak's brother came into the shop. He was a nice looking older man and they got chatting – just generally passing the time of day and asking how each other was getting on, coming to a strange new country. Mum said she was sewing for people, but really needed a proper home for herself. Mum also spoke of being a bit worried as a few English words had been changed in America. She had noticed these words in the newspapers, especially the adverts, and had, at first thought, that they had been misprints, such as wagon instead of waggon, color instead of colour and traveled instead of travelled. But then, asking around, was told that an American dictionary had been devised by a Mr Noah Webster back in 1828. This Mr Webster believed that English spelling rules were unnecessarily complex, especially with so many nations, speaking their own languages, having entered America. These new emigrants wanted a language everyone could understand and to create their own identify. The American language was growing, new words were made up also, as the equivalent didn't exist in English, with some taken from these other languages.

He travelled around the U.S. giving lectures about standardising the English language, and in his travels he met

133

Benjamin Franklin, who shared Webster's concerns about language reform. Franklin proposed deleting the letters c, w, y, and j and adding six new letters to the American alphabet. Webster, however, did not like the idea of adding or subtracting letters, but rather he wanted to simplify the spelling of words— changing favour to favor, for example, or replacing words ending -re with -er as in centre/center and theatre/theater, and words ending ...'ising', with 'izing' in order to match spelling with pronunciation, as well as 'wagon' for 'waggon'.

"So, George, I must take on this new way of writing. I am in a new country, one that speaks English but I can well understand that the Americans want their own identity. If I had emigrated to a non-English-speaking country I would have to learn that language, so to adapt my writing of a few odd words, will be a lot easier. I have already noticed that you George are saying curtailed words, such as 'didn't' for 'did not' – so I must take that on as well, although it seems very strange to me."

"You will get the hang of it in time, Ann." George responded.

George and mum met up another time and George asked her if she would partake of a coffee with him. "Oh, I am not sure if I like coffee. I am used to English tea."

"Well, I'm sure English tea can be provided, if you so wish ma'm."

And so they went and talked about the family and their troubles and their journey over. They obviously had a lot in common as everyone had done the same journey at some time and had their own experiences."

George had his own story to tell. "Our company, the Darwen Richardson Company, arrived in Utah on 30 September 1854, after travelling over on the SS Windermere. I started out with my wife, Sarah and seven children. The youngest is now 19 and married to William Lefevre. She married at the tender age of 14. I know you think that's young, but that's what she wanted and they are quite happy and live here in Parowan. Unfortunately my wife got the cholera on our journey and died on 26 July 1854. Also, two others of my children, Mary, died in Missouri – she was 27, and Ann, who was married, died in Wyoming – she was just 22."

"Oh, really sorry to hear that George." I replied.

"Well, it was a tough journey, as you know too well yourself. I am on my own now, the children have all made their own lives and some have moved away.

I did make friends with someone called James Moyle, on the journey. We had about fifty wagons with ten people in each wagon. We started with two yoke of oxen and one yoke of cows. One of the yoke of oxen was Texas cattle, and very wild, with two long sharp horns, which you had to be really careful of as they could be dangerous. Yes, I can see you wondering who got injured – well, James Moyle got hit by one of these horns that made a hole in his upper lip."

"Oh, nasty."

George continued, "We had a great time with them until they were thoroughly broke, and then they were not worth much.

135

We had a tent to each wagon, where the most of us slept at night.

As we come near Fort Kearney, we began to see signs of buffalo that we had heard so much about. About four miles west of the Fort we saw about ten that the men at the Fort had killed a few days before. They were strange looking animals to me as they lay there swelled up in the hot sun, but I soon after became familiar with such sights as we were now getting into the buffalo country, and as we come into the Platte Valley the buffalo trails were paths about three feet wide, and sometimes eighteen inches deep. These paths would lead to and from the river. Sometimes we had seen several herds of buffalo at the same time and some of them would seem to extend for miles in length and breadth and the plains would appear black with them. Sometimes they would come and run right through our train. One day James and a fellow called Tripp came very near catching a young calf. Some of our men shot a number of them, but I did not like the meat so well as our beef."

"We did not really see all that many buffalo when we travelled, George, but that was six years later, just skeletons."

"Yes, I believe white trappers and traders have been killing the buffalo for their hides. I don't know if you've heard of 'Buffalo' Bill Cody - I hear he's been hired to kill bison and has slaughtered more than 4,000 in two years. What makes matters worse, is that buffalo are being killed off systematically by the US army in what they say is an attempt to defeat the native Americans, who are resisting the takeover of their lands by white settlers. This is to deny them an important source of food."

"So, that is why we came across a party of first nation Indians, who were begging for food?"

"Quite so, although, on our trip, the Pawnee Indians did bother us some. They would come and demand presents from us for traveling through their country. After we left them we come into the country of the Cheyenne Indians. I have a vivid recollection of how they looked on their horses and dressed for mischief. We camped one day at noon in a good place and the Captain said he would stay there for the day and do our washing. The cattle were turned out with no-one to watch them. We had been camped an hour or more and the Captain noticed that the cattle were straying off into the low foot hills. He asked James to run and turn them back as he was afraid that the Indians were watching, thinking to run them off, and that he would send some more to help him. So James ran off alone with nothing but a small whip in his hand. He found that some of the cattle had got over among the low hills. Two or three men were sent after him, so he carried on among the hills. After running among the hills for some time he found about twelve of them in a bunch together, and ran around to try to turn them back. There, he discovered six Cheyenne Indians on their horses looking at him and talking to each other. Obviously, they wanted the cattle and it looked like they were going to shoot him. When he got back to camp, he told us how frightened he had been but didn't want them to see that and started hollering to the cattle and managed to turn them back. He'd had to pass the Indians but, luckily, they did not attack. He'd had a narrow escape.

We found buffalo all the way up the Platte valley for over three hundred miles. There were some days we would estimate that we had seen over ten thousand buffalo. Some days we wouldn't see any.

Our cattle would have a mind of their own and, if they got frightened, would cause a stampede, so we put guards around at night, on four-hour shifts."

"Yes," I interrupted, "Ours stampeded once, and my poor little granddaughter got hit by a waggon wheel and got her collar bone broken."

"Quite, it's really dangerous when they stampede. Anyway, one night I was out guarding and it was raining and very dark, all at once the cattle stampeded. I thought they were coming towards me so I ran to one side and they rushed past where I stood - but they ran over one man and he was badly hurt. It was late the next day before we found them all. Some of them were found twelve miles off, so we didn't move that day.

When we came near Chimney rock, which had loomed up on the horizon three days' travel away, we camped as I thought about two miles from it, so I thought that I would get up early and go and see it before breakfast. I started early the next morning, as soon as it was light. I walked and ran and I must have been about four hours before I got there and I found it so different from what I expected that I was angry with myself for coming so far to see nothing but a pile of gravel in layers, one above another, about sixty feet high. It was a lonely quiet place, I didn't stop long, but started back to find the camp, and it took me until noon before I caught up with it and I was almost dead with thirst.

When about six miles east from Fort Laramie, we came to a very large camp of Sioux Indians. Some of our people said there were two thousand of them. They were camped in a fine meadow, some of them were horse-racing and, as our train passed along the road, they stood on both sides of us. They were a fine looking lot of people, great tall fellows and clean-looking squaws, but they did not molest us, so we passed on and stayed at the Fort a little time. Then we went on and camped about six or eight miles west of the fort and crossed the North Platte and camped near the river. Soon after we camped a man rode up and said the Indians had killed two soldiers that had been sent to their camp on some business and that they intended to attack us. There was a large Danish company just behind us, and we were afraid they would attack them before they caught up to us, but we soon saw the Danes coming, which lightened our hearts. The poor fellows were in a great hurry as they understood the Indians were coming, so we made a large corral with the two companies. That is we made a circle with our wagons and chained them together, so that our cattle could be safe on the inside. We got all the old guns and cleaned them and sharpened our knives expecting the Indians any minute, but they did not come. During the night we had several parties come and beg to be allowed to stay with us. I remember a small party with two wagons with horse teams who were going to Oregon. They came after night and I heard them pleading with Mr Richardson. 'For God's sake Mr. Richardson give us shelter for the Indians are after us'. We also had a mountaineer that stayed with us for over a week, but we were not molested nor did we see any more of the Indians. However, the Indians did attack Fort Laramie and killed a number of the soldiers. Soon after this we got into the Sweet-water country and our cattle began to fail and die. Before we got to the City our food become scarce and we were met by some teams with flour from the valley which was a great help to us."

So, we got on very well, telling our various stories.

Ann enjoyed the discussions and found herself talking of William and poor Emma dying after so much agony on the journey. "But William found himself a nice wife, someone who had been with them from the ship over, and they married. They both seem to be very happy. .

George then, very unexpectedly said, "Ann, I would like to make you happy too." Ann raised her eyebrows, wondering what was coming next. "Forgive me for startling you. I had no wish to do that, but I know the difficulties you have been having and I think I have the answer to your problems. I have a house, and no wife, and I would like you to come and live with me, as my wife."

"Mr Holyoak..."

"George, please."

"George, this is so sudden. I had no idea you thought of me in that way. I mean, I am an old woman, I am 63. You cannot possibly love me?"

"Love may come, Ann, but I admire you greatly and I would be honoured if you would marry me. You would make my life complete in my old age. Please say you will. You will have no worries as I am financially stable."

"George. All I can say is that I will think this proposal over."

Ann then left the establishment. This was certainly a lot to take in. What would the family think of it?

"Well, mum I think your toast has landed with the butter uppermost." This was George.

William, Ann's brother said, "Well, you seem to get on well enough. I have no objection."

The women of the family were a bit more anxious for Ann but, in the end, agreed that, if she liked George well enough, she should accept his proposal, "I mean, he has a house and everything. What more could you want?" This was Caroline.

So, Ann finally agreed to marry George and a wedding was planned for 29 December 1860.

1 William Gunn   Emma Baker

John Gunn and Ann I. Brazier Family

9 Benjamin Gunn   Alice Bowdidge

2 Lois Gunn   6 Mary Ann H. Gunn   7 Lois Brazier Gunn   8 Alfred Gunn   Rachael Ann Fenton

3 John Gunn   Caroline Barham   4 George Gunn   Ann Munford   5 Thomas Gunn   Ann Houghton

142

r William Brazier

Eiza Rogers

Caroline Brazier

Thomas Gunn

Elizabeth Judd Gunn

MaryAnn Paramore Adey

William Dyer Gunn

Alfred Gunn

143

Benjamin Gunn   Lydia Munford

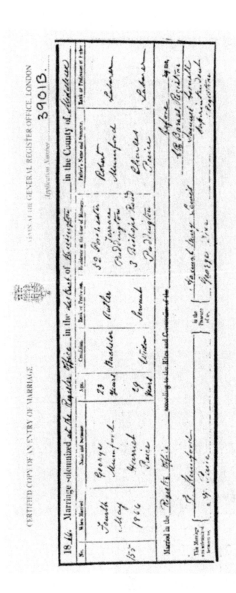

Wedding Certificate - George Munford and Harriet

145

Ann Gunn home in Parowan

George Holyoak

146

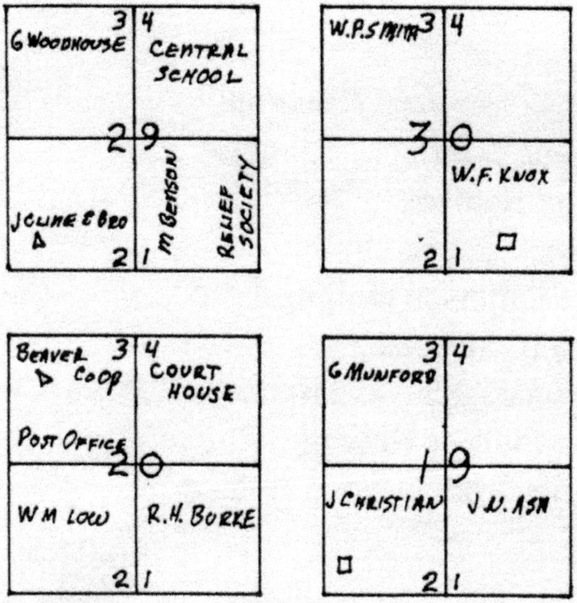

George's property in Beaver

THE MUNFORD FAMILY

149

The Munford Family

Father	Robert Munford
Mother	Lydia Morphew
Son	John Morphew Munford married Albinia Duffell
Daughter	Mary Morphew Munford
Daughter	Sarah Ann Morphew Munford married Wm Murrell
Son	William Morphew Munford – (died, aged 30)
Daughter	Jane Morphew Munford
Son	James Munford – (died, aged 19)
Daughter	Ann Munford and son William Stubbs
	Ann married George Gunn
Daughter	Margaret Munford
Daughter	Mary Munford
Son	George R Munford – (died, aged 7 months)
Daughter	Sarah Ann Munford
Daughter	Lucy Munford married Joseph Stevens
Son	George Munford married Harriet Paice
Son	Thomas Munford

See translation from the Norfolk dialect from Page 323.

Ann Munford

Daughter of Robert Munford and Lydia Ann Morphew

* Born: April 24, 1832 in Costessey, England
* Died: April 30, 1922 in Parowan, Utah
* Married **George Gunn** March 1864 in Parowan, Utah

Children (5): **Lucy Albena**, George Robert, Lydia Ann, John, & Alfred James Gunn

* She grew up in a little farming village. She was well educated and her family was "well off."
* Ann wanted to marry William Stubbs, but her family objected – so they eloped! Shortly after their marriage, William "went to sea" and was never heard from again.
* She came to America as a 'widow' with her four year old son.
* Ann was one of the first school teachers in Parowan.
* She did beautiful embroidery work. Her handwork always took first place at the county fair.
* She did much in helping clothe the poor and afflicted.

151

ANN MUNFORD

CHAPTER 11

"Oi wo'a call a family meeting." This was my father, Robert Munford, a sprightly-looking 63-year old, speaking in his broad Norfolk dialect. We lived in Costessey, or Cossey as the locals called it. The year was 1863.

The meeting was duly called. I was there, with my four-year-old son, William – I am Ann, by the way and 31 years old now – pleased to meet you. My mother, Lydia Morphew Munford, was obviously there. She was 52 at the time. Lucy my sister (aged 24) came along, my brother George Morphew (23), my brother Thomas Morphew (20) and my brother William Morphew (36). My siblings had taken mum's name as well as our father's as part of their surname, that is Morphew Munford.

There had been more of us at one time but William, James and Jane had all died, unfortunately. This had been terrible for my mother, having three grown children die, and not even in childbirth, which was a regular occurrence in those days. Maw did have one child, two years after Margaret was born, but he only lasted two months. James had been 19, so young - the death certificate said 'congestion of the left lung'. Jane died of consumption. William died of an abscess of the liver – he was 30. Well, it's not good to have your children die before you – it's not the way of the world.

My sisters, Mary (10 years older) and Margaret (3 years older than me), and brother, George, had all been servants in the same household in Surrey, 1 Kennington Lane, Upper

Lambeth, if I can recall correctly, which was really fortuitous, all living together. Mary was a cook and George had started off as a footman but had made his way up and was now the butler for a family in Paddington, London. It was difficult for Mary and Margaret to get away at the same time and take the long journey back to Cossey, so only George managed to make the journey. Luckily we had the steam trains now to cut his journey significantly, otherwise he would never have been able to get enough time away.

George was dating a lady six years older than him, Harriet Paice. Harriet had a daughter, Louisa, and said she was widowed, but none of us thought she had actually been married before as little Louisa still bore her mother's maiden name. Harriet's parents were Charles Paice and Deborah Butter. Still, that sort of thing happened, although it was very frowned on and George seemed to think the world of her, although they were not living together. George was living at 52 Porchester Terrace and Harriet lived at 3 Bishops Road, in Paddington, London. Harriet was a servant and Louisa was being looked after by her grandparents in Herriard in Hampshire.

John had gone to find work in London when he was still a young man. He started off as a servant in Kennington Cross. There he met and married Albina, who's father was a maltster and he was now a victualler at Marquis Grange, High Street, Epsom, Surrey. He was doing quite well for himself, very smart-looking last time I saw him, which I suppose must have been for Williams' funeral in '57. I know he had an impressive beard, which suited him well.

So, basically, most of the family had moved away. There was no work in Norfolk to be had and they took the only jobs open to them – mainly servants, getting one day off a week, if you were lucky, and skivvying from dawn to dusk, getting only pocket money for their time. George was going steady with someone called Eliza Rogers. How George managed to meet Eliza, I've no idea, as servants had so little free time to themselves and most were not allowed to marry.

I suppose you must be wondering about little William's father and why he was not there at this meeting. Well, the blighter had gone and left me – hooked up with some floozy or other. I suppose I must have loved him at one time, and we wanted to get married. My parents did not like him, though, and did their best to persuade me out of it. I was having none of it though – I suppose I was naïve and thought everything would be rosy once we were married – so we eloped. Well, I did not see much of him after he'd found I was pregnant, then he finally scarpered off. I had to come back to live with mum and dad. He left me penniless. I did see him again. He turned up on the doorstep after William was born and snatched the baby away from me. I was screaming at him to bring him back and that he needed his mother. He said that was the law and if I wanted him back so desperately, I'd have to fight him in court, adding that that would cost a fair copper and, as I had none, I'd never get him back. I cried and cried for weeks. Dad couldn't help – he had no money either. I obviously did get him back but that is a story for later on. We were all gathered here together, seated in the front parlour, to hear what father (or daw, as we called him) had to say.

"I hev some gri' news. as yow know, from thur many meetings we hev had, and our discussions, as a family, on thur possibility f emigrating to America, oi hev finally got backing and finance fur us all tuh goo."

A big cheer went up, with claps on daw's back by his sons. We were finally going to America. I felt like dancing and actually got up and did a jig with Lucy. We'd been waiting so long for this news – it seemed like years. Our lives had been put on hold for so long, so we could now look forward. We'd had enough of just scraping by, searching every day for a few pennies for a crust or a potato to eat, with no work, or intermittent work. There was just nothing for us anymore in Norfolk. So many people had gone before us already – friends that we'd never see again.

When we'd all calmed down, it was George who posed the question, "Daw, who's putting up thur kew'er fur us tuh goo?"

"Well, I're managed to gi' assistance from thur Nair'av – food, clothes and travel kew'er – but tha' ois thur Mormons, their church, son – thay hev ariddy set up in America and thay are planning a big move to Utah. Thay wo'a as many families as thay ken get, Mormon families, to set up new towns. Thay are durn all thur arranging, transport and provisions from their base in Florence, Nebraska. We jist need to gi' ourselves to Liverpool and on thur ship. Tha' ois thur roight toime to goo."

There was a lot of excitement. Most of the family had been inducted into the Mormon faith, changing from the Catholic faith. The families in the area were deep into their religion but we'd had a visit from one of the missionaries, back in 1851, telling us about their beliefs and extending a helping hand to us. Mormons seemed to be a great community of like-minded souls who wanted to escape the tyranny of the Church of England or Catholics and set up their own church, offering assistance when we needed it. We felt like we were being taken under their wing. I mean, what had the Catholics given us apart from penitence, forever asking for forgiveness, just for

155

being alive, or so it seemed. They did not give us any hand-outs of help in any way.

They believe that Jesus' atonement (death and resurrection) provides immortality for all people regardless of their faith. Christ thus overcame physical death. Because of his atonement, everyone born on this earth will be resurrected, they will become immortal. All people who ever lived will be resurrected, 'both old and young, both bond and free, both male and female, both the wicked and the righteous'. So, they gave us something to look forward to, not like the Catholics, basically condemning us to a life of hell, should we do something bad – it was always talk of hell and damnation.

So. My parents, Lucy, George, Thomas and I were all baptized in the Wymondham Branch at Norwich. We couldn't persuade Margaret to change faiths – so she kept with her hell and damnation.

......

Daw continued, "Thass a ooj amount f things tha hev got tuh be done in preparation afore we leave. Thass a ship, "The Amazon" ois sailing from Liverpool to New York in June and oi suggest we aim to be on it. Atwin me, yew an' the geartepost, tha' ois gorn to be a long, owl' journey – taking weeks to gi' from Liverpool to New York, and months afore we gi' to our final destination. We are gorn to Utah. We do not know waa we will come up agin, there are mountains, hundre's f moils f vast plairns to cross, dangerous countryside an' orl. Thass jist thur beginning – we hev got to tairke possession f thur land we are allotted and work and toil until we ken mairk a gorn f thur land. Howsomever, oi hev to say, and oi know yow do not wo'a

156

to hare this, but, we may navver mairk it. Think on waal oi hev said and let me know do yow are coming wi' me and yar maw."

We were all a bit hushed at hearing what dad had to say about the journey. I mean, I had a young son. Lucy asked dad if he felt he was strong enough to undertake such a harrowing journey but dad just said, if he was not, he was not, but nothing was going to make him stay.

"Hold yew hard, everyone". This was my brother, George, speaking, "Oi know thur situation 'are in Norfolk, ois desperate, and getting worse, but oi hev not bairn able to persuade moi Harriet to leave. She ois worried about her little one, Louisa. She's oolly 4 yares owl' and she ois delicate. Oi think we will hev to put this on hold, at this toime. Oi will keep begging and pleading wi har, but oi think thur oolly way to persuade Harriet to tairke thur journey ois do we gi' news from yow tha yow hev all arrived safely. Oi am sure yow ken understand our worries."

Yes, we could all understand William's worries. Yes, I had my young William, but Louisa had been poorly. We agreed with him that maw, daw, Lucy, Thomas and I with young William would make the trip and, all being well, and God having mercy on us, we would send for William and his family at a later date. I say, William and his family, but William and Harriet hadn't actually tied the knot, and not actually living together, even though they'd had a child. They'd 'jumped over the broom' so they say. They hadn't got to know each other properly and the situation between them was not good. I did not even know if William had proposed! Our brother, George, said he wanted to come, with his then girlfriend, Eliza but they would be coming later too, as they needed to get some money together.

157

"Sorry.....Oi think oi hev changed moi mind." This was Lucy. "Yes, oi wo'a tuh goo, but oi think oi wo'a to know yow are all safe first."

"Thass alright, dear," maw replied, "Oi am sure we all understand. Tha' ois scary. We are all scared. We dunna know waa to expect and waa dangers we will come acros. Yar daw and me, well, we be getting on, so tha' will not be all tha bad do we do not mairk that'. But yow are young and yow hev your whole life ahead f yow. We are putting our loives in God's hands."

"Tell yow what, Lucy," I piped up, "If we mairk it, and oi know thass a big iff, tairke thur next ship wi' George and Harriet and Louisa. Oi am sure Harriet would appreciate thur company and hev someone to 'alp her with Louisa."

"Yes, tha zounds a good plan."

So, it was all agreed.

EAST ANGLIA

CHAPTER 12

Robert Munford's home in England with Ann and Lucy in the doorway.

Daw had told us the background of the great emigration of the people from East Anglia, i.e. Essex, Suffolk and Norfolk. Lucy, Thomas, George and I hadn't been born when the problems started, and to a certain extent, we hadn't known the difference. We knew we were hungry most of the time and daw had been doing his best, going from job to job, but the work had been piecemeal, that is, if there was news of work on a farm, he made a run for it, even if it meant a lot of travel back and forth. More often, he got there and all the jobs had been taken and he was told to be on his way. He did get a job as a railway gateman for a time, but that did not last either.

He knew the area when it was the crucible of agricultural advancement in Britain, when everyone was crying out for produce from East Anglia. Daw had been born in 1790. The area had been well off, for centuries, but it was hard hit after the Napoleonic wars. The demand for corn, and the large labour force required to harvest it, had always fostered a healthy rural economy. However, with the end of the wars, demand eased and rural England slid into economic depression, burdened by a destitute surplus labour force. To make matters worse, the cottage spinning and plaiting industries collapsed around the same time.

The unemployment, and consequent disorder, got so bad that parish authorities began to explore the possibilities of assisted passages to deal with the rural unemployed. People started to leave throughout the 1830s, increasing in the 1850s, with significant numbers choosing to move overseas to the USA, Canada and Australia, although Australia wasn't popular as people still had memories of the numbers of prisoner ships sailing there.

It wasn't just Norfolk that was feeling the hardships. Emigration was happening all over as a reaction to the destruction of the traditional structures of a rural society.

Government schemes for emigration began soon after the end of the wars in 1815. Daw had seen adverts way back then for 'lands in British America.... where there is a good market for grain and other production from the earth'. Daw had kept all the adverts in a folder, which he would bring out intermittently. In the early 1820s the British government made four large grants to encourage emigration, but the feeling at the time was that maybe things would turn a corner and get back on their feet. Also there was a fear that the Irish, escaping from the famine there, would fill the places left by those emigrating, and there would be wide-ranging vagrancy.

I would ask my father, every so often, if I could look at his folder, being particularly interested in the government advertisements and views on emigration. He was pleased in my interest and, one time, brought out a well-worn and brown-tinged newspaper cutting from 1828.

> *'There is reason to hope for the greatest and most important results from connecting emigration and the repeal of the poor laws, so as to accomplish at once relief for the present and security for the future'.*

Daw had gone on to say, "Yes, things navver picked up, as yow know. pay was cut all oover. We jist navver had thur kew'er to buy anything. Food was scarce and thur Pore Relief wuz not enow to sustain a family. Thur rich folk, those landed gentry and busines owners, did not wo'a t'put their hands in their pockets to increase thur Pore Relief. Do people dint move out, thay were dying f starvation do put in thur dreaded workhouse, navver to return, so thur government explored thur possibilities f assisted emigration."

161

I would listen to daw as he talked about the industrialisation of the area. "Yow know, those land-owners made tha' worse for us farm-hands." He would relate the history of the area and I would sit there listening intently, quite intrigued. He told me, in times gone by, it was realised there was a problem with the soil, especially in Suffolk – the soil was just clay-heavy and was hard to dig over. Innovative farmers here started a six course rotation system, the use of turnips as a root crop and a system of hollow draining, so the area became known for its spirit of innovation and our agriculture was way ahead of most Midland counties. As a consequence, during the high prices and grain shortages of the Napoleonic wars, our farms were able to convert their land use to grain production in a far shorter time. When the wars ended, the depression took hold and East Anglian agriculture was left highly vulnerable to the inevitable slump in grain prices. The farmers here, however, still, continued to plough up dairy pasture to make room for corn, believing that the eastern counties dry climate could not complete with the low price of imported Dutch and Irish dairy products. Then came bad harvest years. "

"We were at thur beck and call f thur landlords. 'Ose land-owners jist employed casual landlords to look ar'er their lands. We hev noo truck with thur landlords and nayther thay wi' us, which made tha' woss for us farm-hands..Thay dint know waa to do for thur best – do thay laid orff thur workers to reduce their losses, tha woulda incurred more debt as thay were required to pay thur nair'av towards thur Pore Relief, which thay were not inclined to do, so waa did we end up with - mas unemployment and depression. Naathins changed."

Daw delved into his folder again. "Oi've got a la'er 'are to Lord Sidmouth dated 27 May 1816.

'The state of the labouring poor is truly miserable. Such is the want of employment that stout active young men are employed by the overseers, at three or four shillings a week, merely to prevent them from starving ...The labouring poor in husbandry (including disabled men from the army and navy) are not four fifths employed. The poor rates ...are higher than at any period in the last forty years.

Daw told me that his wages had dropped from 10s a week to 8s 5d by 1823. "Oi am sorry, lass, but ken yow recall thur larst toime we had meat? Must hev bairn Christmas last, when yar maw and oi did without, jist to give yow childer a good meal, along with bread and potato, washed down wi' a cup f water. We hev survived, but tha ois all. Oi feel so sorry for yow childer, but oi car' do more. Oi hev bairn in touch wi' yar brother, John, telling him our plans. He 'as got some savings and ois gorn to 'alp us out for our move to America. We will need food on thur journey."

I remembered that maw used to do hand-loom weaving in the winter months. I used to help her too, along with my sisters, and doing embroidery. It was seasonal work while the fields were in farrow, but that work had all stopped now as well, so we couldn't bring in any money either.

Daw got out a book on Constable he had been reading. In it there was a letter Thomas Sherlock Gooch Esq, MP Halesworth 1824.

' The labourer is now, in general, the mere servant of the day, or of the season; and is cast off, when the task is done, to seek a precarious

subsistence from other work, if he can find it; if not from the parish rates '

163

"Woss changed fur thur woss, more recently, ois tha dreadful troshin machine. Oh, do there ent enow unemployment as tha' is, why not bring in a machine tha ken do thur work f 20 men? Machines everywhere, putting good, hard-working, men out f work."

Daw related his tale: It seems he was so livid that he even took action himself. He'd got together with about 200 people, all armed with axes, saws, spades and such like – whatever they could use as a weapon and they took it upon themselves to destroy the threshing machines on one farm then, the next morning, went to another farm, where they destroyed a plough. They tried to attack another place but this landlord managed to get together his neighbours of about 20 people and word was got to the local Waterloo force, that rode out and got between us and the barn where the machines were, then the Riot Act was read. We couldn't compete with that, so, with tails between our legs, we, begrudgingly, wandered off.

It seems there were incidents like that all over East Anglia.

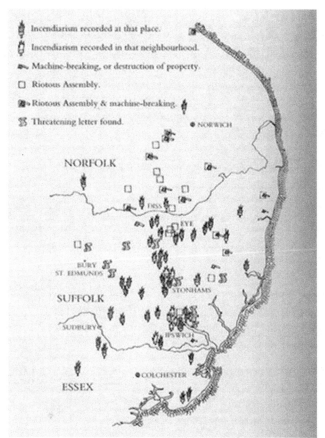

Incendiarism recorded at that place.

Incendiarism recorded in that neighbourhood.

Machine-breaking, or destruction of property.

☐ Riotous Assembly.

Riotous Assembly & machine-breaking.

Threatening letter found.

● NORWICH

NORFOLK

DISS

EYE

BURY
ST. EDMUNDS

SUFFOLK

STONHAMS

SUDBURY

IPSWICH

● COLCHESTER

ESSEX

The East Anglian disturbances of December 1821-1822

Something had to be done and that is when the idea of emigration was decided on by the East Anglian parish authorities. It would be expensive but it was deemed there was sufficient capital available to allow the destitute to consider it as a viable option. Describing how the money had been raised a government report stated that:

165

'The funds were in most cases advanced by the parish, which were either borrowed from private individuals or from country bankers to be repaid by instalments from the rates '.

British Parliamentary Papers, Poor Law session 1834 Appendix A p375 (60-64)

Blything Hundred

Number out of Employment	1001
Wives belonging	602
Children	2399
Total	4002
Cost for the month	£938 s.9 d.4
Outdoor relief for the same month and those maintained in the house	£844 s.11 d.8
Total expense of poor	£1783 s.1

Hoxne Hundred

	Able bodied Men	No out of employment	Monthly Cost
Baddingdon	110	60	£8 s.5 d.4
Denningtone	150	65	£65 s.12 d.8
Wilby	71	32	£80
Laxfield	100	55	£73
Stradbrooke	110	70	£97
Fressingfield	140	110	£176
Framlingham	200	160	£222 s.10

Table from The Agricultural Labourers in Suffolk, Farming in the Nineteenth Century, edited by J Thirsk and J Imray p134

For those able to leave, North America proved a popular destination. A great demand for labour in some parts of United States offered the prospect of employment, there was also the draw of the fertile lands of the Midwest that had become open to agricultural settlement. Assisted and unassisted emigration to the North America took place in East Anglia throughout the 1830s.

Daw had said that he'd being keeping account of the travels to America, reading in the Bury and Norwich Post that men, women and children had been passing through Bury, from local towns, including the Diss Hundred, which had a high area of unemployment due to the introduction of threshing machines. They travelled through in stage waggons, on their way to London to take shipping to America. Others had left for London to board a ship bound for Philadelphia. The parish had provided any necessary shoes and clothing. The poor people of the parishes had been inundated with pamphlets from the United States.

Daw had got a few of these pamphlets and had pinned them to the kitchen wall. I perused through them now. They had gone a bit brown with the heat from the coal fire, as most of them had been up there some years now.

The United States is a country of hospitality, which the wild Arab never violates and where a labourer might raise himself by industry to the level of farmer, were he to head for the countries west of the Allegheny mountains, that is, Ohio, Indiana, Kentucky and Tennessee or the Illinois.

Further on I read a note from John Syring, who was so confident of his prospects that, when he emigrated to Ohio, he took his 80 year old mother-in-law.

> *'Ohio is a great state for growing wheat which they raise in abundance owing to the land being rich...I am about to become a farmer bye and by, I bought a farm last November of 82 acres for 640 dollars of which I paid 150 dollars down and the balance in 5 years ...old Mrs Slackforth is pretty well and had her health remarkably good since coming to America*
>
> *'Bury and Norwich Post April 30th 1851.*

168

So, no wonder the depressed, unemployed people of East Anglia were taking the plunge, when there was a world of opportunity waiting for them over the Atlantic. It was exciting and I was taken up with the prospect of living a life, in a different world, with food and new clothing, and work, so I could buy things, and I couldn't wait to go.

Taking some of the pamphlets off the wall, and reading through, I read that the authorities were making it a rule not to press for the whole of the purchase price at the time of effecting a sale, instead requiring payment over a four year period. Farmers were also able to take advantage of pre-emption acts, offering farms at reduced charges to colonists who would live there for a certain length of time.

There was a piece more from John Styring. He had written home from Plaster Bed Sandusky Bay on March 24th 1851

> *The farming is very rough and slovenly compared to English farming. We have farms around us which has been sown with wheat 5 or 6 years in succession and the last is the best. There are fields in this district which produce 100 bushels per acre. They run a heavy drag over it without ploughing it and sown with fall wheat and it remains without doing anything until harvest. Animals, we have none worth speaking about only horses which are good being light and spirited, cattle are very ordinary, they take no pains in their breeding, all running about the prairies. As for wild animals most or all of them have shared the same fate of the poor Indians and have been forced to fly further west, the only*

remaining are foxes, mink, opossums, racoons, woodchucks, squirrels, skunks and deer etc.

There was another piece:

'On Thursday last, a great number of persons passed through Bury in waggons, many people appeared in great poverty, they were from the parishes of South and North Lopham and were on their way to embark at Liverpool for the U.S.A. Between 100 and 200 are emigrating from these parishes with a considerable amount of money being borrowed on security of the rates to defray expenses of passage (about 6L 10s a head) and to furnish each family a clear sum of 5L when they land at New York. Two couples from each parish married on Monday se'nnight in contemplation of joining the party of colonists and so anxious were some to quit the home of their sires, they sold off their little stock of furniture.

'Bury and Norwich Post March 31st 1830

"These are old, daw, dating from thur 1830s. Why dint we all tairke orff then? Why hev yow waited so long?

"Well, oi will tal you, mawther. Do yow read a bit further, yow willl find tha thur first emigrants wen' to thur eastern coastal cities, where thay orfen found themselves woss off, alonga thur bad conditions, high living costs, disease, epidemics and

170

employment was scarce. Hare, look, thass waa yow need to read."

Daw took another pamphlet off the wall.

> *'So many emigrants arrive at all the principle ports of the United States that there is little chance of procuring employment in them, most of the distress which has been reported to exist in America has been suffered by those who have imprudently lingered in the cities until their money was exhausted '*

Oh, some managed alright, indeed but oi bent be taerkin' moi young family oover to hev them cop-owld diseases and die on me. No, and yow were oolly 3-years-old in 1835. No, mawther, oi wairted. Many returned. Oi haad tha unemployed emigrants were bairn paid in store goods, tha thay could not sal on for a good price. Tha ois thur sairm system thur north ois up in arms about 'are – truck shops. Then oi haad thur west was opening up. A soigh' further to go, indeed, but thass mare chance do we jist pas quickly through New York.

.

MUNFORD FAMILY JOURNEY

The Amazon **London to New York** 4 Jun 1863 - 18 Jul 1863

CHAPTER 13

Lucky for us, the Amazon was leaving from London – the first ship, taking Mormons from England to America, to leave from London. It would have been so difficult for us to have made our way to Liverpool. So we hauled all of our belongings that we felt were vital to have, into wheeled carts, leaving everything else behind, our furniture and carpets and so on, and pulled these carts to Norwich station, where we loaded them on the train for London docks.

In the party were my five year old son, William; my parents Robert (73) and Lydia (52); my younger brother, Thomas (20) and myself, Ann (29). My brother William (23) and his family plus my sister, Lucy (24) were to come later. We also expected my Brother George to join us at a later date.

The Amazon, we found, was a splendid packet ship, captained by H.K. Hovey. There were 895 people on board under the presidency of Elder William Bramall, Elders Edward L Sloan and Richard Palmer as his counsellors.

We found out the ship was a 1,771 ton ship, 216 feet long by 42 feet wide and 27 feet deep, with three decks, three masts with a round tuck and a female figurehead. She was one of the largest and fastest packets of the day and had a reputation as being one of the luckiest of the western ocean packets.

We passed through the Government Emigration Offices on 3rd June, after which President Cannon, accompanied by several elder, held a meeting, organising the company and giving appropriate instructions.

There was a lot of excitement among the passengers. I was spinning around with little William and he was giggling with glee. It was a novelty to us all. None of us had even been much further than Norwich, for shopping for exceptional items. People were waving goodbye to friends and family on the dock side, others were waiting for instructions on where they were to go on the ship. Elder Kay closed the meeting with prayer, with President Cannon pronouncing a blessing upon the ship, her officers and crew and all the travellers.

A brass band, from South Wales, were on board too – the performers being members of the Church, also going to Utah, or Zion, as some people were calling it. Sweet music was coursing through on the poop-deck before and after the meeting, while the sun shone down upon the crowded deck as if the heavens and the earth were coming together to bestow their blessing on us all.

What amazed us still was a fanfare went up and a smartly-clad elderly gentleman boarded.

"Waal's tha all about." I asked to no-one in particular. I then heard people shouting out, "It's Charles Dickens, the famous author – he's coming on board!." He did indeed come on board, with various other dignitaries.

I was overawed seeing Charles Dickens. He was one of my favourite authors and I went to see if I could speak to him. I left little William in charge of his gran and went to see him. His eyes were on everybody and, as he was walking about he was writing all the time. He was watching people bring on their belongings, up and down the two gangways, the men, women and children, with their boxes and bundles containing all their worldly belongings and dock workers carrying boxes full of food being brought on for the voyage, teeming with tins, bread, vegetables, cheese, butter, milk. He watched the to-ing and fro-ing of carts and horse-drawn cans and vans bringing more and more immigrants with their belongings.

I followed him below deck and he seemed disconsolate at seeing so many people crowded in all the nooks and crannies but they were just getting themselves organised with no foul language and no drinking. The Captain approached Mr Dickens and they had a short conversation. "The most of these came aboard yesterday evening from various parts of the nation but they all seem to be ordered and getting on with their neighbours, although they had never met each other before. They have even established their own police, made their own regulations and set up their own watches at all the hatchways."

174

Mr Dickens then spoke to the Mormon agent. He was a short and fairly stout man, but handsome, dressed in black, with rich brown hair and beard and clear bright eyes. To me he had a strange accent but sounded quick and intelligent and had a confident manner about him.

I hid myself, not wanting to interrupt them.

"These are a very fine set of people you have brought together here."

"Yes, sir, they are a very fine set of people."

Looking about him, Mr Dickens continued, "Indeed, I think it would be difficult to find Eight hundred people together anywhere else, and find so much beauty and so much strength and capacity for work among them."

The agent did not follow Mr Dicken's gaze but looked at him steadily. "I think so.--We sent out about a thousand more, yes'day, from Liverpool."

"You are not going with these emigrants?"

"No, sir. I remain."

"But you have been in the Mormon Territory?"

"Yes; I left Utah about three years ago."

Mr Dickens, looking about again continued, "It is surprising to me that these people are all so cheery, and make so little of the immense distance before them."

"Well, you see, many of 'em have friends and family out at Utah, and many of 'em look forward to meeting friends on the way."

"On the way?"

The agent replied. "This way 'tis. This ship lands 'em in New York City. Then they go on by rail right away beyond St. Louis, to that part of the Banks of the Missouri where they strike the Plains. There, waggons from the settlement meet 'em to bear 'em company on their journey 'cross--twelve hundred miles about. Industrious people who come out to the settlement soon get waggons of their own, and so the friends of some of these will come down in their own waggons to meet 'em. They look forward to that, greatly.

Mr Dickens seemed to ponder a bit about this news, then said, "On their long journey across the desert, do you arm them?"

"Mostly you would find they have arms of some kind or another already with them. Such as had not arms we should arm across the plains, for the general protection and defence."

"Will these waggons bring down any produce to the Missouri?"

"Well, since the war broke out, we've taken to growing cotton, and they'll likely bring down cotton to be exchanged for machinery. We want machinery. Also we have taken to growing indigo, which is a fine commodity for profit. It has been found that the climate on the further side of the Great Salt Lake suits well for raising indigo."

Mr Dickens seemed to have so many questions be wanted answers for, "I am told that these people now on board are principally from the South of England?"

"And from Wales. That is true."

"Do you get many Scotch?"

"Not many."

"Highlanders, for instance?"

"No, not Highlanders. They ain't interested enough in universal brotherhood and peace and good will."

Mr Dickens chuckled a bit, adding, "The old fighting blood is strong in them?"

The agent did smile at this but added, more sternly, "Well, yes. And besides; they've no faith."

There were a lot of people pushing and trying to get by, and it looked like Mr Dickens had wanted to speak to someone else, but missed him in the crowd. There were other people who had gathered round, trying to listen in to this conversation. His attention has been drawn to a labourer, a simple fresh-coloured farm labourer of about 38 years old, who had been standing close by.

"Would you mind my asking you what part of the country you come from?" Mr Dickens asked him.

"Not a bit. Theer!" and in a proud sort of manner said, "I've worked all my life o' Salisbury Plain, right under the shadder o' Stonehenge. You mightn't think it, but I haive."

"And a pleasant country too."

"Ah! 'Tis a pleasant country."

"Have you any family on board? Mr Dickens enquired of the labourer.

"Two children, boy and gal. I am a widderer, I am, and I am going out alonger my boy and gal. That's my gal, and she's a fine gal o' sixteen (pointing out a girl who was writing by the boat). I'll go and fetch my boy. I'd like to show you my boy. (Here the labourer disappeared and presently came back with a big shy boy of twelve, in a superabundance of boots. He did not seem at all glad to be presented.) He is a fine boy too, and a boy fur to work! (The boy then ran off).

"It must cost you a great deal of money to go so far, three strong." Mr Dickens enquired.

"A power of money. Theer! Eight shillen a week, eight shillen a week, eight shillen a week, put by out of the week's wages for ever so long."

"I wonder how you did it."

The labourer smiled and seeming to be pleased at Mr Dicken's interest answered. "See there now! I wonder how I done it! But what with a bit o' subscription heer, and what with a bit o' help theer, it were done at last, though I donna hardly know how.

Then it were unfort'net for us, you see, as we got kep' in Bristol so long--nigh a fortnight, it were--on accounts of a mistake wi' Brother Halliday. Swaller'd up money, it did, when we might have come straight on."

"Sir, may I ask you, you are of the Mormon religion, of course?"

Puffing himself up, the labourer replied confidently, "O yes, I am a Mormon" Then repeated himself, but more thoughtfully, "I am a Mormon." Then, looking around the ship, seemed to see a friend and took his leave of Mr Dickens.

I was then called for dinner, along with all the emigrants, so went down between decks to join my family. Then a general muster was called. This muster was for the ceremony of passing the Government Inspector and the Doctor. Those authorities held their temporary state amid-ships, by a cask or two. I saw that Mr Dickens had positioned himself behind them. I was expecting them to be authoritative and commanding but they were good natured and understanding.

Everyone who was coming on board were now all on deck, densely crowded at the stern and swarming upon the poop-deck like bees. There was no rush or disorder, just everyone took their turn with the Inspector, then departed.

The head person of each group or family had their tickets ready, to have checked. I joined the rest of the family at this point.

I heard the names as they were called out from the names on the ticket. "Jessie Jobson, Sophronia Jobson, Jessie Jobson

179

again, Matilda Jobson, William Jobson, Jane Jobson, Matilda Jobson again, Brigham Jobson, Leonardo Jobson, and Orson Jobson. Are you all here?" the Inspector called out, glancing at the party, over his spectacles.

"JESSIE JOBSON NUMBER TWO. All here, sir."

This group was composed of an old grandfather and grandmother, their married son and his wife, and their family of children. Orson Jobson is a little child asleep in his mother's arms. The Doctor, with a kind word or so, lifts up the corner of the mother's shawl, looks at the child's face, and touches the little clenched hand. "If we were all as well as Orson Jobson, doctoring would be a poor profession."

Jessie Jobson took his ticket and passed on

The next group approached the inspector, with their ticket ready, "Susannah Cleverly and William Cleverly. Brother and sister, eh?"

"Yes, sir," the sister replied. She seemed to be a young business women, jostling on her brother, who seemed to be of a slower disposition.

"Very good, Susannah Cleverly." The inspector said, "Take your ticket, Susannah, and take care of it."

And away they went.

The next group were Sampson Dibble and Dorothy Dibble. The inspector surveyed a very old couple, over his glasses). "Your husband quite blind, Mrs. Dibble?"

"Yes, sir, he be stone-blind." Mrs Dibble replied.

Mr Dibble answered too, but looking in the direction of the mast, not the inspector. "Yes, sir, I be stone-blind."

"That is a bad job. Take your ticket, Mrs. Dibble, and don't lose it, and pass on."

"ANASTASIA WEEDLE." Anastatia was a pretty girl, in a bright Garibaldi, elected by universal suffrage as The Beauty of the Ship. "That is me, sir."

"Going alone, Anastatia?"

Shaking her curls. "I am with Mrs. Jobson, sir, but I've got separated for the moment."

"Oh! You are with the Jobsons? Quite right. That'll do, Miss Weedle. Don't lose your ticket."

Then it was our turn, "The Munford family." Looking at the ticket and reading, "Robert Munford, Lydia Munford, Thomas Munford, Ann Munford, and William Munford Stubbs.

Dad retrieved the ticket and we all went off, letting the inspectors continue the long process.

The next I saw of Mr Dickens was when he went to view the dancing on the top deck, with the band playing. There he met the captain.

""I fully believed that I would bear testimony against them, but to my great astonishment they do not deserve it. Some

181

remarkable influence has produced a remarkable result. Had I not known they were Mormons, I would describe them, in their degree, the pick and flower of England. They merit praise instead of the censure I had been prepared to give them.

When the captain had departed, I took my opportunity, "Sorry, to disturb you, Mr Dickens, but oi am a gri' admirer f your work, and am so excited to see yow."

I introduced myself, "Ah, a Norfolk girl, I hear. I have visited East Anglia many times and have indeed visited Norwich and was in Great Yarmouth in 1849, staying at the Royal Hotel on Waterloo Road. I used Great Yarmouth as my setting for David Copperfield…. I saw an upturned boat on the beach, used as a house, which provided me the inspiration for Peggotty's house. I shall quote you David Copperfield's first reaction on seeing the upturned boat, 'I looked in all directions, as far as I could stare over the wilderness, and away at the sea and away at the river, but no house could I make out. There was a black barge, or some kind of superannuated boat, not far off, high and dry on the ground, with an iron funnel sticking out of it for a chimney and smoking very cosily; but nothing else in the way of habitation that was visible to me.' I was overwhelmed when Mr Dickens then gave me his autograph and wished me a good trip. I thanked him profusely and ran back to join the family to show them the autograph. I then went to investigate further as he was only staying on board for a few hours, quietly observing us.

It was time for him to leave. He raised his hat and wished us all a safe voyage.

The excitement grew as the ship upped anchor and slowly made its way out of the dock and moved down the river. The people on the wharves were cheering and also people on the banks of the river and on their anchored vessels – waving their handkerchiefs and hats and cheering in response to the singing of the people and the music of the band.

We found out later that the chartering of this vessel was not a matter of choice but of necessity as a suitable vessel could not be obtained in the port of Liverpool. It was the first Mormon ship to leave from London.

However, the happiness soon turned to tears for a few of the passengers, as they saw England fading away out of sight and they were leaving loved ones behind, not knowing if they would ever see them again. I admit I wept a few tears and certainly mum had a tear in her eye too and said, "Stop yar blaring, dew yer'll mearke me blar an'orl."

Thomas and my William and I had the upper berth and mum, dad and mum had the lower berth. On the whole, it was a good journey. The brass band would play when the weather was fine, and there was singing and dancing. Brother William Brimall held meetings. Elijah Larkin soon organised a choir. The brethren looked in all the girls' berths every night to see that no sailors had got in them.

The ship's officers passed out provisions, helped the emigrants settle comfortably between decks and fastened down loose luggage.

A baby girl was born three days after departure and was christened 'Amazon Seaborn Harris', which was obviously quite fitting.

At 3.30 each morning we were to rise, receive water, clean out our berths, scrape the decks and prepare for prayers in the various Wards at 7am. However, many had got seasickness early on so that rigorous schedule rule was relaxed. The crew were bringing out boiled gruel to the sick.

At times the ship was becalmed; at times the crew fought headwinds. One Sunday, the ship was hit by a violent squall while Ward meetings were being conducted on the lower deck. One sail was torn into ribbons like paper and water poured down the hatches before they could be closed. Then it seemed as if we were shut in a prison, dark, dismal and eerie and everyone was quiet, just listening to the storm, or tending to their families. The second mate was heard to exclaim, "I am astonished at the nonchalance displayed by the sisters in such a season of apparent peril."

The English outnumbered the Welsh five to one, but that did not deter some members of each group from squabbling over the relative merits of their homelands. The ship's presidency tried to calm the rivalry by preaching against nationalism. A little irritation which developed, over family cooking arrangements, also had to be smoothed over and, apparently, a few were guilty of 'finding' articles that had not been lost.

On Saturday 6th, it was blowing a gale, almost dead ahead. We anchored in the evening near the Isle of Wight, about 6 miles off Portsmouth. The crew were kept busy attending the numerous cases of sickness and suffering. My family were all feeling poorly and I was making cups of tea for them as they couldn't keep down the gruel. I did not know what the crew had done to the gruel, but it tasted burnt. The ship's doctor ordered pale ale for mum to give her strength, as she was feeling quite weak. This seemed to help, thank goodness. I had quite a scramble to get food cooked for the family, without mum's help.

The anchor was not raised until the Monday. People were beginning to feel a lot better and were making up for their sickness and inability to keep anything down by crowding out the cooking galley. Eating seemed to the most important business of the day and we all enjoyed tasty puddings and pies. The return of sunshine and calm weather had a wonderful effect on the appetites of the company.

While anchored, a boat visited the ship twice, from Portsmouth, bringing bread and other fresh provisions on board. There was a general rush for this fresh produce but, from what I heard the cost was well over the top. We did not have that sort of money to waste and were keeping all we had for necessities on our onward journey. I heard many of the crewmen shouting out to the company, "Save your money, you will need it for the journey ahead," and a man was placed beside the cellars to counsel people. Still, I saw some changing gold to buy a trifle such as a loaf of bread and others digging deep into their purses to take out the last shilling they had. I told mum and dad. "Oi car' believe thur foolhardines f some people on board. Do thay not realise tha thay will need kew'er jist to gi' from New York to Florence, let aloon thur journey on from there. Thay will hev to find provisions do starve, do be dependent on others for food."

There was one death on board, on Tuesday 16th - a child, Heber Franklin Tavey, aged 5 months, child of Peter and Frances Tavey of London. The child had died of diarrhoea. It seemed a sad sight to see it buried at sea. They dressed the baby and then sewed it up in sacking, with a weight attached to it, then lay it on a board and put one end on the railing of the ship. This all took place on the port side, the leeward side. Two verses of a hymn were sung by those present, then a prayer and a few remarks. Then the carpenter upended the board and the body slid into the sea.

About eleven o'clock I had to go up for the doctor for William, who kept coughing in a strange way, and couldn't seem to catch his breath. The doctor administered a mustard plaster to his throat and what he said was an antimonial emetic, containing both. Poor William was suffering with a touch of croup. Luckily William got a good deal better by morning.

On Saturday 20th, it was blowing and raining a gale and people were getting sick again. There were quite a few cases of diarrhoea, my family included as well as myself. The doctor came again and tested my pulse, saying it was strong – then looked at my tongue. He gave me two grains of calcium and 10 grains of something beginning with 'rhu'… I did not get what he said. As I was in quite a bit of pain, he administered chloric ether, about 8-10 drops.

The crew were kept busy looking after the sick. One of them was a black steward. I had never seen a man from Africa before and he looked sort of exotic in my eyes. I found out his name was Joseph. He came with some gruel for me and asked how I was. He was very pleasant. I asked if I could do a sketch of him when I was feeling better, but he said, "No Miss Ann, I's too busy to sit for you. Got so much work looking after these

186

sick people." I said that was a shame and thanked him for his kindness.

In the afternoon it cleared up and most people were asked to go up on deck as the crew tar burned between the decks.

The winds blew hither and thither up until 25th and we were being tossed and turned. Tins and cans and luggage not tied down were scuttling across the lower deck.

"I fare badly terday, I dew, an'orl." I told mum. I was feeling quite unwell and was given some brandy and water by the doctor with order to go to bed. I dreamed I had gone back to Costessey again. The dream was so much like reality, seeing my sister, Lucy, again, that I felt very unhappy while asleep to think I should be so foolish, to leave my family here and go back, but when I awoke mum was sitting in front of the berth and I felt she was as a guardian angel to me and fairly clasped mum for joy, with tears running down my cheeks. Mum was very comforting after I told her my dream,

It ois jist tha yow ent tew ferce terday, moi love, and we do not know waa thur future holds, but we'll gi' there, together, don'' yow worry, we'll gi' to our Zion. 'Owld on tuh thur dream f thur future, not yar dream f thur parst."

Mum was a tower of strength, even though she had been ill herself.

I managed to get up, still feeling very weak and ill. Luckily I had the rest of the family to look after my William. I felt a little bit better as the day wore on. It was a perfect calm, the ship lying on the bosom of the mighty deep, unmoved save as she

187

gently rose and fell when the swell of the ocean passed under her. The water was like a vast sea of molten glass. For the first time since we left London, we experienced warm weather, the thermometer standing at 72 degrees on the Spar Deck. Some whales appeared in sight, and created quite a sensation as they cast water up through their nostrils or blow holes to a great height. Towards evening the ship gathered way and began to move, the wind being almost dead ahead.

We heard that a young lady was very sick – not seasick, but she had a tumour in her side. She was in great pain and was being administered to by the Elders. I found out she was called Ann Bowing and was only 17 years old. We felt really sorry for her but, obviously could do nothing to assist. Her mother and sister were present. We all said a prayer.

On 22nd there was a head wind and the sea was rough. We made very little progress. A drove of black fish passed the vessel, which the sailors said indicated bad weather. Provisions were served out. I was still feeling very sick with diarrhoea and had a severe headache and went to bed. I had a dream that we were all in the Utah Valley and Ann Bowing and her family were with us. That gave me a good feeling and hoped it was an omen that Ann Bowing would survive.

Dad told me that a school of porpoises had surrounded the ship. Mr. Williams, first mate had struck one with the harpoon but did not get it. Mum put mustard plasters on my chest and loins and I felt much better. I slept and, when I awoke, I was free from pain.

On the 2nd, I couldn't sleep and went on deck at about 5am. Hundreds of porpoises were in sight, and looked beautiful as they raced and splashed along. This evening we had dancing on deck, the band played first rate. The water was rationed to two quarts. We were becalmed so I suppose the captain was just being careful with rations.

On 4th, being the American Independence Day, the American flag was hoisted at the mast's head. The band played the Star Spangled Banner, Hail Columbia, and other such tunes. There was dancing & singing on deck during the day.

The Captain gave a little speech when the flag was raised, "On 4th July, 1776, the Declaration of Independence declared that the thirteen colonies at war with the Kingdom of Great Britain regarded themselves as thirteen independent sovereign states, no longer under British rule and thus the United States of America was formed.

The Captain then introduced an American officer, to give us a potted history of the latest events in the recent Civil War. "I don't know how much you have gleaned of what has been happening in America recently and what has become known as the 'Civil War'. However, there has been much fighting between the Union forces of the north and the Confederate forces of the south. To the west, the Union had destroyed the Confederate river navy by the summer of last year, 1862, then much of its western armies, and seized New Orleans. The siege of Vicksburg has been going on while we have been at sea – May 18th to 4th July. I am pleased to say the Union has won, by splitting the Confederacy in two at the Mississippi River." We hadn't known much of this while we were on the ship, and hadn't known the significance of the flag being raised on 4th July. Also, the names of these strange places meant nothing to us, although I had heard of the Mississippi River. The Officer continued, "Major General Ulysses S Grant and his

Tennessee army had crossed the Mississippi River and drove the Confederate Army of Mississippi, led by Lt. Gen. John C Pemberton into the defensive lines surrounding the fortress city of Vicksburg. After holding out for more than forty days, with their supplies nearly gone, the garrison surrendered on July 4 – quite significantly on our Independence Day. The successful ending of the Vicksburg campaign has significantly degraded the ability of the Confederacy to maintain its war effort. There is at present fighting at the down-river Port Hudson with Maj. Gen. Nathaniel P Banks leading the Union troops. If they succeed the command of the Mississippi River will revert to the Union forces. Approximately 3,000 Confederate troops have been killed, injured or are missing and 29,000 captured, so far. So, ladies and gentlemen, hopefully our Civil War is coming to an end, although there are still skirmishes and I endeavour to plead with you all to be vigilant."

We thanked the officer. I wondered how he had got his information, but we had passed numerous ships and there had been flag semaphore communication between the ships and then I remembered that a small boat had been rowed over to us and someone came on board. The small boat was then rowed back with that same person on board.

This was definitely something to worry us all. Would we be safe when we landed? What sort of danger would we be in? We didn't expect to arrive in the middle of a Civil War. Poor dad thought this would be the right time to travel, thinking his family would be safe, as long as we got out of New York quickly. I commenced writing a letter to Lucy, telling her all of this news, then packed up my things. We were 330 miles from New York when a thick fog set in about 4pm. Everyone was ordered off the Poop Deck but one of the ladies refused to go. The black steward, Joseph, who had been very helpful to us, very kindly persuaded her to go below. At midnight a steam ship passed us so close that we could hear the bellow of both vessels that were used as fog signals, ringing very violently.

Soundings were taken the next day. We were 180 miles from Sandy Hook by the next day and the fog looked like it was beginning to clear.

Fire Island was sighted at 6pm.. A pilot came on board at 6:30. The New York Papers were read on board informing us of the riots that were going on there, which caused great deal of turmoil on board. None of us knew what to expect and if we were heading into danger. There was a lot of commotion amongst the crew and it looked like they were arming themselves.

As the American officer had said, the Siege of Port Hudson, Louisiana from 22nd May had been the Union campaign to recapture the Mississippi River in the Civil War. This would have yielded command of the Mississippi River to the Union forces. However, we read in the newspapers that Gen. Nathaniel Banks had been ordered to capture Port Hudson then go to Gen. Gran's aid. This didn't happen as his assault failed, so he set up a siege around the port, the longest siege in history – 48 days in total. It was only after the fall of Vicksberg that Gen Franklin Gardner surrendered the port.

It seemed that the northern states, known as the 'Unionists' had been in a civil war with the southern states, known as the 'Confederates', since April 1861. This civil war had begun primarily as a result of the long-standing controversy over the enslavement of black people when secessionist forces

191

attacked Fort Sumter in South Carolina, just over a month after Abraham Lincoln had been inaugurated as the President of the United States. The loyalists of the Union in the North, which also included some geographically western and southern states, proclaimed support for the Constitution. They faced secessionists of the Confederate States in the South, who denounced this strategy as infringing upon their Constitutional rights. Southern whites believed that the emancipation of slaves would destroy the South's economy, due to the large amount of capital invested in slaves and fears of integrating the ex-slave black population.

The Confederate army surrender on July 4, 1863, is sometimes considered, when combined with Gen. Robert E. Lee's defeat at Gettysburg by Maj. Gen. George Meade the previous day, the turning point of the war. It cut off the Trans-Mississippi Department (containing the states of Arkansas, Texas and part of Louisiana) from the rest of the Confederate States, effectively splitting the Confederacy in two for the rest of the war. Lincoln was calling Vicksburg "The key to the war."

There was also notification on the gallantry of black soldiers in the Union service. Captain Robert F. Wilkinson had written, "One thing I am glad to say, that is that the black troops at P. Hudson fought and acted superbly. The theory of negro inefficiency is, I am very thankful at last thoroughly exploded by facts. We shall shortly have a splendid army of thousands of them." General Banks also noted their performance in his official report, stating, "The severe test to which they were subjected, and the determined manner in which they encountered the enemy, leaves upon my mind no doubt of their ultimate success."

On June 11, 1863, an editorial from the influential and widely read *New York Times* stated, "They were comparatively raw troops, and were yet subjected to the most awful ordeal... The men, white or black, who will not flinch from that, will flinch from nothing. It is no longer possible to doubt the bravery and steadiness of the colored race, when rightly led."

The talk on board was that the anti-coloured antagonism was not just going to go away because the negros had acted so bravely in the war and a few generals had approved their entry into the army. This was deep-rooted and neighbour would be up against his own neighbour for their beliefs for or against slavery. The bit in the paper "The theory of negro *inefficiency*..." by Captain Robert F Wilkinson had jumped out at me – that was obviously the general feeling. I couldn't help thinking of Joseph – he had been so good and helpful – definitely not inefficient!

Confederate batteries fire down onto Union gunboats on the
Mississippi.

The papers also referred to 'The New York City draft riots',
which had been going on from 13th July to 16th. There had
been violent disturbances in Lower Manhattan, regarded as
the culmination of working-class discontent with new laws
passed by Congress to draft men to fight in the ongoing Civil
War. These riots were regarded as the largest civil and most
racially-charged urban disturbance in American history.

A drawing from The Illustrated London News showing armed rioters clashing with the Union Army soldiers in New York City.

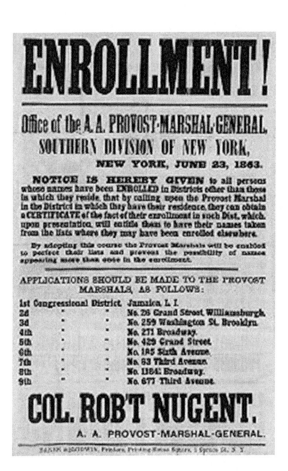

Recruiting poster for the Enrollment Act or Civil War Military Draft Act of the fderal government for the conscription of troops for the Union Army in New York City on June 23, 1863

Just to enhance my thoughts, I read further that U.S. President Abraham Lincoln had diverted several regiments of militia and volunteer troops to control the city and, according to the papers, the rioters were overwhelmingly white working-class men who feared free black people competing for work and resented that wealthier men, who could afford to pay a $300, (an exorbitant fee of possibly six years' earnings), commutation fee to hire a substitute, were spared from the draft.

Initially intended to express anger at the draft, the protests turned into a race riot with white rioters, many of them Irish immigrants and black people erupting in violence throughout the city. The official death toll was listed at either 119 or 120 individuals. Conditions in the city were such that Major General John E Wool, commander of the Department of the East, said on July 16 "Martial Law ought to be proclaimed, but I have not a sufficient force to enforce it."

The military did not reach the city until the second day of rioting, by which time the mobs had ransacked or destroyed numerous public buildings, two Protestant churches, the homes of various abolitionists or sympathizers, many black homes, and the Coloured Orphan Asylum at 44th Street and Fifth Avenue, which was burned to the ground.

There was a lot of discussion on the ship, but though we knew that the Mormon doctrine was that no man should be a slave. However, one of the American officers said "Actually, this was not true when the Mormons first went to Utah. Utah then was under Spanish and Mexican rule, it was a major source of illegal slave raids by Mexican, Ute and Navajo slave traders, particularly on Paiute tribes. When Mormon pioneers entered Utah, they introduced African slavery and provided a local market for Indian slavery. After the Mexican-American war 1846-48, Utah became part of the United States and slavery was officially legalised in Utah Territory on 4th February 1852. It was repealed on 19th June 1862 when Congress prohibited slavery in all US territories. This caused a great deal of conflict with the Mormon neighbouring states that had a slave-owning culture at the time, and they were persecuted as they no longer kept slaves, and they were seen as a threat."

He seemed to be knowledgeable on the facts so we were loath to dispute what he said, but then President George Q Cannon joined our conversation and confirmed this as fact. "In April 1847, Brigham Young consulted with members of the Quorum of the Twelve Apostles who had recently returned from the British mission. Chosen members of the vanguard group were gathered together, final supplies were packed, and the group was organized into military companies. The group consisted of 143 men, including three enslaved African-American men, and eight members of the Quorum of the Twelve Apostles, three women, and two children. The train contained 73 waggons, one cannon, and carried enough supplies to fully provision the group for one year."

We listened intently as President Cannon went on to say, "So, Brigham Young was not opposed to slavery but he tried to conform to the views of the Unionists. However, the local Indians they encountered used slaves to trade. Brigham Young and the first pioneers had developed a good understanding with the Indians - they helped each other, especially in that severe winter of 1849, when a measles epidemic broke out. The first pioneers used their limited medicine to nurse the Indians, and likewise when Mormon supplies ran low, the Ute shared their food supply. In 1850, the Indian chief, Walkara agreed to be baptized into the LDS

Church with his son. However, Walkara regularly traded women and children as slaves in order to trade for horses, guns, and ammunition. Mormon settlers tried to stop this practice, but their efforts only angered the tribe for interfering with their Indian slave trade. Relations with the Mormon settlers deteriorated rapidly."

....

On the 18th, several pilot boats were in sight, pulling toward vessels that were making for the harbour. We passed Sandy Hook at 12pm. A tug steamed up to us and the captain made arrangements for them to tow us into harbour.

The scenery was splendid on both sides of the river. A transport ship, loaded with troops for the city, passed us, and we were informed there was 4,500 troops already there to quell the riot. We anchored in the harbour about 2pm. Our band played the Star Spangled Banner, and we gave several hearty cheers. The government doctor came on board examined us all and passed us all alright. The officers of the customs came on board this evening and we started to disembark. A perfect forest of ships were in sight. We had been at sea 6 weeks and 3 days.

Six New York runners came on board, but finding they were watched by our guard, four left the ship and the other two were arrested by the guard. Brother Pinnock was called and I tried to listen in, although my family were urging me to get my things together and join the disembarkation queue. One of the guards and Brother Pinnock questioned one of the runners, "I keep a boarding house and have come on board to see if anyone wants to stay in New York." The other runner said, "I have come on board to engage seamen." The officer replied, "We are not a prey for land sharks." Then ordered the two of them to be kept under guard behind the poop deck. They were placed on the first boat that came alongside to take them ashore. One of them shouted out in a threatening manner to the officer, "We'll be waiting for you in New York." The officer shouted back, "I am well acquainted with blacklegs and thieves in the old country and I know how to deal with the likes of you in the new."

The officer then placed a guard of 12 men to prevent any more such characters coming aboard.

This had all been bewildering to everyone trying to disembark. Women were holding their children tightly to them and the children were crying, reacting to the tension they felt in their parents. The men, hearing these threats, were relying on the armed guards to keep their families safe, but were willing to fight, if the worse came to the worse.

We had to spend two days at Castle Garden in lower Manhattan, taking turns to be registered. As we were standing in a little group, the black steward, Joseph, who had befriended us on the trip, came off the boat. Father was grateful and as a matter of courtesy, shook hands with him and gave him his blessing. Onlookers, not understanding, grew very much animated over father's shaking hands with this black man. They had witnessed the draft and black rights convulsing New York City. We did not know but, only that day, blacks had been chased and hanged by mobs. A crowd had gathered round and were now threatened to hang both father and Joseph to a lamp-post. We were all so taken aback with this reaction and tried desperately to defend father, shouting out, "Leave us alone", and trying to fight off the crowd. Luckily guards came and broke up the gathering, warning my father to beware and stay clear of blacks.

SAMUEL WHITE COMPANY

CHAPTER 14

That was a narrow escape and we all gathered around poor father to console him. Mother had some brandy on her, just for medicinal purposes, which she gave to father. He needed it as he was physically shaken. We led him away from the crowd to a bench, where he could sit down and regain his composure.

So, we finally passed through Castle Garden and we were to make our way to Florence, Nebraska, continuing our journey by rail to Albany, New York. There were 1002 people in the company. Because of the civil war, the army had seized the passenger trains, leaving us all stranded near the Mississippi River. We heard that the Army was afraid the good cars would be burned by the Confederates. A string of dirty cattle cars were finally able to be chartered, which people tried to clean out and make them bearable by covering the floors with straw. We just had the straw to sit on. Food was not easy to come by and we were all hungry. Poor little children were whimpering with hunger but we couldn't leave the cars to get provisions. There was no place to cook. In the three days we were travelling, we saw some people actually get off the train when it stopped. We heard their family shouting out to them not to go, "We're frightened you'll miss the train and not be able to get back on." They managed to get back, however, by the skin of their teeth, with the whistle blowing. They had managed to procure a sack of bread scraps that they shared out. Someone else produced a dozen eggs.

Also, one of the baggage cars caught on fire and Brother Athay's family's clothing got burned and they had nothing but what they stood up in.

We were all hungry.

We finally arrived at Hannibal, Missouri, then regular train to St Joseph. From there we took a steam boat to Florence, Nebraska. We were on this boat for three days, on the Missouri River, and it was crowded. We had to sleep just where we could get space to sit down. It was cramped and very uncomfortable and the sailors were a rough set of men, making us quite afraid for our safety. We had no idea America was going to be full of such coarse men. We daren't say a word or even look askance at them, in case we got a clip around the head or even a kick. We were like prisoners, being treated harshly by our jailors, and starved into the bargain.

When we landed, we were met by the brethren from Utah with their teams, and they took us to Florence, where we had to camp until the waggon trains were ready to take us the long journey over the Plains. We were going to be travelling with Samuel White's waggon train of 46 waggons (the 10th Church waggon train of the year). The teams of oxen and waggons were waiting in a large open plain.

We left Florence on 15th August. There was a young boy, John Hayes, who seemed to be travelling on his own. Mr Morris' son was being cruel to him, for some strange reason, which made me mad and I went up to him, "Leave pore john aloone, you're jist bairn a bully. yow should be koind to everyone. do oi see yow bairn unkoind agin, oi will tal yar daw." He looked at me strangely. I can't understand you miss, are you Dutch?" I hadn't realised before that, that my Norfolk accent was so strong. Anyway, I told his father about his son bullying John Hayes and Mr Morris was very kind to John all the way and appeared to take the place of a good kind father. John was much happier and a good friendship grew out of that journey. I am sure John will never forget Mr. Morris. We were all looking out for John, knowing that he had no relatives with him.

We would sometimes give him a ride. He was only ten years old and very small for his age. Thomas would take him fishing with him. John nearly got adopted by a family near Echo Canyon. Their name was Peck and they had boys, cows and a horse. They, and the boys, took kindly to John. They would take turns in riding and driving the cows and the Pecks would give him milk, which he very much enjoyed. The Pecks wanted John to stay with them but John insisted that he wanted to get to Salt Lake City.

Everyone would look out for each other. Elijah Larkin, who was running the choir on board the Amazon, organised his family, consisting of 9 persons, and added five others to it, Ruth Coe, Hannah Webb, Martha Larkins, William and Charles Read, in order to pool their resources and rations together.

We managed to get fresh plums at Wood River but had to be careful to ration them.

We would camp for the evening, walking about 9 miles a day. I was not feeling much fatigue, although the heat was intense and the road hilly.

The next day the heat was very intense and we were all so thirsty. There was an occasional farm house along the way, where we managed to get shelter from the sun and water. We reached and crossed Elk Horn Bridge about 6pm August 16th. We camped about one mile from the bridge on the bank of the river. People took the opportunity to bathe in the river. Several other teams joined our train this evening.

We saw buffalo along the way. One day a large herd came into sight. The Captain ordered the train to halt and all the women and children to get in the waggons, clambering over their belongings. Then the men rode out toward the herd, where they fired a few shots at the buffalo to try to turn them away from the waggon train. Thomas was saying, "Do yow think they ken taan them? Someone else answered, "They have been known to run over waggons in their mad race." So we were all holding onto each other tightly, frightened that we would be killed or dreadfully maimed in the stampede". Luckily, the buffalo swerved to the right and missed the waggons. We all praised God for being our saviour. Several of the buffalo were shot and brought back for meat for the camp.

. . . .

I saw quite a number of people buried on the plains, This reminded with of Brother Clayton's hymn.

"And if I die before my journeys o'er
Happy day all is well
We then are free from toil and sorrow so
With the just we will dwell."

I was thinking that the last two lines were beautiful and true, but it was a sad scene, placed in a shallow grave, a wrap, no coffin, with a hymn and a prayer of dedication, covered over with dirt, then the waggons would roll on, with the relatives mourning, leaving an unmarked grave.

Many times there was a scarcity of fuel for the fires. Men started gathering dried droppings from the buffalo (called buffalo chips) and cattle. They had heard that these could be burnt down to a hot bed of embers and, when the smoke had dissipated, the food could be cooked, leaving no bad odour. We also had iron kettles and baking skillets to cook on.

We travelled on for several days in the blistering heat, passing through Fremont, then onto the bank of the Platte River, trudging, trudging, trudging with the heat searing my lungs. On the third day, dad said to us, "Tha' looks loike a tempest brewing, looking at thur clouds." We needed rain to bring the temperature down. I was looking forward to standing out in it, to be able to cool and wash my body and clothes. It would be such a relief. We would also be able to put buckets out to catch the rain for fresh water. Sure enough, about 5pm a thunderstorm broke out in all its fury. The heavens were perfectly black and the thunder rolled fearfully, but strangely enough the expected torrents did not materialise where we were, so we just continued.

The storm had been raging for about ½ an hour when, all of a sudden a tremendously loud thunderbolt broke immediately over our train. The women started screaming, me included, but strangely enough all of the cattle stood still in their tracks - we all had expected them to stampede but they did not. Then a cry went up, "Fire". We all rushed in the direction of the cry to find that 5 of Charles Adams team of 6 oxen had been struck dead on the spot and he himself had been knocked out.

The team happened to be at a point of the road where the telegraphic poles were crossing it and the lightning had been conducted to Charles Williams' waggon as they were passing underneath. The lightening had struck the hind end of the waggon, making a hole in the cover as large as a hat and set some hay on fire and then travelled along the chains to the cattle. We knew there were several hundred pounds of gunpowder and stoves in that same waggon. Men ran to pull off the cover and get the gunpowder off. Captain White shouted out a warning. "It's gonna blow – get back," but the teamsters had energetically and bravely already removed the contents, so preventing and possible danger of an explosion

The train moved on about 500 yards from the scene of accident and camped for the night. Providentially to say that none were hurt or injured by the storm although several were somewhat stunned. The thunder and lightning continued all night

It was lucky the lightning hadn't struck one of the waggons loaded with people, as they would have all been killed. As it was, Charles was in a right state, and had to be tended to for burns. The waggon was burnt out. After the fire died, we looked to see if anything was salvageable, but not much, most of the stoves being red hot still and damaged. Charles was put in one of the other waggons and his remaining ox used to help pull another waggon.

The storm had caused many of the cattle to stray, so that it was late the next morning before we started out. We reached Columbus, Loup Fork, on the Platte River about 6pm.

Everyone had to get out of the waggons. The mud was so soft, even the sick were taken across on horseback for fear the weight in the waggons would cause them to sink. A long string of oxen was used to bring each waggon across without stopping. Men, on horseback, rode on each side of the ox team to urge them along. I studied the naturally flowing water, which although not overly deep, could be waded across easily enough by foot. Still, we all needed to cross. I crouched and rested on the bank, removing both boots and tying them around my neck by the laces. I saw the children taking off their shoes and carrying them into the frightening water. I tied my long dress up in a knot above my knees and hesitantly dipped my left foot first into the clear-flowing river. Soon, my right foot was given the same tortuous treatment, and I carefully waded through the river. The flow hit the top of my knees, and with each step, its force attempted to push me farther downstream. I held hands with others and the children, to try to steady ourselves. Arriving at the other bank, I sat down and let the sun dry my skin.

It took all day to cross the river. It took about 3 hours to ferry our train over. Another train joined us, F Little & Company, just with 2 mule waggons.

News had spread of the narrow escape and the amount of gunpowder they were freighting into Utah, and word was received that the United States Military officers were coming. Captain White approached a number of waggons and gave instructions, "Each of you take a crate of gunpowder and stow it in your waggon, under whatever you can find to hide it." The officers came and searched the train but could not find as much as they expected and let the company proceed. But for the wise course of the Captain the powder would have been

208

confiscated, and this would have been a great loss to Charles and the trade he hoped to make in Utah with the Indians.

Charles told us a story about his father. "In the summer, trouble had begun on the plains with the Sioux Indians. One company of six waggons was destroyed, all the men killed, and one woman taken prisoner. The teams were killed and the waggons burned. My father, Adam, had been detained for two weeks at Fort Kearney by order of the Military. While he was kept there a company of soldiers returned having had to retreat with the loss of one man and one cannon, and were nearly surrounded and destroyed by the Sioux. There were five hundred waggons collected at Kearney City before they were all permitted to pursue their journey."

Of course we all had been listening intently and began to be worried about possible Sioux attacks but Captain White said that they hardly attack waggon trains, and only attack in retaliation, including the Military, of course, who had destroyed so much of the Indian way of life.

On Friday 21st August we left Loup Farm about 8am. F Little & Co went on separately. We had now travelled about 100 miles. Much to our surprise, on getting to the River Platte, the river was quite dry. "This has never been known before" Captain White advised us. "We shall have to find a small stream or dig into the bed of the river to get water." So, spades were taken out and wells were dug. Luckily, by the evening we had found a small stream.

On Saturday, 22nd August it was a fine morning, but much colder. Mum and I got shawls out of the waggon. Little William was bleating, "I am all on a-dudder," so I got a jacket for little

William to wear. "There, William, tha will keep yow a bit warmer." It was such a change from the blistering heat, but meant that we could walk in some degree of comfort. We started out at about 7.30am and travelled until 1pm. It had got warmer by then. Mr Sands and John Hayes went down into the bed of the river to see if they could get any fish. The river was still fairly dry but there were still little ponds of water. In the meantime, mum, little William and I went searching for what we could find and came back with a quantity of wild grapes. "Where's thur waggon train, maw". It was nowhere in sight. I started to get a bit frightened. "Well, ent that a caution." Then "Look, Ann, yow ken see its trail. It's left a haardy-daardy cloud f stew. We'll hev to run to cop-owld wi' 'em."

I couldn't see maw running at her age, just a quick hop and step, then have to rest. Little William would just run ahead, then run back, but he soon got tired of that and nearing the end of our tramp we had to take turns in carrying him, piggy-back style. "Oh, hew could thay goo withou us. surely daw would hev known we weren'' on board?" We picked up our pace, but we couldn't keep that up, especially as it was hot now. The grapes came in handy as we did not have any water with us. We did not manage to reach them until about ½ hour before camping for the night. We had had to walk another 8 miles or so. We were both quite sick, dehydrated and exhausted by then and I gulped down loads of water. Daw got a real telling off. "Yew duzzy shanny waarmin, yew. Do yow were a child, you'd gi' a roight clip round yar lug.

Dad said he was sorry, over and over and in the end came out with, "For Gawd's searke, gi yar tongue a rest an stop goin on – yew do run on, yew do, an' thass a fact."

210

So, enough said, and mum then turned on Thomas. "You're not anarl big, bor, to put oover moi knee and give yow a good hiding"

"But, maw, oi didn" know yow weren" in thur waggon. oi didn" see yow goo orff. Oi thought yow had fallen back with thur following waggons and were talking to friends you'd made."

Ann made a move towards him with her hand raised. Thomas, took to his heals and ran into me.

"Maw didn" harf ding moi lug!"

"No more than yow deserve, bor. That'll larn yow to be more observant."

I arose on Sunday, 23rd August feeling quite unwell, feeling cold and with a pain in my stomach. We started off about 8am, walking, but then I asked to get in the waggon, "Hitch up bor, then there'll be room for me an'orl on the seat. My stommick's givin; me jip." I remained there all day, feeling too sick to walk.

We camped at about one for about 2 hours, during which time Mr Sands and his children and a great many others caught a quantity of fish in the ponds and bed of the river, which they shared round for supper.

During the day it has been very cold, and this afternoon a high wind arose from the north and made it very cold indeed. In fact we all had to put on heavier clothing to keep from freezing. The wind fell about 9pm but the cold continued all night.

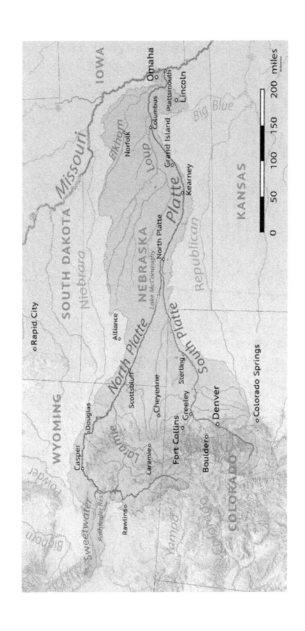

212

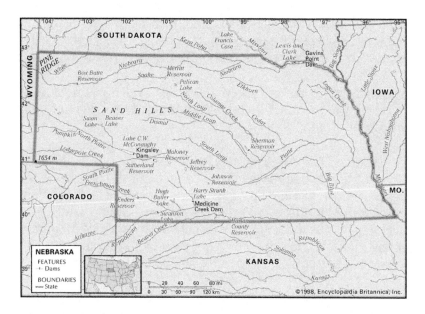

On Monday, 24th August, the day started out cold but got warmer towards noon. We started out about 8am, camped at noon and crossed Wood River about 6pm. We camped about 2 miles from the bridge on the bank of the river.

The next day there was a delay in starting as the captain's horses couldn't be found. A search party went out and they were finally found. We did not start out until 10am, reaching Wood River Centre about 5pm, where we camped for the evening. I wrote to my brother, George and posted it that evening. I am still not feeling great, having trouble with diarrhoea, so was feeling very sick and weak. I could scarcely walk without pain in the lower part of my stomach, so I travelled in the waggon again.

We carried on and, unfortunately, heard on Friday 28th August that Catherine Morwick had died last night. She'd been suffering with diarrhoea. We buried her on the banks of the Platte River about 2 miles east of Elm Creek, in Nebraska.

We had now travelled about 260 miles and by Sunday was beginning to feel a lot better. We had plenty supplies of both wood and water.

On Monday 31st August, Mary, the wife of John Falkner, died and was buried before we left the camp ground. The trees were not growing in this part so we're having to use the buffalo chips. We camped in the evening at the Pawnee Spring and had a visit from Sioux Indians. We were obviously wary of them and a few men got their guns out, but they were friendly and just wanted to barter with us, food for buffalo hides.

On being bombarded with questions about the Indians, how dangerous they were; was this their land we were traversing, and so on, Captain White told us, after the Sioux had departed, "I'll give you a potted history of recent events. A treaty had been signed at Fort Laramie in 1851 between the United States and representatives of 8 Indian tribes. The treaty set forth traditional territorial claims of the tribes and that all the land covered by the treaty was Indian Territory, and did not claim any part of it. The Native Americans, in return, guaranteed safe passage for settlers on the trail and allowed roads and forts to be built in their territories, in return for promises of an annuity in the amount of fifty thousand dollars for fifty years. This treaty should have made an effective and lasting peace among the eight tribes.

There was uproar between the various tribes immediately after this treaty was signed. The Lakota Sioux had received exclusive treaty right to the Black Hills, to the consternation of the Cheyenne and Arapohoe, who claimed this area as their home country. The Cheyenne and Arapaho, the southernmost of the treaty tribes, held an area southward of the North Platte, basically, the land we have passed through.

However, there was then the mass immigration of miners and settlers in western Kansas and southwestern Nebraska territory during the Pike's Peak Gold Rush of 1849. An estimated 100,000 gold-seekers prospecting and mining. This broke the Treaty as they had taken over Indian lands in order to mine them, found towns, start farms and build roads. The Indians' protests went unheard, basically as the US Government had the upper hand and the greater manpower and arms to fight the Indians, against which the Indians knew they could not compete. They had lost their lands and their livelihoods. The Cheyenne and Arapahoe found themselves driven from the mountain regions down to the waters of Arkansas, where they were competing with the miners for game and water. So, we are basically travelling on Indian land that had been signed over to them in the Treaty, with hundreds of thousands, such as yourselves and many more before you, coming in to settle the land. The situation escalated with the Grattan Affair in 1854 when a detachment of US soldiers illegally entered a Sioux encampment to arrest those accused of stealing a cow, and in the process sparked a battle in which Chief Conquering Bear was killed.

What is more appalling is that the white settlers and government agents started killing thousands of bison. The US army did not enforce the treaty regulations and allowed hunters onto native land to slaughter buffalo. One hundred thousand buffalo have been killed each year, thus forcing the tribes into each other's hunting grounds, and more inter-tribe fighting. By the summer of 1862, all tribes had been forced out of their shared treaty territory. The Arikara were driven from the other side of the Missouri River by the Sioux; the Yanktonai Sioux moved into Assiniboine hunting grounds in North Dakota and Montana; and, on top of all this, the US Government have not paid the promised annual amount to the Native Americans for the land."

The Lands of the 1851 Ft. Laramie Treaty

"So, this promised-land we are making our way to, has bairn stolen from thur Naitav Americans." I interrupted.

"Well, not quite as easy as that. The Indians are roaming tribes with no settled land. They owned nothing, had paid for nothing, just been living off the land from time immemorial and considered the land theirs. The Mormons were petitioned by Indians for recompense for land taken, however, Heber C. Kimball, first counsellor to Brigham Young, responded that the land belonged to "our Father in Heaven and we expect to plough and plant it."

Land has since been allocated to the Mormons by the Government, and is being bought bit by bit.

The Indians are still fighting their corner with various skirmishes, but they know they cannot win. Thousands have been killed by the US army - so many have just accepted their lot and turned to trading, just to get food. Many are traipsing off to camps set up for them, where they are learning English and learning American ways and having to put off their native ways of dress and customs."

I knew they looked fierce, these Indians, I thought to myself, but there was also a sadness in their eyes, and no wonder. What had Brigham Young brought us to and what an awful country we had come to, with such a shameless, licentious government.

Looking at my sad expression, Captain White added, "It's the way of the world, ma'm – the rich will get rich, the poor get poorer, the mighty overthrow the weak and the weak will have to conform."

....

There was another death on Tuesday 1st September. The young son of William Crystal died and was buried. He was only one year old. He had had the measles, which he got while on the ship.

It was very hot again and loads of flying ants were troubling us. Also the ground was sandy, which made the travel hard-going.

One of the waggons broke an axle the next day, so we had to stop. While the waggon was being repaired we had another visit from Sioux Indians.

There was great rejoicing when the day came when the company could see the distant mountains! We encamped in the wood on the west side.

The going was tough now, crossing large sand hills. It was very hot and the cattle were struggling.

At night on Friday, 4th September, the wind got up so fierce that it blew down the tent. We all had to get in the waggon to try to get some sleep. We passed Rattle Snake Creek the next day

Started again about 2 pm & travelled on till about 7 p m when we camped on a small creek. The road had improved as well as the weather. The nights were cool but the days were not oppressive.

The next day we came across another sand hill but Captain White directed us to travel the dry river bed to avoid this hill.

In the night, we experienced a heavy thunderstorm, which lasted for about 3 hours. The wind and rain were so heavy it beat in the side of our tent, making it very disagreeable and uncomfortable for sleeping and our bedding, as well as ourselves, got a good soaking. A great many tents were blown over during the night. After repairing the tent we started out again and reached Ash Hollow by about 7.30pm. The weather was fine, but cloudy. Flour had been left here by some of the former companies, which was picked up and stored. It seems the flour had been too heavy to get the waggons over the sand hills.

We had plenty of water, but no wood, except willows & chips. We could see Court House rock this evening. The weather was cool and cloudy with the odd shower.

Chimney Rock was seen for the first time this afternoon. Had it been less cloudy we should have seen it before. Camped in the evening about 5.30pm immediately opposite Court House Rock. The last three days we have made good travelling.

On Wednesday, 9th September, about 4.30pm the sky became very cloudy and it immediately began to blow very hard. What with the roads being dusty, it was most disagreeable. The wind was followed immediately by rain, accompanied by thunder and lighting. Captain White advised us to corral up, which we did about 3 miles west of Chimney Rock. The storm continued in intervals throughout the night, but had cleared by the morning. Loads of people were getting ill, not just with the diarrhoea but a burning rash. John Hayes was suffering too.

We reached Scotts Bluff and camped nearby. In the afternoon the same burning rash broke out all over my body, accompanied by a sickening weakness and I felt very ill. I managed to whisper to maw, "Oh maw, I dun't harf feel queer." I lay down by the side of the fire in camp, feeling too ill even to sit up. I felt I was dying. I'd been ill since being on the ship, then the long walk I had to do after the waggon train left mum, William and me stranded, the diarrhoea, the sickness, the stomach cramps, the burning rash, the oppressive heat, then cold, then the lightning storms. It was just too much. I couldn't go on. I felt that I wanted to die - to lie peacefully in my grave and let the world pass me by. Strangely enough, and I do not know what brought it on, but I suddenly started laughing, laughing hysterically and then crying. I couldn't stop. People came to my assistance, trying to comfort me with camomile tea and whatever medications they had - calamine lotion for my skin, a. tartar emetic – which was a crystalline salt of sweetish metallic taste; and brandy. I could hear someone crying, it might have been mum.

I slept and rose the next morning, strangely feeling better and somewhat elated that I had survived, although I was still troubled with the rash on my body, which causes a swelling in my flesh wherever it appears. I thanked everyone who came to my rescue.

A few days later, after a restless night, and after riding in the waggon, I woke to find my body bloated. The rash had all but gone leaving this dropsy-like swelling. "It's Water Blash." Mrs Bennet informed me. "It's because you got overheated and were drinking too much water but, do not fret, it will go away in time." Others said the sickness may be because of the fish we ate or even the grapes, but I was not sure about that as no-one else in my family had got sick through eating the fish and little William and mum ate the grapes and they were alright.

I still had no energy to walk, so rode in the waggon again.

On Saturday, 12th September another child died, Ellen Duncan's baby and was buried this morning. The baby was another child who had caught measles on board the ship

We did not have enough feed for the cattle and the next morning found that over 40 head was missing. The night guard and others went searching for them, on horse-back. They were eventually nearly all found - except 4 - back the way we had come. We yoked those up and proceeded on the road, while 3 men, mounted, went back to search for the missing 4. At about 9pm they brought them to camp, having found them where we had camped two days previously. The cattle had gone looking for food.

On Monday, 14th September we passed Fort Laramie. The fort seemed to be run by volunteer regiments with the troops originally located there, having been withdrawn to fight the Confederate States Army in the east, in the American Civil War.

John Hayes enquired at the Post Office for letters, then accompanied Captain White to the telephone office where he sent the following telegram to President Young. I just happened to be there and heard him stating aloud what he wanted to put on the telegram. "Passed here today. All well. Cattle in good condition, none lost, health of passengers generally good, 5 deaths only. Expect to make the City in 5 weeks."

We crossed the river about 11 miles above Laramie. It was a difficult to wade over, the bottom being small stones and pebbles which cut into people's feet. The river had to be crossed three times that day.

On Tuesday, 15th September we had to collect the cattle again as they had strayed, looking for food. After leaving camp we saw, on a high tree on the edge of a high cliff, the dead body of an Indian, wrapped in his blanket and strapped to the branches of the tree. Captain While commented, "He was there last year, so I've been told."

We crossed many sand hills. At the foot of one was a nice spring of water, so the cattle could get water, if not food. The wind began to blow hard and rain started falling. It remained squally all afternoon while we were travelling over the sand hills and the dust was insufferable- between the wind and the dust, we could scarcely breathe and we all got scarves, or whatever we could find, to put over our mouths and noses. It was so bad you could barely discern the waggon in front of you. It was also very cold. This carried on for some days. We left the hills and travelled along the river bottom

The weather did not improve until Saturday, 19th September. We passed Deer Creek and Station. One of the oxen had died.

We travelled on the rough, broken and dusty roads to where the road leaves the Platte River and strikes over to the Sweetwater River, where we had a rest for the remainder of the day, this meant we had to travel 15 miles the next day before we reached water and we wouldn't have got there, if we'd carried on, without having to travel by night.

After we camped a large herd of deer and antelope came near to the camp. Some of the men went out to shoot a few for food for us all. "Oi'll hev a sleep time yow cook thur dinner, maw. Oi'll mow in wi' the washin-up, arter"

"Yes, that be fine." Mum replied. It was the best meat I had ever tasted really succulent.

Strong wind was blowing from the south west and made it very unpleasant walking. The most conspicuous object today was the snow-capped mountains. The roads were good but hilly which made it hard traveling for those who walked and also for the teams with their heavy loads. We just tramped on, one foot after the other, holding up hands against our faces to try to ward off the wind. I remember stumbling a few times and my legs were shaking and throbbing. Tired, hungry, and in desperate need of a rest we carried on. We finally camped by a creek surrounded with mountains.

"Blass me, thass a right ole rimer this morning." Dad said. The weather was cold with a strong cold wind blowing in our faces all of the way. In the afternoon we camped in a hollow at the mouth of the great gap of the south pass. When we passed over the rocky ridge we could see the Wind River range of mountains which the teamsters said were covered with perpetual snow, and on the left hand we could see the mountains on the other side of the pass. It was a calm but cold night. It was a bad camping ground, all covered with sage brush, which had to be cleared before we could pitch our tents.

Adjacent to the camp ground was a quantity of Brush wood in which wild buffalo berries were growing and which the people were gathering when, at about 4 pm, a big brown bear was discovered, up in a willow tree, something none of them wanted to face and they all ran back to the camp. When everyone was back a team of men, with firearms, entered the wood to hunt down the bear. The hunt lasted about 3 hours. Thomas and I took a vantage point from a high bluff at the back of the brush wood. There was a huge scuffle with the bear defending itself. Even though I was at a distance, I held onto Thomas, as the animal's growling and roars sounded ferociously fierce and loud...... and frightening. Anyway, in the skirmish, one man had his wrist torn by the animal's teeth – he was lucky not to have had his hand bitten off. Another had the seat of his pants ripped by the bear's long nails and another got knocked down by the bear and would have been savaged to death, if the others hadn't taken aim and shot the animal. He was brought into camp, skinned and hung up on a telegraph pole by two log chains for everyone to look at, with various exclamations as to the size of it and its claws.

The bear was cut up the next morning and divided among the messes in camp, before we started out. We left the Platte River. There was no water and the weather was very hot, but we travelled on until 8pm when we camped on Greasewood Creek. Here we were met by Ebenezer Farnes, who had come direct from the City by horse team with five church tents for the use of the camp. These will prove very acceptable as the nights have turned very cold.

We camped on Sweetwater River. John Hayes was asked by Captain White to write an account of the bear fight to the Editor of the Deseret news. This was handed to Mr Farnes, who left us the next morning to return to the City. We had to go hunting for the cattle again, as they had roamed off. In the meantime, Thomas walked to Independence rock, being a little over a mile from the camp and ascended it. There he met up with two others from the camp. He was excited on his return.

"We wen' all oover it, and in thur southern portion f tha' we found a cave formed by thur rocks, and thur walls and roof were covered with nairms f different persons who had bairn there. And there was a note painted on with tar. One nairm had bairn there 18 years! We didn" hev any tar with us so we took choifs f wood and bones, which we found in thur cave and wri' our nairms and dates on them and stuck them in chinks f thur rocks. There were a ooj mor' f other nairms elsewhere on thur hill, cut with a chisel."

On nearing Devils Gate, I and some others left the train to see for ourselves and, as the water was low I hitched my skirts up and we waded through the water, over the boulders of rock lining the bed of the creek. It was a beautiful sight. While there a man fired a pistol twice & each report echoed from peak to peak about a dozen times before it died away. Each side of the Cliffs were also covered with names & dates of persons who had been there. We met the train again the other side of the gate. We camped that evening, 15 miles from Independence Rock and were met by the stray cattle which had roamed on ahead.

Elizabeth Stackam died on Monday, 28th September. She was 64.

The next day we lunched on the river near to a soldiers' fort at the foot of a high hill. Shortly after corralling, a company of 5 soldiers with their officer, came into the camp and made us all take the Oath of Allegiance to the U.S. government. One man proved obstinate and would not take the oath. He was initially put under guard but relented before we broke camp, and took the oath.

This evening we travelled on until 9 pm when we reached and camped on Strawberry Creek. The weather the last few days has been very cold indeed, showing unmistakable signs of a snow storm and, about 7pm, the snow began to fall & fell about 2 inches deep. It cleared off towards 10 pm and it was a clear night. "That snew an' snew all day!" young William commented. He had enjoyed playing in the snow. "Dunt yow hull a snewball at me, bor?" I had reprimanded him as he looked like he was about to throw one in my direction.

We were entering high ground now, going up and up. The incline was steep. Each step upward became more exhausting that the last, my knees buckling with tiredness, my body fatigued. We were all exhausted. It was very cold and we had to wrap ourselves up, but the snow had disappeared as the sun rose. I pushed myself consistently to reach the next goal ahead, the next rock on the horizon, stopping every so often to rest on a rock or fallen tree. Over the next couple of days, we travelled on through the South Pass and crossed Pacific Springs, passing by Little Sandy, then Big Sandy, crossing the Green River. We did not have much water and little feed. At Hams Fork we loaded with flour. We travelled on through the dust to Blacks Fork, where we spent the morning shoeing the cattle.

By 8th October we had reached Fort Bridger. I posted a letter to George but hadn't received any in return. I did not know if he had even got my first letter so was not too disappointed.

By the time we got to Quaking Aspen Springs, the cattle had found some grass to feed on.

We were entering the mountains now, and the cattle found it hard going. We all had to get out of the waggons and walk. It was a fine morning and nature seemed to smile down on us. We all began to get more cheerful with our thoughts of soon arriving in Salt Lake City for we were now only about 70 miles away. We entered Cache Cave and Echo Canyon and continued down the canyon, getting almost to the mouth of it. The scenery was varied and changeable, with many curious-looking rocks of different shapes and forms on the right-hand side. On the left we could see mountains covered with brush and grass, while the rocks were adorned with pine trees, growing in abundance in all kinds of places – so, unexpectedly great grazing for the cattle.

We still had a way to go though and had to get over Big Sandy Creek. The men waded in and the women and children rode in the waggons.

We then came across the Green River. It was about 2½ft deep and about 50 yards wide. Still, it looked beautiful.

We carried on across barren and hilly country, stopping at Mud Creek. The air was cold and frosty plus dust was being swirled around in the wind. We wrapped ourselves in scarfs and shawls, but they weren't enough, so we got the blankets out to put round our shoulders.

We travelled on over barren, hilly country. Some of the hills looked like mine pit mounds back in England, and seemed to contain ironstone and limestone. The roads were narrow and thick with brush in some places, which made it very difficult walking. We camped and mum baked some bread.

The scenery was becoming more verdant now, with fir trees and grass. One of the ladies went into labour. We had to stop for about two hours, pitch the tent and attend to her. Mum, dad, Thomas and William went on with the train but I stopped behind. One of the men stayed behind too and made a fire and cooked some bacon and pancakes for everyone, which were delicious, albeit we had to eat whilst being 'serenaded' by the screams of the poor woman giving birth. In due course, the lady was delivered of a fine boy and we carried on the journey, trying to catch up with the others. It was a very steep descent and rather dangerous in the dark. The sun set when we were about half way over the mountains. We should have stopped but we carried on the difficult and dangerous downward trail – in the dark, to try to join the others.

The next day, we continued, covering very mountainous country, but it was pleasant and beautiful, being adorned with fir trees and willows. When we came to Bear River, the teams forded the river but, luckily, there was a bridge for foot passengers. We camped at Yarrow Creek. We had two little hail storms in the afternoon and a sharp frost at night. We were all so cold and miserable and huddled around the camp fires.

The creek ran down about the middle of the canyon, and in some places it made the road very narrow. On both sides of the creek willows grew in great abundance - their leaves now indicating the season of the year had turned to a beautiful orange-yellow colour. We travelled on, going round a great mountain by the side of the Weber River, shining in the sun. We started to see signs of civilisation, with one-storey houses.

Trees were growing by the side of the foot path at regular distances from each other. Everything appeared neat and pleasant. This, we found out was Chalk Creek.

We passed more houses the next day, with their stock grazing in their pastures. It all seemed to us very encouraging. We continued our journey onward through Silver Creek Canyon but found it very difficult going as the path was so narrow. Many of us had to get out and walk, even the small children, and I held little William's hand, to keep him close by. It was very wearisome and dangerous. The men were required to walk on the upper side of the waggons and hold onto them in an attempt to prevent the waggons from tipping over. Thomas was trying to get dad to climb up the rock face to hold onto the waggon but dad replied, "Let thur younger men do tha. No, I dissent do that, do I do, I might blunder down." I didn't blame him, it was dangerous. In many places the men also had to lock the wheels of the waggons and put on brakes as it was so very steep and rocky. We women and children stayed well back, keeping out of their way and praying there wouldn't be a disaster. We heard Thomas shouting out orders, "It be on the sosh" and "Thur wheel ois twizzlin'." I was sure the others couldn't understand his dialect, but they could see what he was pointing to came to help.

The creek rushed wildly through the canyon, first to one side and then the other. Another time it would be picturesque, but not in these dangerous conditions. We camped at Parley's Park for the night where I made myself busy, with mum, washing, sewing and cleaning, as did the other women.

We then entered Emigration Canyon. It was very steep and difficult to climb. The wind blew up clouds of dust, which made the going very unpleasant. We were all covered in dust. I said

229

to dad, "I've navver seen miners, but oi ken imagine this ois waa thay looked like coming out f thur pits."

"Well, yes Ann." and he laughed. "Somewhat, oi suppose, but thur coal stew would be black – you'd be covered oover with black soot. And tha would be a soigh, that's a fact!" We both had a laugh at the thought of what we'd all look like.

On October 17th Salt Lake City came in sight. I thought it was the most beautiful sight I had ever seen. Then I began to feel very lonesome. "Oi wonder waa thur family at hoom will be durn now, maw. Oi know George and his family are coming oover but will we ever see thur rest f thur family?" I could not help shedding tears. I knew the people we had travelled with would also go different ways.

"Oh, Ann - Margaret, Mary and John hev meard thur own loives, gone thur own way, so we navver saw much f 'em anyway. Yow ken allus write. Hush now and cheer up, we hev a new loife to create now."

Waggons from Salt Lake City brought fresh food and supplies for the remainder of the trip. The company finally travelled down Immigration Canyon. When we got in sight of the mountains, the Utah boys gave a great shout and up went their hats in the air. The mountains and canyons looked wonderful to us.

We entered the Great Salt Lake Valley on 15th October 1863, went down into the city and camped. The trip across the plains took 3 months and 25 days.

We, as a family, were called by Brigham Young to help settle Parowan in Utah and were received into the Parowan Ward on Sunday, November 18th, 1863.

In the spring of 1864 dad was among the pioneers who were asked to help settle the area called Panguitch.

George Morphew my brother, with his wife, Harriet, and my sister, Lucy, arrived in the winter of 1864, went to help dad, along with my brother, Thomas. They helped build the road over the divide between Little Creek Canyon and Bear Valley.

I received letters from the family back home, expressing their concern for us all in this wild new country with its many hardships, and I wrote back with all the news, saying we were managing.

GEORGE GUNN AND
ANN MUNFORD

CHAPTER 15

I went into George Gunn's leather shop, basically looking for cottons for my sewing. I thought he might stock them as harnesses and such needed to be stitched.

I came in with little William. George was standing there behind his counter. My first thought was that he was really handsome and smart, and clean, although dressed in his work trousers and white shirt, with no jacket. He had wavy brown hair and he seemed to have an air about him, as if to say that he was in charge, but his friendly smile that drew me into his dark eyes, showed that he was approachable. He was, I supposed, just a couple of years older than me.

"Can I help you ma'am." I stuttered a bit, "Mmm, mm" I don't know why but he continued, "We have a good collection of leather work, harness, saddles and similar items. I wonder if I could interest you in anything we have in our store."

He was so well spoken that I felt conspicuous about my Norfolk dialect all of a sudden. I tried to say something, trying to adjust my accent, but it came out all wrong, "Oi, (going to say, "Oi do be") oh I am looking for soo…sewing thread, bo…sir."

"Well, ma'am you have come to the right place." And he directed me to another counter where there were a range of coloured threads and needles. While I was looking, George started chatting to little William. He was very easy with him. "What's that you have behind your ear young sir" and he produced a lolly pop, seemingly out of the air, from behind my William's ear, which he gave to William.

"Say thank you, William." I said, and William said, "Thank yow."

"Begging your pardon, ma'am, but I notice a slight accent. People have come to Utah from all over the globe, ma'am, and I manage to understand most of them, although the Scots and those from Newcastle in the north can be a bit arduous. I believe you originate from Norfolk. Am I right? There is no reason to deny your origins here.

"Thank you sir. You are correct in that I come from Norfolk. A little town called Costessey, near Norwich." I continued trying to speak properly "but, I am trying to tone down my accent a bit, as I would like to get a teaching post, if possible and I do not think a strong accent would go down well with any future employers.

"That may be true, ma'am." Let me introduce myself. I am George Gunn, originally from Bishops Stortford, in Hertfordshire."

I introduced myself as Ann Munford.

"I must apologise if I seem impertinent, I do not wish to be but, may I ask, did your husband manage to survive the long journey here. I know so many people died. In fact, my own wife did not survive."

I thought for a moment before answering. I did not want to go into great detail at so brief an encounter but, in the end, came out with, "Yes, my husband did not survive. I almost did not survive myself, being drastically ill."

"I am sorry to hear that, Mrs Munford. I trust you are well now?"

Mrs Munford did not ring true, it was my mother's name, so although seeming a bit forward, I said, "You may call me Ann, if you wish, and yes, thank you, I am well."

"In that case, Ann, you may call me George. A pleasure to meet you."

I nodded, then paid for the items I had selected and left the shop.

"Tha war a strange encounter, William... but he seemed rare noice – giving yow a lollypop an'orl. Oi think oi would like to encounter him again."

"Why did yow speak so strangely maw?

"Oh, so people not from where we were born ken understand us. You'll larn tha' by and by."

....

The little town of Parowan was only 13 years old, but already there were homes and industries.

There was a dance organised for Christmas 1863, which my family were looking forward to. Everyone was coming and a band would be playing with singers and choirs. I was not surprised to see George there and waved. It was a time to let your hair down enjoy yourselves. Naturally, there were plenty of religious carols, but, there were fiddlers later on, fiddling up a storm of dancing. I was surprised how vibrant the music was and found my feet tapping to the music.

Just then, over my shoulder, George appeared and asked me if I wanted to dance. We'd had barn dances in Norfolk, so agreed.

There we were, kicking up a storm, in and out of other couples, swirling around, then falling back, clapping as other couples took their turn, one by one to sashay between the clapping rows on either side. Then it would all start again.

We finally sat down, exhausted, panting and laughing. Then, after getting our breath back, we were up again, twirling round, being passed from one man to the other, and the men passing from one woman to the next, then back to your original partner, to start all over again.

"Oh George, this is so much fun, but I've had enough, I need to sit down"

"I am glad you said that." George replied, blowing heavily. "we are not 18 anymore."

So, we laughed and joked and passed the evening away.

"I would like to see you again, Ann. Do, you think we could meet up, preferably soon. I like you Ann."

235

I agreed and George walked me home. We talked, the first time, we could have a proper talk, as it had been too noisy in the barn to hear properly.

"I am in the process of building a home near my mother, on a lot west of Main Street."

"Why George, that is near where William and I are living at present, where we are going to now. I live there together with my parents and brother, Thomas. We moved there on 18 November."

"Yes, I know, I've seen you going to and fro. Have you seen what I am building? It's going to be lovely, with a garden and fruit trees. I am going to get furniture for it, real good-looking furniture and every room with have those lovely sheep-skin rugs – both black and white – adorning the chairs and the floors. I can just imagine it – cute as a sweat pea. But, sure, it's going to happen. I am going to make sure it's going to happen. We're doing pretty well in the shop."

George continued, "I started farming in the Valley when I first arrived, acquiring land there and planting crops. I didn't have much of a place to stay in – just basically a mud hut, but then I got together with William Holyoak and John Brown and started setting up this harness shop and tannery.

George carried on, "You mentioned your brother Thomas. I have a brother over here too, William. He married Elizabeth Judd on 26 February 1861 as his wife, Emma, sadly died as soon as we arrived.

236

William has been working for the church and, as payment, he receives food supplies from the Tithe Office. He has been helping build the first road in Parley Canyon and Silver Creek Canyon. He moved his family to a camp in the canyon where Elizabeth has been cooking for some of the workmen. It's a bit bleak out there, basically living in a mud hut, with no windows and doors. Indians, miners, and wild animals looking for food, so a guard has to be kept, but they're doing alright.

I've just heard a contract has been won to settle Hoytsville, a little town near the Weber River, 40 miles east of Salt Lake City, and William will be on the team – hard work but he will be paid well and be able to buy himself some land."

"My father, Robert, has been asked if he wants to work at Panguitch, to clear the land and build a settlement there. He might start when the weather improves in the New Year. Thomas is going to go with him too. There's discussion of a road being built over the divide between Little Creek Canyon and Bear Valley"

"Well, hopefully, they know what they are getting into. Leaving your house in Parowan for mud huts, and hard back-breaking work."

"Well, they are of a like mind. They came here to create a town and that is what they intend to do. They hope my brother, also called George, will join them next year, when he and his lady friend, Harriet Paice, and my sister, Lucy, plan to come over.

"So, Ann, we are here." As we stood outside where I lived. "It looks like our families have a great deal in common, and I would like to get to know them better, and you." Then George

237

kissed me, on the lips, tenderly – a wonderful feeling that made my spine tingle. I hadn't been kissed in that way for so long, and even my so-called husband, was not such a good kisser, in fact he hadn't been a kisser at all. But, why was I thinking of that so-and-so, when this handsome, funny, intelligent, lovely man was kissing me?

So, we started dating and naturally, George, wanted to meet my family. This took me unawares. I'd told George that my husband had died on the waggon trail. That was a lie, and if George met my family, the truth would come out. I would have to tell him the truth now.

"George, I need to tell you something before you meet my family…..I do not really know where to begin…. I told you a lie, George."

George's eyebrows rose at this and a frown appeared on his face.

"Please do not be angry with me. It's just that, when we first met, I did not know exactly what to say when you asked about little William's father and I did not want to go into detail at the time. I mean, I did not know that we were going to start courting and I wanted to keep that bit of information to myself."

"You're not still married are you? Did your husband die or not?"

"Oh, it's not as bad as you think, George. Yes, my husband is still alive – he did not die on the trail. However, when I was pregnant with William, he left me and went to sea. I returned home to mum and dad. Then I heard that he had set up home with someone else. He'd obviously heard that he had a son

238

and, two years later, he appeared at my door, demanding the baby. I was so scared, George. I tried to slam the door in his face but he put his boot in to stop the door closing. I tried to fight him off, but he was too strong and he came in and seized hold of William and went off with him. There was nothing I could do to stop him, George. And I was so heartbroken, I cried and cried. Dad said I needed a lawyer and that there was a new Divorce Act that had been approved in 1857. I did not know anything about this Act. I mean, before then, women were not allowed to divorce their husbands and the husband could take the children. I thought I had no leg to stand on – everything I had belonged to him, no matter if he had deserted me. Anyway; we saw a lawyer. The lawyer explained that women could now divorce if her husband had been adulterous, but they also needed to prove desertion for two years or physical cruelty, so yes, he had deserted me for over two years, but it would still be so costly, and we would have to go to Court in London, so there was no way we could afford it – he had won and taken William."

"How did you get William back?"

Well, we all got together, my brothers and dad, and neighbours and we went to hunt him out. After a lot of investigation, we, eventually, found him down by the docks in Ipswich, in an old, damp, decrepit boarding house. We could hear little William crying and broke down the door, en masse, and grabbed William back. The poor thing had not been looked after and had a cold and was sitting in a soiled nappy. I then had to go in hiding with William in case he came after us.

"So, are you still legally married?"

"Well, dad contacted the Mormon brethren and told them the whole story. The brethren, knowing that we wanted to emigrate with the church to Utah, came to our assistance and put up the money for one of their own lawyers to represent me in Court. It meant going to London. I was overawed seeing the huge building and the many marbled corridors and huge winding staircase, then finally entering the Court, that my legs were shaking and I just wanted the ground to swallow me up, but the lawyer stood by me. I had to take the stand and tell my story. My husband had been subpoenaed to attend and I could see him, staring evilly at me, in the front row with his own lawyer. He took the stand and told a lot of lies about me, saying I was an unfit mother, but my lawyer had friends and relatives to give affidavits on my behalf. The state of the premises he was living in was taken into account and that William had been left unattended and uncared for, and that I had family around me and a good house. So, thankfully, the judge agreed to the divorce and William was put in my care."

"What a relief, Ann, and what a nightmare to go through."

....

So, George came to visit and was introduced to my family. They got on well, talking about the new plans for Panguitch.

George also said that his brother, Benjamin had gone back to Florence in 1861 and 1862 to assist other emigrants to Utah. "On his last trip he met a young emigrant girl, named Alice Bowdidge, and it seemed to be love at first sight. Alice had enquired of Heber C Kimball about the character of Benjamin, especially as she was thinking of marrying him, and he told her that, if she married him she would marry a good, honest, hard-working man. So Alice agreed to marry Benjamin and Brother Kimball married them in the Endowment House, saying that, his holy impression was that they had been engaged to each other, in the Spirit World, before they were born."

I suppose, the talk of marriage, had some influence on George's thoughts at the time and he asked my father if he could have a personal talk with him, away from the main gathering.

"I know I have only known Ann for a short time, but I believe we are of the same mind. I grateful admire her and would go so far as to say, I am enamoured of her. I would like to, with your agreement, ask for her hand in marriage."

"Do Ann agree to this marriage?"

"I have not actually brought up the subject. I thought it prudent to ask for your permission first."

"Then, by all means, do Ann ois happy, oi give moi agreement."

Naturally, I was over the moon when George proposed. A wedding was planned for 1st March.

CHARLES DICKEN'S REPORT

CHAPTER 16

I started to tell George all about my journey, and that I had actually met Charles Dickens on board the Amazon. I had been so excited to get to talk to him, no matter how briefly.

"He had been scribbling all sorts of notes about the people on board and the loading of the ship."

"My, I didn't know you actually met the great Charles Dickens. That is certainly something. I am a great admirer of his too and used to read his books, when I could get them. You mentioned he was writing notes. They were probably the notes he used for his report about the Mormon travels. I actually managed to get a copy – well delayed on getting here, but yes, I was going to make sure I got a copy."

"You did not! How wonderful? Have you still got it? May I read it? I was so excited, I was jumping up and down and clapping my hands. George, please tell me you still have it."

"Quieten down now, Ann. In answer to all of your questions – the answer is yes."

"Oh, I could kiss you, George."

"Well, there's nothing stopping you, we are engaged to be married." So, I gave him a big hug and a kiss.

George retrieved the report for me, which I read avidly.

Charles Dickens: The Uncommercial Traveller; No Thoroughfare

Bound For the Great Salt Lake

Behold me on my way to an emigrant ship, on a hot morning early in June. My road lies through that part of London generally known to the initiated as "Down by the Docks." Down by the Docks, is home to a good many people--to too many, if I may judge from the overflow of local population in the streets--but my nose insinuates that the number to whom it is Sweet Home might be easily counted. Down by the Docks, is a region I would choose as my point of embarkation aboard ship if I were an emigrant. It would present my intention to me in such a sensible light; it would show me so many things to be run away from.

Down by the Docks, they eat the largest oysters and scatter the roughest oyster shells, known to the descendants of Saint George and the Dragon. Down by the Docks, they consume the slimiest of shell fish, which seem to have been scraped off the copper bottoms of ships. Down by the Docks, the vegetables at green grocers' doors acquire a saline and a scaly look, as if they had been crossed with fish and seaweed. Down by the Docks, they "board seamen" at the eating houses, the public houses, the slop shops, the coffee shops, the tally shops, all kinds of shops mentionable and unmentionable-- board them, as it were, in the piratical sense, making them bleed terribly, and giving no quarter. Down by the Docks, the seamen roam in mid street and mid-day, their pockets inside out, and their heads no better. Down by the Docks, the daughters of wave-ruling Britannia also rove, clad in silken attire, with uncovered tresses streaming in the breeze, bandanna kerchiefs floating from their shoulders, and crinoline not wanting. Down by the Docks, you may hear the incomparable Joe Jackson sing the Standard of England, with a hornpipe, any night; or any [p. 220] day may see at the waxwork, for a penny and no waiting, him as killed the policeman at Acton and suffered for it. Down by the Docks, you may buy polonies, saveloys, and sausage preparations various, if you are not particular what they are made of besides seasoning. Down by the Docks, the children of Israel creep into any gloomy cribs and entries they can hire, and hang slops there--pewter watches, sou'wester hats, waterproof overalls--"first rate articles, Jack."

Down by the Docks, such dealers exhibiting on a frame a complete nautical suit without the refinement of a waxen visage in the hat, present the imaginary wearer as drooping at the yard arm, with his seafaring and earthfaring troubles over. Down by the Docks, the placards in the shops apostrophize the customer, knowing him familiarly before hand, as, "Look here, Jack!" "Here's your sort, my lad!" "Try our sea-going mixed, at two and nine!" "The right kit for the British tar!

"Ship ahoy!" "Splice the main-brace, brother!" "Come, cheer up, my lads. We've the best liquors here, and you'll find something new in our wonderful beer!" Down by the Docks, the pawnbroker lends money on Union-Jack pocket handkerchiefs, on watches with little ships pitching fore and aft on the dial, on telescopes, nautical instruments in cases, and such like. Down by the Docks, the apothecary sets up in business on the wretchedest scale--chiefly on lint and plaster for the strapping of wounds--and with no bright bottles, and with no little drawers. Down by the Docks, the shabby undertaker's shop will bury you for next to nothing, after the Malay or Chinaman has stabbed you for nothing at all: so you can hardly hope to make a cheaper end. Down by the Docks, anybody drunk will quarrel with anybody drunk or sober, and everybody else will have a hand in it, and on the shortest notice you may revolve in a whirlpool of red shirts, shaggy beards, wild heads of hair, bare tattooed arms, Britannia's daughters, malice, mud, maundering, and madness. Down by the Docks, scraping fiddles go in the public-houses all day long, and, shrill above their din and all the din, rises the screeching of innumerable parrots brought from foreign parts, who appear to be very much astonished by what they find on these native shores of ours. Possibly the parrots don't know, possibly they do, that Down by the Docks is the road to the Pacific Ocean, with its lovely islands, where the savage girls plait flowers, and [p. 221] the savage boys carve coconut shells, and the grim blind idols muse in their shady groves to exactly the same purpose as the priests and chiefs. And possibly the parrots don't know, possibly they do, that the noble savage is a wearisome impostor wherever he is, and has five hundred thousand volumes of indifferent rhyme, and no reason, to answer for.

Shadwell church! Pleasant whispers of there being a fresher air down the river than down by the Docks, go pursuing one another, playfully, in and out of the openings in its spire. Gigantic in the basin just beyond the church, looms my Emigrant Ship: her name, the Amazon. Her figure- head is not disfigured as those beauteous founders of the race of strong-minded women are fabled to have been, for the convenience of drawing the bow; but I sympathize with the carver:

"A flattering carver who made it his care
to carve busts as they ought to be--not as they were."

"Oh, he paints such a picture, just with words, George. Oh, he's now talking about the emigrant ship – the one I was on."

My Emigrant Ship lies broadside-on to the wharf. Two great gangways made of spars and planks connect her with the wharf; and up and down these gangways, perpetually crowding to and fro and in

246

and out, like ants, are the Emigrants who are going to sail in my Emigrant ship. Some with cabbages, some with loaves of bread, some with cheese and butter, some with milk and beer, some with boxes, beds, and bundles, some with babies--nearly all with children--nearly all with brand new tin cans for their daily allowance of water, uncomfortably suggestive of a tin-flavour in the drink. To and fro, up and down, aboard and ashore, swarming here and there and everywhere, my Emigrants. And still as the Dock-Gate swings upon its hinges, cabs appear, and carts appear, and vans appear, bringing more of my Emigrants, with more cabbages, more loaves, more cheese and butter, more milk and beer, more boxes, beds, and bundles, more tin cans, and on those shipping investments accumulated compound interest of children.

I go aboard my Emigrant Ship. I go first to the great cabin, and find it in the usual condition of a cabin at that pass. Perspiring landsmen, with loose papers, and with pens and inkstands, pervade it; and the general appearance of things is as if the late Mr. Amazon's funeral had just come home from the cemetery, and the disconsolate Mrs. Amazon's trustees found the affairs in great disorder, and were looking high and low for the will. I go out on the poop-deck, for air, and surveying the emigrants on the deck below (indeed they are crowded all about me, up there too), find more pens and inkstands in action, and more papers, and interminable complication respecting accounts with individuals for tin cans and what not. But nobody is in an ill-temper, nobody is the worse for drink, nobody swears an oath or uses a coarse word, nobody appears depressed, nobody is weeping, and down upon the deck in every corner where it is possible to find a few square feet to kneel, crouch, or lie in, people, in every unsuitable attitude for writing, are writing letters.

Now, I have seen emigrant ships before this day in June. And these people are so strikingly different from all other people in like

247

circumstances whom I have ever seen, that I wonder aloud, "What would a stranger suppose these emigrants to be!"

The vigilant bright face of the weather-browned captain of the *Amazon* is at my shoulder, and he says, "What, indeed! The most of these came aboard yesterday evening. They came from various parts of England in small parties that had never seen one another before. Yet they had not been a couple of hours on board, when they established their own police, made their own regulations, and set their own watches at all the hatchways. Before nine o'clock, the ship was as orderly and as quiet as a man-of-war."

"I was listening in when he spoke to the captain. I heard him say this, George"

I looked about me again, and saw the letter-writing going on with the most curious composure. Perfectly abstracted in the midst of the crowd; while great casks were swinging aloft, and being lowered into the hold; while hot agents were hurrying up and down, adjusting the interminable account; while two hundred strangers were searching everywhere for two hundred other strangers, and were asking questions about them of two hundred more; while the children played up and down all the steps, and in and out among all the people's legs, and were beheld, to the general dismay, toppling over all the dangerous places; the letter-writers wrote on calmly. On the starboard side of the ship, a grizzled man dictated a long letter to another grizzled man in an immense fur cap: which letter was of so profound a quality, that it became necessary for the amanuensis at intervals to take off his fur cap in both his hands, for the ventilation of his brain, and stare at him who dictated, as a man of many mysteries who was worth looking at. On the larboard side, a woman had covered a belaying-pin with a white cloth to make a neat desk of it, and was sitting on a little box, writing with the deliberation of a bookkeeper. Down upon her breast on the planks of the deck at this woman's feet, with her head diving in under a beam of the bulwarks on that side, as an eligible place of refuge for her sheet of paper, a neat and pretty girl wrote for a good hour (she fainted at last), only rising to the surface occasionally for a dip of ink. Alongside the boat, close to me on the poop-deck, another girl, a fresh well-grown country girl, was writing another letter on the bare deck. Later in the day, when this self-same boat was filled with a choir who sang glees and catches for a long time, one of the singers, a girl, sang her part mechanically all the while, and wrote a letter in the bottom of the boat while doing so.

"A stranger would be puzzled to guess the right name for these people, Mr. Uncommercial," says the captain.

"Indeed he would."

"If you hadn't known, could you ever have supposed?"

"How could I! I should have said they were in their degree, the pick and flower of England."

"So should I," says the captain.

"How many are they?"

"Eight hundred in round numbers."

I went between-decks, where the families with children swarmed in the dark, where unavoidable confusion had been caused by the last arrivals, and where the confusion was increased by the little preparations for dinner that were going on in each group. A few women here and there, had got lost, and were laughing at it, and asking their way to their own people, or out on deck again. A few of the poor children were crying; but otherwise the universal cheerfulness was amazing. "We shall shake down by tomorrow." "We shall come all right in a day or so." "We shall have more light at sea." Such phrases I heard everywhere, as I groped my way among chests and barrels and beams and unstowed cargo and ring-bolts and Emigrants, down to the lower-deck, and thence up to the light of day again, and to my former station.

Surely, an extraordinary people in their power of self-abstraction! All the former letter-writers were still writing calmly, and many more letter-writers had broken out in my absence. A boy with a bag of books in his hand and a slate under his arm, emerged from below, concentrated himself in my neighbourhood (espying a convenient skylight for his purpose), and went to work at a sum as if he were stone deaf. A father and mother and several young children, on the main deck below me, had formed a family circle close to the foot of the crowded restless gangway, where the children made a nest for themselves in a coil of rope, and the father and mother, she suckling the youngest, discussed family affairs as peaceably as if they were in perfect retirement. I think the most noticeable characteristic in the eight hundred as a mass, was their exemption from hurry.

Eight hundred what? "Geese, villain?" EIGHT HUNDRED MORMONS. I, Uncommercial Traveller for the firm of Human Interest Brothers, had come aboard this Emigrant Ship to see what Eight hundred Latter-day Saints were like, and I found them (to the rout and overthrow of all my expectations) like what I now describe with scrupulous exactness.

The Mormon Agent who had been active in getting them together, and in making the contract with my friends, the owners of the ship, to take them as far as New York on their way to the Great Salt Lake, was pointed out to me. A compactly-made handsome man in black, rather short, with rich brown hair and beard, and clear bright eyes.

From his speech, I should set him down an American. Probably, a man who had "knocked about the world" pretty much. A man with a frank open manner and unshrinking look; withal a man of great quickness. I believe he was wholly ignorant of my Uncommercial individuality, and consequently of my immense Uncommercial importance.

After a noontide pause for dinner, during which my emigrants were nearly all between-decks, and the Amazon looked deserted, a general muster took place. The muster was for the ceremony of passing the Government Inspector and the Doctor. Those authorities held their temporary state amid-ships, by a cask or two; and, knowing that the whole Eight hundred emigrants must come face to face with them, I took my station behind the two. They knew nothing whatever of me, I believe, and my testimony to the unpretending gentleness and good nature with which they discharged their duty, may be of the greater worth. There was not the slightest flavour of the Circumlocution Office about their proceedings.

The emigrants were now all on deck. They were densely crowded aft, and swarmed upon the poop-deck like bees. Two or three Mormon agents stood ready to hand them on to the Inspector, and to hand them forward when they had passed. By what successful means, a special aptitude for organization had been infused into these people, I am, of course, unable to report. But I know that, even now, there was no disorder, hurry, or difficulty.

All being ready, the first group are handed on. That member of the party who is entrusted with the passenger-ticket for the whole, has been warned by one of the agents to have it ready, and here it is in his hand. In every instance through the whole eight hundred, without an exception, this paper is always ready.

251

The faces of some of the Welsh people, among whom there were many of old persons, were certainly the least intelligent. Some of these emigrants would have bungled sorely, but for the directing hand that was always ready. The intelligence here was unquestionably of a low order, and the heads were of a poor type. Generally the case was the reverse. There were many worn faces bearing traces of patient poverty and hard work, and there was great steadiness of purpose and much undemonstrative self-respect among this class. A few young men were going singly. Several girls were going, two or three together. These latter I found it very difficult to refer back, in my mind, to their relinquished homes and pursuits. Perhaps they were more like country milliners, and pupil teachers rather tawdrily dressed, than any other classes of young women. I noticed, among many little ornaments worn, more than one photograph-brooch of the Princess of Wales, and also of the late Prince Consort. Some single women of from thirty to forty, whom one might suppose to be embroiderers, or straw-bonnet-makers, were obviously going out in quest of husbands, as finer ladies go to India. That they had any distinct notions of a plurality of husbands or wives, I do not believe. To suppose the family groups of whom the majority of emigrants were composed, polygamically possessed, would be to suppose an absurdity, manifest to anyone who saw the fathers and mothers.

I should say (I had no means of ascertaining the fact) that most familiar kinds of handicraft trades were represented here. Farm-labourers, shepherds, and the like, had their full share of representation, but I doubt if they preponderated. It was interesting to see how the leading spirit in the family circle never failed to show itself, even in the simple process of answering to the names as they were called, and checking off the owners of the names. Sometimes it was the father, much oftener the mother, sometimes a quick little girl second or third in order of seniority. It seemed to occur for the first time to some heavy fathers, what large families they had; and their eyes rolled about, during the calling of the list, as if they half

252

misdoubted some other family to have been smuggled into their own. Among all the fine handsome children I observed but two with marks upon their necks that were probably scrofulous. Out of the whole number of emigrants, but one old woman was temporarily set aside by the doctor, on suspicion of fever; but even she afterwards obtained a clean bill of health.

When all had "passed," and the afternoon began to wear on, a black box became visible on deck, which box was in charge of certain personages also in black, of whom only one had the conventional air of an itinerant preacher. This box contained a supply of hymn-books, neatly printed and got up, published at Liverpool, and also in London at the "Latter-Day Saints Book Depot, 30, Florence-street." Some copies were handsomely bound; the plainer were the more in request, and many were bought. The title ran: "Sacred Hymns and Spiritual Songs for the Church of Jesus Christ of Latter-Day Saints." The Preface, dated Manchester, 1840, ran thus: "The Saints in this country have been very desirous for a Hymn Book adapted to their faith and worship, that they might sing the truth with an understanding heart, and express their praise, joy, and gratitude in songs adapted to the new and Everlasting Covenant. In accordance with their wishes, we have selected the following volume, which we hope will prove acceptable until a greater variety can be added. With sentiments of high consideration and esteem, we subscribe ourselves your brethren in the New and Everlasting Covenant, Brigham Young, Parley P. Pratt, John Taylor." From this book--by no means explanatory to myself of the New and Everlasting Covenant, and not at all making my heart an understanding one on the subject of that mystery--a hymn was sung, which did not attract any great amount of attention and was supported by a rather select circle. But the choir in the boat was very popular and pleasant; and there was to have been a Band, only the Cornet was late in coming on board. In the course of the afternoon, a mother appeared from shore, in search of her

253

daughter, "who had run away with the Mormons." She received every assistance from the Inspector, but her daughter was not found to be on board. The Saints did not seem to me, particularly interested in finding her.

Towards five o'clock, the galley became full of tea-kettles, and an agreeable fragrance of tea pervaded the ship. There was no scrambling or jostling for the hot water, no ill humour, no quarrelling. As the Amazon was to sail with the next tide, and as it would not be high water before two o'clock in the morning, I left her with her tea in full action and her idle Steam Tug lying by, deputing steam and smoke for the time being to the Tea-kettles.

I afterwards learned that a Despatch was sent home by the captain before he struck out into the wide Atlantic, highly extolling the behaviour of these Emigrants, and the perfect order and propriety of all their social arrangements. What is in store for the poor people on the shores of the Great Salt Lake, what happy delusions they are labouring under now, on what miserable blindness their eyes may be opened then, I do not pretend to say. But I went on board their ship to bear testimony against them if they deserved it, as I fully believed they would; to my great astonishment they did not deserve it; and my predispositions and tendencies must not affect me as an honest witness. I went over the Amazon's side, feeling it impossible to deny that, so far, some remarkable influence had produced a remarkable result, which better known influences have often missed.'

'After this Uncommercial Journey was printed, I happened to mention the experience it describes to Lord Houghton. That gentleman then showed me an article of his writing, in The Edinburg Review for January, 1862, which is highly remarkable for its philosophical and literary research concerning these Latter-Day Saints. I find in it the following sentences:--"The select Committee of the House of Commons on emigrant ships for 1854 summoned the

Mormon agent and passenger-broker before it, and came to the conclusion that no ships under the provisions of the 'Passengers Act' could be depended upon for comfort and security in the same degree as those under his administration. The Mormon ship is a family under strong and accepted discipline, with every provision for comfort, decorum, and internal peace."

BIB: Dickens, Charles,*The Uncommercial Traveler and Reprinted Pieces etc* (Oxford: Oxford University Press, 1987) (CHL)

That was wonderful George. I am glad you kept it – and gave him another kiss.

WEDDING AND DEPARTURE

CHAPTER 17

We had a great shock, in late February, on receiving a letter commissioning my father, my husband to be, George, and my brother, Thomas to report for work in Little Creak Canyon to make a settlement on the Upper Sevier River. They were to report on 1st March 1864 – the day of our wedding! Everything had been arranged for the wedding, with guests invited. We couldn't re-arrange at this late notice. The church had been booked and the vicar.

"Oh waa are we gorn to do, maw? Oi do so wo'a to gi' married."

Mum thought for a while, then said, "Ol'll tal yow what, sweetnes. We will hev yar wedding, say yar goodbyes, then yow and George, daw and Thomas ken mairk their way to thur site. Oi will stay ahoind to see to thur guests and keep thur plairce hare."

I gave mum a hug, then went to tell George. We would need to prepare for the journey and for living in a barren place with no facilities, nothing – so, cooking stoves and fuel, pots and pans, cutlery, crockery, food, warm clothes, tools, such as spades, rope, axes, pickaxes, nails, hammers, and anything else we would not be able to do without.

So, the wedding was a quieter affair than expected, although all the neighbours, relatives and friends came. Luckily we had arranged the service for early in the day, so that meant we could get off soon. People weren't amazed at our intrepidness

– we had all been through the mill with the journey over, many losing their loved ones as well. We all knew we had come to build our Zion, but they wished us all well and warned us to be careful of the wild animals and Indians. Loads of men and families were going too, so we wouldn't be on our own.

A town site had been surveyed and the first job was to dig ditches for irrigation. We were back, living in tents. The settlement was called Panguitch, meaning Big Fish. The next big job was to clear a field and fence it off. It was only then that it was possible to construct log houses on the site. These were gruelling times, and hard work, cutting trees, clearing ground. I worried about my father – he was 74 now – he should not have been doing hard labour. Thankfully, the people in charge realised this and put him on lighter labour, exempt from sawing and digging, plus he got an active job assisting with the planning and putting forward ideas. He still had to muck in, although, with ploughing the land with a team of horses and such like.

The plan was to raise a crop in the cleared fields, but that first winter the wheat was frozen before it was fully ripe. We had to survive on what meat was available – 'frosted wheat' and milk. We women had the job of grinding it up in an old coffee mill to make bread. Sometimes we boiled the wheat and ate it with milk. We were all hungry, especially the men, doing all that back-breaking tree-felling, log splitting, sawing, scything, hammering and so forth – all on a bowl of wheat and milk! It was freezing too, especially at night, so we were wrapped up in all the clothes we could possibly wear with coats thrown over blankets. We were so pleased when the log houses were finally built and we could get shelter and build indoor fires in the hearths.

Even then, in the log cabins, the winter chill would engulf us. I would sit watching, out of the window, at the first snow falling harshly, sticking to the ground almost instantly. The snow-laden white sky would soon turn to dusk, and any light would have disappeared into blackness. The lamps would flicker aggressively, with the fire spitting and popping, sending flickering shadows around the room.

We were still in dire need of food and my stomach cramped around my sunken belly.

George confided in me one day, "It is a good job my first wife, Eliza, never made it here. She would have hated it and probably would have stayed in Parowan. She never had the pioneer spirit. I'm glad you are nothing like her. You and I were made for each other." and he gave me a hug and kiss.

The men had their guns with them to protect themselves from prowling wolves and the odd grizzly bear. There were also packs of Indians, mainly just coming to look what we were doing. Some came down, looking for food but then realised we had none and we had nothing to trade.

We heard about the atrocious Bear River Massacre. Although it was nowhere near us, being up in Nova Scotia, our local Indians were uneasy. Five hundred and thirty one Shoshone were slain by the US Army under the control of Colonel Patrick Edward Connor – among them, old men, 90 women and children. After the slaughter ended, soldiers went through the Indian village raping women and using axes to bash in the heads of women and children, who were already dying of wounds. The troops burned 75 Indian lodges, stole their food and horses. The troops then returned to Camp Douglas in Salt Lake City with their wounded, and buried their dead. Hundreds of Indian bodies were left on the field for the wolves and crows. Brigham Young obliged the federal government's request by supplying cavalry troops from the Utah Militia. The Mormons in Cache Valley in northern Utah were grateful for Col. Connor's intervention, seeing it as him working with the Almighty on their behalf, while they were trying to plant their fields and settle in the area. No-one knew, at the time, the far-reaching explosion of Indian ferocity that would take place and that Col. Connor would be blamed for the atrocities.

Our local Indians had been quite peaceable, even coming for talks, smoking pipes with our men. George made friends with some. He was trying to tell them, through drawings and interpreters, what they, as a group, were planning with the area. The Indians didn't mind us clearing the area but started to get angry when they saw that log-cabins were starting to be erected. These talks turned into arguments. They said that more and more white men were settling in their land, hunting and fishing, so there was not enough game to share. They also did not understanding our way of living, ploughing fields and growing corn and wheat. Their way of life was nomadic, travelling from summer quarters to winter quarters, hunting buffalo. Likewise, we didn't understand the Native American way of life and the Native Americans rejected the settlers' culture of property rights. To them, cattle were for sharing and land was not for buying and selling – it was not our land to sell.

We, as a group, tried to say that seven years ago, Chief Walkara offered the ground to us settlers and we believed the land now belonged to us. Chief Walkara believed that we Mormons were friendly and promised us many comforts and lasting friendship. This, angered the Ute's even more as they said that the land offered was just one area, Chief Walkara's

259

own summer hunting ground, but we whites had taken over land that was occupied and used by tribes, destroying pasture and grazing. "You whites were friendly for a short time until your numbers grew, then you changed, you people started abusing us severely. We have been driven from our homelands from place to place. Settlements have been made on our hunting grounds in the valleys and the graves of our fathers have been torn up by you whites."

Co-existence seemed unattainable. The talks stopped. It was a sight to behold when groups would swarm down on us, riding through our newly-planted fields, waving tomahawks, threateningly, towards the settlers in our group. They were shouting out that it was their land and we were expanding onto it, building more houses for the white man.

The Utes had been pushed out of their traditional hunting and foraging areas by Mormon towns and they couldn't survive. Some were actually starving.

At this time, we saw this as only threatening behaviour but we knew it would not be long before they attacked. We decided, as a group, that it was too cold and dangerous to work during these harsh winters. We didn't have enough food or supplies, plus the Indians were getting more and more aggressive, So, we left, saying we would return in the spring, which we did.

So, after the winters of 1864/5 and 1865/6, we travelled back there and continued the work. Every so often, the Indians would fire lit arrows at our settlements and we had to have water on hand to put out the fires.

We returned to Panguitch in March 1865. On 10 April 1865 we heard there had been an attack, on the Mormon settlement in Manti, just north of Panguitch. This was to be the first incident of what was to become the Black Hawk War in Utah. Black Hawk, a young chieftain, had led sixteen Utes to drive off a cattle herd outside Manti. Several young men rode out to see what was going on and ran into the Utes, who began to shoot. One of the young men was shot and killed the rest fled back to Manti. The Indians around Manti had already struck camp and left.

It seemed that, on Saturday, 8 April 1865, Ute war chief, Black Hawk and Chief Jake Arapeen of the Timpanogous tribe and a group of other Utes appeared to attend a council meeting in Manti, some distance north of us. It was believed this meeting would lead to some understanding, but Arapeen demanded restitution for his father's death from smallpox in the winter of 1864-5 epidemic. There was a great dispute as the settlers were accused of using supernatural means to dispose of natives and thought they could stop the sickness and death by destroying white leaders. Settler John Lowry, an interpreter for the Superintendent of Indian Affairs for Utah, believed in being peaceful and friendly, when friendship was possible, and had learned Ute and Shoshone languages. However, he also believed the settlers could survive only if they were quick to punish for the loss of cattle and to revenge the death of their friends. Lowry, who may have been drunk, claimed to be protecting an unarmed family and himself; Chief Arapeen began to argue back. Chief Sow-ok-soo-bet and Toquana, Chief Sowiette's son, reminded Arapeen that the Mormons had often helped the natives with food and clothing, and urged a peaceful settlement of the issue. Arapeen set an arrow to his bow; Lowry instantly grabbed Arapeen by the hair and dragged him from his horse. There was a brief scuffle in the dirt and anxious associates on both sides dragged the two apart. Arapeen was badly beaten. Utes at this point had endured 15 years of white encroachment and 10 years of reservation life. Two days after this incident, a small group of riders from Manti was ambushed at Nine Mile and Peter Ludvingson was killed.

This started a spree of fort-building by the army in Manti and other nearby communities.

The Utes started to form groups to try to scare us off – with parties swooping down on us, threatening us. Telling us to go and that we were not welcome. The started stealing our cattle and horses,   George, in one of his, now infrequent, talks with the Utes, managed to find out that they were doing is as a kind of 'rent' payment for the settlers use of the land where the Utes had lived for centuries.

This stealing of cattle and horses persisted and grew with Black Hawk taking thousands of heads of livestock, transporting them out of Utah and selling or trading them for goods and money. They saw this as the quickest way to interfere with the growth of settlements.

GEORGE MORPHEW MUNFORD

CHAPTER 18

We got news from mum that my brother George Morphew Munford was finally coming to join us. He would be travelling with his new wife, Harriet, Harriet's daughter, Louisa, from a previous marriage, and my sister, Lucy, on board the ship Hudson. George and Harriet had got married on 4 May 1864 in Middlesex, and had been living in Paddington, London, England. George was 23 and she was 29. George had been a footman in a "Gentleman's" family, at 52 Porchester Terrace and Harriet lived at 3 Bishops Road, as a servant.

We were all overjoyed that they all seemed to be safe and sound but none of us could return to Parowan as we had to stay on at Panguitch. We would have to wait until winter set in again before we could see them, to see Harriet and Louisa for the first time, but mum would update us with letters. There would be so much to catch up with, about their wedding and the journey over.

Mum was there to greet the family. George had lost his Norfolk accent as he had to refine his speech for getting the job as butler in London. He sounded very refined now, according to mum. George told her, "Cap'n Isaiah Pratt was the master of the ship. It was built, just last year, in New York City and this was the ship's first passage. The ship was a full-rigged packet with three decks, a round stern and tuck, and a billet head. We started off in London. On board were Mormons from the British Isles, Switzerland, Germany and Holland. It took us 46 days. I can tell you, it was not all plain sailing though, as you can imagine from your own recollections. Measles broke out among the children and nine died and had to be buried at sea. One woman from Switzerland died and there were three births."

"Ah but there war boo-ful sunsets when thur sea wuz calm and glossy." This was Lucy.

"Nevertheless, I was not in a fit state to appreciate the lovely views as I was unwell most of the journey." Answered Harriet.

"And we saw a school of porpoises following the ship." This was Louisa."

"Anyway," George continued, "we docked at New York on 19 July. We were warned, on board, about the Civil War, which made on-going on our planned route, rather impossible. We had to take a detour through Canada by steamboat and railroad. The railway tracks came to an end so all had to disembark and continue our journey across the plains – which took about two weeks."

"It wuz pouring down wi' rairn most f thur way. A rafty tempest" Lucy commented.

"Yes, so our journey was made even more difficult. We finally joined William Hyde's Company on 9 August at Wyoming, Nebraska. Poor Harriet was still too ill to walk alongside the waggon, so we had to make room for her inside. Then the company was advised to wait, because of the Indian hostility, and travel with the Warren G. Snow Train. We only travelled about 10 miles that first day.

We camped overnight when we managed to lift Harriet out of the waggon, to rest. On one occasion, it was decided to travel on through the night.

"Yes, dear, "Harriet exclaimed – firing a fiery look at George. "You forgot about me – left me sitting on a rock."

"I have begged your apology so many times now Harriet. It's over and done with and I cannot go back and repeat the journey. Please let it rest. As you know, I was asked to go ahead of the waggon train to search out a good trail. We had travelled nearly 15 miles when the waggon train caught up and I found that you were missing."

"Oh, George," mum butted in. "Thur sairm thing 'appened to Ann and me. Yar daw had gone on withou us and we had such a trek, with little William wi' us too, trailing ar'er 'em in thur blazing sun with noo water. We were so quare afterwards, Ann 'specially so. We thort she was gonna die at one point."

"Oh, sorry to hear that, but thank you, I do not feel nearly as bad now. I am not the only silly fool in the family." Giving Harriet a stare back, but with a sort of smile too.

"Anyway," George continued, "I gave the alarm and I went back with a friend to find Harriet. We had gone a number of miles when we heard the rumbling of waggons. It proved to be an independent company on its way to California and, luckily, Harriet had thumbed a lift and was in one of the waggons. I was so relieved to see my Harriet safe." And he kissed her forehead."

"Yes, while sitting on that rock, feeling wretched and ill, I heard coyotes howling around me and was terrified they would attack. I was so pleased the other waggon train turned up."

"Rations were low, as you can imagine, but there was game to be had and, on one hunting trip, we managed to decoy one antelope just with a red handkerchief, would you belief." And George laughed."

"The water tasted awful though – it tasted of bicarbonate of soda and earthy metal and it gave us bad stomach aches." Harriet commented, "and we ran out of flour on 8 October. Luckily a mule train arrived from Salt Lake, bringing a load of flour, then a group of people came from Coleville and traded butter and potatoes for their tea and rice. "

"It took us four whole, gruelling months to cross the plains. We were travelling down Weber Canyon, within one day's travel of Salt Lake. There was snow on the ground when we entered the Great Salt Lake Valley, so we could not have been any later in getting here, otherwise we would have been snowed in. We then arrived in Beaver on 3 November and the following morning journeyed here. And here we are, on 6 November."

The bad weather was setting in in Panguitch now, so we decided to join George and his family back home Parowan. My brother, George, was asked to join the work team at Panguitch the following spring. He and his family went on to live at Old Fort Sanford on the Sevier River, 7 ½ miles north of Panguitch, where their first daughter, Lydia was born on 6 February 1865. She was the first white girl born at that place, still being Indian country.

In June 1865 Brigham Young took a personal interest in settling what was perceived as a squabble between Sanpete Valley's settlers and resident Utes. He called all of the old-guard chiefs that he had negotiated with in previous Ute/Mormon conflicts to meet at Spanish Fork's Indian Farm to figure out a peace settlement. Sowiette, the aging chief of the Northern Utes, Tabby from the Uintah Utes, Antero (the namesake of Mount Antero) and Kanosh from the Pahvant Utes, Mountain, Black Hawk's brother, and Sow-ok-soo-bet agreed to meet the first week in June. Consequently, the chiefs, accompanied by 500 Utes, showed up to see what would happen next. Sanpitch came at the last minute. The superintendent of Indians for the territory read out the terms of the treaty which simply asked the Utes to sign away any and all lands in the territory except for the Uintah Basin; that all attacks on settlers, miners, and others; cease warfare among themselves except in self-defence; and they were to turn in renegades who sought shelter among them. In return the US government promised to pay the tribe an annual payment of $25,000 for ten years, then $20,000 for twenty years, $15,000 for 30 years thereafter. They were promised $30,000 for unnamed improvements in the Uintah Basin and $10,000 for a vocational school. They were promised grist and sawmills, and personal homes for signers of the treaty. The chiefs listened and then asked for a private meeting with Brigham Young.

Brigham Young met with them and urged them to accept the treaty as the best deal they could get. He saw it as a way to help the destitute Ute who were being pressed out of the landscape year after year with nothing to show for it. The chiefs then went to their tents to think about what had been said. The following morning the chiefs were asked for their views of the treaty. The older chiefs suggested that Brigham Young would not mislead them and encouraged the others to sign. Kanosh and Sanpitch simply refused to give up their land, wanting to keep things as they had been for all time. After additional consultations the chiefs, except for Sanpitch, agreed to the treaty and set their marks to the paper on June 8, 1865. Sanpitch remained in his tent, refusing to sign. The rest of the chiefs lined up to receive the obligatory presents from the superintendent and church leaders. Sanptich was persuaded to accept his presents but refused to put his name to the paper. The Ute chiefs were reminded it was their duty to turn in anyone who broke the peace and the assembly broke up. In the meantime, Black Hawk had attacked Thistle Valley, not ten miles from the location of the treaty negotiations.

These treaties, made between the Utes and the Church of Jesus Christ of Latter-Day-Saints, were never ratified by the US government, they were only agreements. Only the United States Government had the authority to make Treaties with the Native Peoples. So, all these promises were pie in the sky. They meant nothing and were not going to be honoured.

On July 14, 1865 word was received at Manti that two more men had been killed at Glenwood in Sevier Valley and over 300 head of cattle driven off. This could not be tolerated and once again the militia was called out by Brigham Young himself and ordered to bring the Indians responsible to justice. Under the leadership of Warren Snow the Legion marched to Glenwood under cover of darkness so they could surprise the raiders. They coerced Mountain, Black Hawk's brother, to be their guide in the dark. He slipped away and went directly to warn Black Hawk of the Legion's intentions. They followed an Indian, who said he could lead them to Black Hawk. They made their way into Grass Valley on July 18. As they rested after the night's march, a guard noticed a large grove of junipers that hid a Ute camp. Thinking them to be a small part of Black Hawk's band, 13 Ute men and boys resisted when surrounded by the 100 militiamen. After a four-hour fight, ten were killed, two escaped and a third captured. The rest of the encampment consisted of women, children and old people. Several women and children had been wounded or killed during the fight leaving several prisoners. When one of the captives attacked one of the men with her knife, he shot her dead. This sent the other women into a violent panic and the men simply shot them down. The whole incident was later referred to as the 'Squaw Fight'. The militia set about looting the camp of anything of value. Snow shouted them back into order, threatening to arrest and court martial anyone who refused to follow his orders. Indian oral history paints a colder version that most of those killed were shot down including women and children and feeble old people. One boy managed to escape saying that the camp had a paper from the Bishop at Salina stating that they were good Indians; the militia apparently had failed to ask to see their pass. The Squaw Fight was a grim precedent that would be repeated again and again.

. . . .

I had gone back to Parowan, in the latter stages of pregnancy with our first child. I had missed Mum, who remarked on how much weight we had lost. Yes, I was just skin and bone, apart from the lump that was my daughter to be. Mum made sure we ate hearty meals and kept warm. Lucy Albena Gunn was born on 4 September 1865 in Parowan. It was nice to get us all back together again, to see mum and our friends and relatives. We had seen my brother and his family over the winter of 1864/5 for the birth of their daughter in February, but they had now gone onto Old Fort Sandford now.

George and I returned to Panguitch in March the following year, 1866.

My brother, George, had been called up to serve in the Black Hawk Indian War. George was one of Beaver's minute men. They were prepared with horses, ammunition, bread and a little hardtack candy for immediate call to arms. When called, they served from ten days to two weeks and then were relieved by a group of men from another settlement.

Knowing that hostilities were about to begin. The Utes had rounded up forty cattle and drove them toward Salina Canyon.

Black Hawk sent runners out asking Jake Arapeen's band to join Black Hawk's band in Salina Canyon. The settlers at Salina did not even notice that the Utes who had been living in the valley had all disappeared. The two bands together had about 90 men. They killed two white men in Salina Canyon and drove off Salina's entire herd of cattle and horses, bringing the total to about 125. Calls for help went out from Salina to the territorial militia, then known as the Nauvoo Legion from Gunnison, Manti, Ephraim and Spring City.

Chief Sanpitch, who had been so reluctant to sign the treaty drawn up and presented to his fellow chieftains at Spanish Fork on June 8th of the previous year, 1865, was quick to violate his pledge when opportunity offered and when Black Hawk's successes proved sufficient to seduce him from his allegiance, he joined in some of the depredations planned by the renegade chiefs.

The eighty-four men of the Legion headed by Colonel Reddick Allred started up Salina Canyon on April 12. Thinking that the

270

Indians would flee before such an imposing show of force, the militia failed to anticipate an ambush. In a narrow stretch of the canyon the Utes poured down arrows and bullets onto the mounted militia below. The instant panic that ensued among the untrained militia was a disaster. Only their speed of retreat prevented more of the Legion from being shot. They left one wounded young man to his fate and the body of another behind. They didn't stop until they reached Salina and had to listen to the jeers and taunts of Black Hawk and his men that night. Allred was relieved of command and Colonel Warren S Snow was appointed to take over during the emergency.

Too afraid to go back to the canyon to retrieve the bodies, Snow persuaded Sanpitch, a Sanpete Valley Chief to scout Salina Canyon for them so the settlers could retrieve the bodies of the two young men. When Sanpitch returned with word that Black Hawk had gone over the pass into Castle Valley the Legion returned to the canyon and brought back the dead: Jens Sorenson who had been terribly mutilated, and William Kearnes, the son of the Mormon bishop of Gunnison, who had been carefully protected. They also came back convinced that Sanpitch had met with Black Hawk and sent him over the pass, implying that Chief Sanpitch was the architect of the whole affair.

One day in 1866 we got a visit from a group of men from the Iron County Militia. They had received orders to build a fort and a stockade to protect us all from the Indians. The order was given on 22 March 1866 and, under the direction of George A Smith and his military companions, a drill was held at Panguitch, commencing at 9am. Forty men met, with 22 guns – although we found out they were not the best guns with various accidents and maiming incurred when a gun would backfire or blow up in the face of the poor soldier. Some men also had revolvers.

General Smith was going to make a speech to the forces. A meeting was commenced at 10am addressed by George A Smith, Silas S Smith, John Steele and Z B Decker.

At another meeting held in the afternoon, the rest of the brethren, who had accompanied George A Smith from Parowan spoke, including Wm. H Dane. After the meeting Colonel Dane, pursuant to military orders issued by George A Smith, got the soldiers to lay out the ground area of a fort that was going to be 28 rods square.

Another meeting was held in the evening, which was addressed by Jesse N Smith and George A Smith. At that meeting military orders were read out to everyone:

Panguitch, March 22, 1866.

Special Order No. 7, to Col. W H Dane, Commanding 1st Regiment Iron Military District

1   *You are hereby directed to order a fort surveyed in the town of Panguitch, sufficiently large to accommodate 30 or 40 families.*
2   *You will remove all the building in the town which are built of logs and place them on the fort line and locate the inhabitants inside the fort. The importance of these measures must not be overlooked.*

This was signed by George A Smith, Aide de Camp on Lieut. General's Staff.

As you can imagine, there were a lot of disgruntled faces amongst the pioneers. All their hard work, clearing the area and building the log cabins to house their families, was for nothing. The cabins were going to be pulled down and the families made homeless again.

Elder George A Smith then issued the following:

Panguitch, March 22 1866

To: Wm Wilcock, Jos. W. Paramore, Wm. Williamson, Morgan Richards, Henry Payson, Jos. Simkins, Horace Thornton, Daniel Allen, Samuel Connell, Wm. Holyoak, Wm. Morris and George Gunn.

Oh, I pricked up my ears to that, my George's name had been read out plus his partner in the tannery, William Holyoak.

Brethren: I understand that you claim land at this place and yet continue to absent yourselves, depending upon others to defend your property here during the Indian War.

This is to notify you that you are expected to either come here and help to defend your property or, failing to do so, must submit to such measures as may be taken in the premises, as it is manifestly unjust for the brethren here to bear the expense incident to an Indian Campaign, while you remain quietly away and attempt to reap the benefits of their labours.

Feeling confident that this notification will meet with a hearty and immediate response, I subscribe myself.

Your brother in the Gospel George A Smith.

Well, we weren't having any of that. "Surely they know it's impossible to work here during the winter with little to no supplies?" I enquired of George.

A discussion ensued amongst the workforce and it was decided we would have nothing to do with the building of the fort. We had had enough. They were trying to kill us with extremely hard labour, and then would not even defend us, wanting us to join their war against the Indians.

So, we all upped sticks and abandoned Penguitch, going back to our various homes in Beaver, Parowan and Paragonah.

We had heard that, as a ploy suggested by Brigham Young to bring Black Hawk to the bargaining table, the elderly Chief Sanpitch and other Indians were taken into custody on April 12th and incarcerated in the jail in Manti.

They broke jail on April 14, 1866. From Wm. A. Cox of Manti we learnt the following:

"The Indians broke jail late in the evening, and five of them got away. Andrew Van Buren and an Indian by the name of Aukewakets ran over a pile of rocks and leaped over a fence. As they ran over the rock pile each stooped and picked up a good sized rock raised up ready to strike. Van Buren being little and the quickest brought the Indian to his knees, and then took an old jack knife with a broken backspring from his pocket, after which he and the Indian clutched each other by the throat.

Van Buren succeeded in opening the knife with one hand and his teeth and cut the Indian's throat.

When W. A. Cox in the darkness of the night passed the end of a pile of fence posts, he thought he saw something move under the end of the posts; he kicked under and an Indian jumped up with a loud screech. Cox stepped back and with his revolver shot the Indian in the bowels. The Indian coming at him he fired again and shot the savage in the breast.

When Warren Snow passed a shed that night an Indian came out after him. Brother Snow heard him, but it was so dark he could not see him; he struck the Indian with his gun, breaking the stock, but killed the redskin.

Five Indians, including Sanpitch, got away and made for the West Mountains; a posse went in pursuit and on the 18th of the month Chief Sanpitch was found hiding in Birch Canyon, between Moroni and Fountain Green and was killed. The other four were tracked into the mountains between Fountain Green and Nephi, south of Salt Creek Canyon. On the 19th, Amasa and George Tucker and Dolph Bennett struck their tracks on the side of the mountain, where some men from Moroni joined them, and they followed the trail nearly to the top of the mountain where they overtook and killed three of them. They followed the track of the other one, whose name was Tackwitch, over the mountain and down some distance. Bennett stopped and sat down while the others followed the tracks. The Indian doubled on his tracks and came back to a point near where Bennett was seated and crawled into a patch of oak brush where he covered him-self up with leaves. Bennett saw him, and when the men missed his tracks they came back. Bennett motioned to his comrades pointing out where the

Indian was hidden. At once they surrounded the place and one of the men shot and wounded the Indian who jumped up and came at Bennett with a large butcher knife. Bennett emptied his revolver at him without bringing him down or stopping him. When within a few feet Bennett threw his pistol hitting the Indian on the temple and knocking him down. The Indian had no more than struck the ground when Bennett was on top of him, wrenched the knife from his hand and cut his throat. This finished the jail-breakers."

The two Mormon men responsible for the chief Sanpitch's death buried his body under a rock slide by shooting at the canyon wall

We heard many stories of atrocities committed, on both sides. The father of a settler, called Richard Ivie, was murdered outside Scipio for Richard's murder of a Ute nicknamed Old Bishop in Utah Valley sixteen years earlier. There was also the murder of Black Hawk's family at Battle Creek in 1849; the killing of 70 of his kin including beheadings at Fort Utah in 1850; the Bear River Massacre in 1863; and the "Squaw Fight" Grass valley massacre in 1865. In addition there was a local drought in 1864, and the food shortage in Mormon settlements and the US Indian agent's failure to provide enough supplies to Utes on the new Uintah Reservation brought many native bands to the brink of starvation. It is believed that Ute leaders, especially Chief Black Hawk, were aware that within a few years life as they knew it was about to end and forcing them to go into these newly-created "reservations" for tribes was a death sentence. Chief Black Hawk's personal agony was due to his people becoming increasingly famished, sick, and their alarming death rate while being forced to live in the conditions of the reservations. Typically tribes were given the least habitable areas within Utah territory, making livestock or agriculture impossible.

Black Hawk had personally experienced the settlers' distrust and contempt for his people. He had been beaten, with a bucket, for a supposed theft, his family members had been shot, and supposedly their heads taken as trophies in the Fort Utah War. He had been forced to lead Mormon militia against his own people. He was not alone; other natives had badly suffered physical and emotional torment due to white settlers who were on their lands.

29 January 1863 –Bear River Massacre Five hundred thirty-one Shoshone people were slain by the U.S. army, just north of the Utah-Idaho border.
1864 - Twelve Mile Creek Reservation dissolved when Indians had stopped maintenance.

1864 - Act of Congress required Utes to give up all land and title rights and move to Uintah Reservation within a year.
1864–1865 (winter) -Smallpox epidemic sweeps through Ute band. Chief Arapeen (senior) was among casualties.
July 18, 1865 - The Grass Valley Massacre, The Old Timpanogos Chief was Beheaded, U.S soldiers then surrounded the camp and opened fire on the tribe killing women, men, and children.

8 April 1865 - Chief Yenewood (aka "Jake Arapeen") and interpreter John Lowry contended with each other. Official beginning of the war.

10 April 1865 - Peter Ludvingson from Manti was killed in an encounter between Utes and settlers at Nine Mile.

26 May 1865 - In the early morning hours John and Elizabeth Given, along with their children John Jr., Mary, Anna, and Martha were killed by a band of Utes on the Utah-Sanpete county border.

1865 - Black Hawk and his band killed 32 whites in Sanpete and Sevier Counties, and stole over 2,000 cattle and horses.

1866 - Mormon leaders consolidated settlements and cattle in Sanpete and Sevier Counties to forts in Manti, Ephraim, Mount Pleasant, Moroni and Gunnison. Tabernacle fort built in Manti.

18 April 1866 – Chief Sanpitch (father of Black Hawk) was killed near Fountain Green.

. . . .

Mormon officials ordered the Paiutes to be disarmed. Black Hawk and his band had killed many during the year before. A determined camp of Paiutes remained in Circle Valley (now Circleville), trying to be friendly with the Mormons. However, the Mormons felt that they were in danger every moment, as some of the Natives were so aggressive that the Saints believed danger was imminent.

On April 21, 1866, an express from Fort Sanford reached Circleville, Utah, telling of a Paiute who, pretending to be friendly, had shot and killed a white man belonging to the militia stationed at the nearby fort. The people of Circleville were told to protect themselves against the Indians who were camped in their valley. Upon receipt of this information, the people of Circleville called a town meeting. After much discussion, it was decided that they should arrest all the Paiutes that were camped nearby and bring them to Circleville for confinement.

278

Every able-bodied man in the town set out to take custody of the Indian camp, and they surrounded the camp at night. James T. S. and Bishop William Jackson Allred went to the Indian camp and persuaded the Indians to come to a meeting at Circleville. They told the Indians that they had received a letter and they wanted to have it read to them. All of the Indians agreed, willingly, to go to Circleville with the men, except one young Indian warrior who refused to go and began to shoot at the posse. The posse returned fire, killing the young man. The rest of the Indians were then taken at gunpoint to Circleville and the letter was read to them. The Indians were told that they were to be retained as prisoners.

The Indians were taken into custody and placed in the meeting house that night under guard. On the evening of the following day, some of the Indians were able to cut themselves loose from their bindings to escape. Guards shot and killed two Indians who were attempting an escape. The remaining imprisoned Indians, totalling 24, were moved to an underground cellar. In a subsequent town meeting, the settlers decided to kill the remaining imprisoned Indians. The Indians were led out of the cellar, including men, women, and children. They were struck on the back of the head to stun them and then their throats were slit, leaving them to bleed to death. Two young boys and girl prisoner managed to escape before execution.

The following day, the three children were found in a nearby cave and taken by James Allred to Marysvale. Allred intended to sell or make a trade for the children. The little girl was killed by a violent bludgeoning. While the fate of one of the boys is unknown, the other was adopted by the Munson family of Spring City.

The town of Panguitch was abandoned in May 1866. Residents left their homes and crops and sought safety in Parowan and other communities.

After the Indian wars were over, the Church Presidency advised the people to return to their homes in Panguitch, but many of the original company had made permanent homes elsewhere.

George went back to his tannery with William Holyoak and John Brown and my husband, George, began to finish off his house – our house.

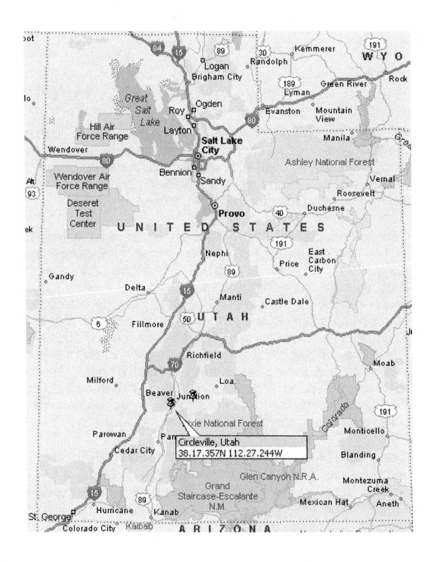

Circleville, Utah
38.17.357N 112.27.244W

281

1866

CHAPTER 19

My sister, Lucy, had found herself a nice young man, Joseph Stevens and they got married on 5 November 1865 at St. George in Utah, a couple of hours carriage drive south west of Parowan. It was a fine affair, with dancing and singing in the church hall. My George loved these affairs.

George had built a lovely two-room house with a lean-to kitchen. We even had a hand woven carpet on the floor in the living room. There was a fireplace with a sheep skin rug in front, which George had tanned. In fact, every room had a sheep-skin rug that George had tanned. I had decorated the mantelpiece with interesting pictures and ornaments. We had a central table, a sofa, a big rocking chair and two other chairs. The kitchen had a cook stove in the corner, a kitchen table and chairs and a cupboard full of pretty dishes. The door to the cellar was a trapdoor in the kitchen floor. It had to be lifted up for anyone to go down the stairs to the cellar, where I kept fruits, vegetables, cured meat and other foods.

I had started braiding a big rug to go by the door. The bedroom had a big four-poster bed, a small rocking chair and a black dresser. In time, I was going to make a bedspread and pillow cases. I had this all in my head as an idea. It would be beautiful.

Outside was a garden and an orchard or apple trees that George had just planted. I could see us having lovely applies from them in the future. Under one of them, I had dug a pit to put my cheeses to age.

Benjamin, George's youngest brother, had bought a lot on the corner of Wall and Elm Street (now 5th Avenue and J Street), ten by ten rods, for which he paid $5. Jedediah M Grant, first mayor of Salt Lake City signed the deed. It was a patch of sagebrush and a southeast corner he thought but, when the streets were laid out, he had a southwest corner. They were living in a tent while Benjamin was building a two-room log house, one of the first houses built on the north bench.

One night, a storm came up and blew the tent down and, as the cellar had been dug, they huddled in a corner, trying to keep warm and dry. Unfortunately, his baby, Benny, had the whooping cough and took another cold and died from exposure.

....

George was brilliant with the children and William had taken to him like a son to his father – he had no memories of his real father anyway, thank goodness. George loved playing games with them, taking William for piggy-back rides and he would pretend to be a bear or a roaring animal and scare them both silly. Lucy would start crying, but George would then just pick her up and swing her round, until she started giggling, then give her a big kiss. He would also read to them and help William with his reading – he was doing pretty well. George would also tell them stories – mostly made-up fairy tales with ghosts and goblins – though some were memories of his journey over, which had their own ghosts and goblins of a kind. I had my own stories to tell, but tried to make them heroic, telling him that he was surrounded with heroes and heroines in his own village. "You're my little hero, William, and one day you will be big and tough, and be able to fight off the baddies, like your dad."

Unfortunately, my father, Robert Munford, died just four months after Lucy's wedding. He was 76 years old. He was given a good send-off, which speeches saying what a wonderfully strong pioneer he had been and that he would be greatly missed. I just remember thinking that, if they hadn't pushed him so hard with all the digging, scything and mowing at Penguitch, he could have lived longer. I remembered going through his paperwork back home in Costessey, planning our journey to get here, getting everything packed up, the long journey over on the Amazon, and the waggon train over the desolate prairies and frozen mountains. He was a great man, a far-thinker. I cried. I would miss him greatly.

BLACK HAWK WARS

CHAPTER 20

By June 1866 the people of the Sanpete and Sevier settlements were scared silly. These settlement were about 140 miles north of us, just north east of Salt Lake City. So, some distance – a couple of days' travel by horse and cart, but we were worried. The stories of the proposed massacre had expanded out of all proportion. Black Hawk had threatened to bring enough men to destroy Manti and Warren Snow that year. 125 additional militia were sent south from Salt Lake to prevent such an attack. However, hearing of the show of strength in the Sanpete Valley, Black Hawk shifted his focus to Scipio. Scipio was the home of the James Russell Ivie family. Stories abounded that one of his sons had been responsible for hostilities in the Fort Utah war, when he murdered a Ute called Old Bishop and sank his weighted body in the Provo River. Another son, James Alexander Ivie, was blamed for starting the Walker War when he hit a Ute over the head with his gun and also participating in the Tintic war, which resulted in the death of Black Hawk's friend Squash Head and the wounding of Chief Tintic.

A band of 100 Utes and allies began herding together 350 head of cattle from pastures near Scipio. They killed a 14-year-old herd boy and shot the elderly James Russell Ivie full of arrows and stripped him of everything except his boots. Gathering up 75 horses the Utes and their allies moved the herd through Scipio Gap into Sevier Valley. Scipio's men charged out after the herd, but were forced back when the Black Hawk's rear guard moved to attack the town, which had been left virtually undefended. The Utes withdrew moving toward Salina Canyon with the largest single capture of livestock in the conflict.

The Scipio settlers sent runners to Gunnison (to the east) and Fillmore to the south, (just west of Salt Lake) to get help. William Pace of the Nauvoo Legion gathered up 20 men, hoping to catch Black Hawk before he could make his escape. They left Gunnison and marched through the night to reach Salina before the herd could be driven away. He could see the herd head for Gravelly ford on the Sevier River and rode there to stop the Utes from stealing the cattle and horses. Upon approaching the ford he found about 60 Utes guarding the ford. He sent for help from Richfield and tried to delay the fording of the herd with a prolonged gun fight. Realizing he could not sustain the attack, he ordered his men to pull back out of range. Several Utes tried to force them farther back from the ford by charging the nearly defenceless militia. Black Hawk himself and his chief lieutenant, Tamaritz, were two of these men. Black Hawk's horse was shot from under him and then he was hit in the stomach. Tamaritz, too, had been wounded. Minutes later the Gunnison militia, out of ammunition took to their heels. The Utes drove the herd across the river toward Salina Canyon just as the Richfield militia arrived on horseback to see the herd nearing the mouth of Salina Canyon and the Gunnison militia riding for home. The wounding of Black Hawk and Tamaritz eventually brought an end to the Black Hawk War and Black Hawk himself just four years later. In the interim several other sub chiefs took over, including Black Hawk's brother, Mountain, Issac Potter and Richard James.

We heard another story that James Ivie, the son of the elder Ivie murdered at Scipio, was crazy for revenge against the Utes. An old Pahavnt Ute medicine man by the name of

Panikary made the mistake of visiting Scipio begging for food. He was known as a 'good Indian' with a peaceful disposition. Bishop Thomas Callister of Fillmore who happened to be in Scipio, advised Panikary to leave town because the Ivie's blood was up and there might be trouble. Panikary took the presents of food offered and headed toward Fillmore. Upon returning from the futile pursuit of Black Hawk, the younger James Ivie, hearing that a Ute had been in Scipio just hours before raced after Panikary and murdered him on the spot. The bishop of Scipio had ridden hard to stop Ivie but failed to prevent the killing. Callister was disgusted by the murder and rode directly to Chief Kanosh's camp to inform him of the incident. Up to that point the Pahavant Ute had not been openly involved in the fighting. Kanosh thanked Callister for being honest, but the war chief, Moshoquop and 27 warriors followed Callister to his home in Fillmore angrily demanding justice. Callister convinced the Utes that Brigham Young would be a fairer judge. The Utes agreed and rode away. Later Ivie was arrested and tried for murder by an all-Mormon judge and jury but was acquitted when it was suggested that Panikary was really a spy for Black Hawk. Bishop Callister was so upset by the outcome that he excommunicated Ivie from the church.

Battles of Thistle Valley and Diamond Fork

Up until that time the Uintah Utes, with their Chief Tabby-To-Kwanah (Tabby), had been on their reservation, out of the war. The call for an additional 350 men, in June 1866, from Salt Lake and Davis Counties to strengthen Mormon settlements angered Tabby and his fighters. But Black Hawk's brother, Mountain, Isaac Potter and Richard led separate war parties toward Utah Valley. They found a Nauvoo Legion detachment (at what is now Indianola) and attacked. They pinned the militia down for most of the day, but a second detachment under John

L. Ivie (another of the Ivie family) arrived late and kept the first detachment from being overwhelmed. The soldiers were convinced that Chief Tabby had led the attack. When an additional 130 men under Warren Snow arrived, it was agreed to chase the Utes up Spanish Fork Canyon. Fearing another Salina Canyon disaster, the troops moved cautiously but, on arriving at Soldier Summit Pass, found that the Utes had split up and gone in different directions. He turned his men around and marched them back to Sanpete Valley.

Mountain (Black Hawk's brother) had led his men to Spanish Fork to exact vengeance on William Berry, who years before had beaten Black Hawk with an old bucket for a supposed theft. They killed Berry and drove off about forty cattle and horses and fled into the Wasatch Mountains through Maple Canyon. The militia, who were already on alert, gave chase. They intercepted the Utes at Diamond Fork River but were outnumbered and pinned down by desultory rifle shots and arrows. A second force of eight men rushed the Utes and three were shot dead. The others put the Utes in a crossfire. The Utes quietly withdrew leaving the livestock and camp to be plundered by the militia. Among the gear they found US issued items, which showed the Utes had been accepting food and supplies at the Uintah Reservation. Leaders of the militia swore affidavits that white men had been seen directing the Utes. It was feared that the US Indian officials were aiding and abetting the Utes in their war against the Mormons. We couldn't believe that white men, even possibly soldiers, who we were relying on to defend us, were actually, supplying the Utes and directing them against us.

Brigham Young ordered this time, not just encouraged, all Mormons to build forts and evacuate small settlements, combining livestock herds, under guard.

The Navajo War was not directly a part of the Black Hawk War, but it may have been a source of some of the native warriors who fought in the Black Hawk War. Black Hawk's success drew fighters from other Utes in Colorado, Apaches from New Mexico and many Navojos. In the winter of 1866 Black Hawk and his band went to the Four Corners region where he received many new recruits. So many Navajos joined him that they formed almost half his raiders. The Navajo had been decimated by the U.S. Army under Kit Carson and forced out of their ancestral homeland. The remaining Navajos were eager for a chance to build up their herds at the expense of white settlers. Manuelito, the most important chief refusing to relocate to the Bosque Redondo Reservation, jointly led Black Hawk's raids on Mormon settlements in southern Utah during 1866. The attacks commenced at Pipe Springs, then a Mormon settlement on the Arizona/Utah border. The retaliation for the Pipe Springs raid left four unarmed Paiutes dead for murders they had nothing to do with. This brought some Paiute fighters to Black Hawk's band. Hopis, hearing of the Navajo's movements feared they were to be attacked and struck first, ambushing Manuelito's Navajos. The raids continued at the Paria settlements, and Kanab, who sent pleas for help against the raids.

Chief Kanosh had made a prediction - seen as a threat - that by the following year they would have six thousand Navajos gathered and they would attack and kill all the Mormon in southern Utah.

Black Hawk's Last Raid

In the spring of 1867 hundreds of Nauvoo Legion militia from northern Utah flooded into central Utah determined to maintain the strict vigilance on settlements and their livestock, and

289

patrol routes known to be used by Utes and their allies. There were several isolated attacks, one of which was planned to capture and kill Warren Snow, which was narrowly averted. Dozens of ranches and settlements were closed and more and more settlers moved to towns with forts for protection. With such a military presence in central Utah, Black Hawk moved his forces south. He was planning a raid on Parowan – where we lived! Black Hawk had never raided so far south before and we were in panic. By July 21, 1867 the townsfolk had gathered their cattle and horses together – a herd of 700 cattle – and placed under guard. George had herded his cattle into the stockade as well and stood on guard. I was so frightened that he would be shot and maybe we would all be massacred. I had a rifle too to protect my little ones, William and Lucy, and I had buckets of water on standby, in case the Indians set off flaming arrows at us to burn our houses down. Lucy was just two years old and William was now 9. I had to put Lucy in her cot but she was screaming continuously and William was trying his best to comfort her. She could sense the tension in the air. This made me even more jumpy. I could not go and comfort her myself as I was on guard, looking out for any signs of trouble. William was such a good boy, picking Lucy up and rubbing her back. He even made a bottle for her. He did not ask questions, he knew that danger was just around the corner and this was not the time to disturb me from my look-out position. George had been giving him shooting lessons, but he just was not big enough to hold a rifle. I knew he was frightened and feeling completely helpless, and I tried to give him comforting words – telling him what a good boy he was and that his dad and the people of the village would keep us safe.

As it happened, Black Hawk and his team instead concentrated on rounding up scattered livestock near

Paragonah (a couple of miles north of us). Guards saw them and the alarm was raised. The Utes were chased into a canyon where the Utes were eventually forced to leave their horses behind in order to escape in the steep terrain. Black Hawk retreated recognizing that it would be impossible to get any stolen livestock over the high plateaus above Cedar City and Parowan.

Death of Isaac Potter

Isaac "Ike" Potter was a white man with several wives in Utah County. He was an apostatized Mormon who had turned outlaw. He was a notorious cattle and horse thief and possibly one of the principal brokers in the sale of Black Hawk's stolen cattle. We had heard of white men leading Ute raids against the settlers – supplying them with guns and provisions. Ike Potter was the most notorious of them. In late June 1867, Ike Potter and a band of Utes and allies sent a demand for beef and other supplies to William W Cluff, a Mormon Bishop at Coalville in Washington County. The demand was supposedly rejected and Potter responded that Black Hawk would come down and wipe out the Mormons. Charges were made against Potter for inciting natives to incendiary deeds against Mormon settlements. A raid on a sawmill brought out the militia, which accidentally learned where Potter and his men were camped. They surrounded the camp and arrested Potter, two other apostate Mormons, Charles Wilson and John Walker (19), 16 Utes and Navajos, on the charge of stealing a cow. They were marched back to Coalville to stand trial. Local Danites were afraid that Potter would be freed by a 'gentile' - Judge Snyder (who had previously discharged them after arrest for alleged theft) and decided to take matters into their own hands. On August 1, 1867 while under guard in the schoolhouse at Coalville, ten or twelve armed persons, appeared about twelve o'clock at night at the building and ordered the prisoners to leave.

Upon reaching the street they were placed in single file, a short distance apart, and in each intervening space two of the armed persons placed themselves. The others took positions at the front and rear of the procession thus formed. In this order they marched along the principal street of Coalville, through the mainly inhabited part of the town. Arriving at the outskirts, and their captors continuing to move on, Porter turned around and said to Walker: "John, they are going to murder us! Wouldn't you like to see your mother before you die?" Thereupon one of the armed men marching behind Potter thrust the muzzle of a shotgun against Potter's mouth. Potter in terror, shouted "murder!" The armed man promptly discharged his gun into Potter's cheek, so killing Potter instantly. At the discharge of the gun, both Wilson and Walker broke away and ran for their lives. Wilson was overtaken and killed at the edge of the Weber River. As Walker made his escape, a charge from a shotgun grazed his breast and lacerated his hand and wrist. He was wearing neither coat nor vest, and the charge set his shirt on fire. As he ran, he smeared his own blood from his wounds to extinguish the fire. He was an athletic youth and soon outdistanced his pursuers. Although a number of shots were fired at him in the pursuit, he reached the river without further injury, swam across, and thereby escaped assassination. After numerous hardships he succeeded in reaching Camp Douglas, where the commanding officer, upon hearing what had taken place, gave him support and protection.

The only excuse ever claimed by any of the accused was that Potter, Wilson and Walker attempted to escape, and were shot while running away. In the light of the fact that Potter's throat was cut and his clothes scorched by the charge which killed him, and that Walker's shirt was set on fire by the shot which wounded him, such a claim is absurd. It was shown by the testimony that Ezra Hinkley was in command of the participants in the affair and directed their movements. He was not a resident of Coalville at the time, his home being in Salt Lake City. He went to Coalville shortly after Potter, Wilson and Walker were arrested. After Potter and Wilson were killed he moved permanently to Coalville, was soon installed in the office of probate judge of Summit county in place of Judge Snyder, and served in that capacity for many years. Walker remained for some time at Fort Douglas after the accused parties were committed, but before the time set for the grand jury of the district court to convene he left the fort to visit his mother at Coalville. He did not visit his mother, but mysteriously disappeared, and was never seen or heard of again. It was presumed that he was assassinated before reaching his home. His testimony was necessary to make a case against the accused, and his disappearance gave them perfect immunity.

Black Hawk had never fully recovered from his wound at Gravelly Ford the previous year. He also had tuberculosis and his health was failing. Two weeks later, in August, Black Hawk and a small band of followers rode into the Uintah Reservation and announced to the agent there that he was ready to talk peace with the whites. We were all so relieved.

With Black Hawk and his family at the Uintah Reservation willing to negotiate, the US government finally stepped into its own. Superintendent Franklin Head rode to the Uintah Agency to work out a peace agreement that would bring hostilities to an end. He found all of the chiefs of the Northern Utes already gathered ready to talk. By mid-September the government had everything it wanted from Black Hawk. Not only would he stop raiding, he promised to use his influence to persuade Tamawitz and others to come to the Uintah Agency and stop harassing whites. Black Hawk explained that it was not his band that caused all the trouble blaming Elk Mountain Utes for the trouble.

Sporadic violence still occurred until 1872 when federal troops intervened. Many Mormon settlers who fought and died in the wars are buried in the Manti Cemetery. Most of the Utes were eventually relocated to the Uintah and Ouray Indian Reservation in Eastern Utah.

1868

CHAPTER 21

George's older brother, William, and his family, had moved into a fort by 1867. They could now move back to their homestead. As the years passed, through hard back-breaking labour, the sage brush covering the land was changed to fields of grain and green inviting meadow-land, where cattle and horses grazed. In summer, these animals were allowed to graze on the mountains and in the canyons, but in the winter months, they were rounded up and brought to the farms to be fed hay and straw. Their home was a little low, two room log home, built back quite a distance from the main road. Here, in a kitchen and one bedroom, most of Elizabeth's children were born – their only source of water being hauled in barrels from the Weber River. But, in spite of its inconveniences and crudeness, this little home was a paradise to them.

. . . .

The spring of 1868 began as a hopeful one for displaced Mormon settlers. They clamoured to return to their homes, farms, ranches, and towns. The very first waggon train to take back the Sevier Valley settlements was attacked by Tamaritz and a small force. The resettlement was postponed for at least a year. There were a few attacks on individuals and isolated thefts, but the Mormon vigilance policy prevented Ute success. Black Hawk sent messages to leaders either once under him or allied with him to come in and negotiate with the government. His treatment was a positive example and one or two raiders made their way to the Uintah Reservation. Tamaritz and his band surrendered in August.

Negotiations between local Utes and settlement leaders took place all through the summer. Tabby met with leaders in Heber City, Orson Hyde met with Sowiette, Toquana in Nephi, Indian agent Dimick Huntington met with Ute in the Strawberry Valley, and Hamilton Kearnes met with Ute at Salina to smoke a peace pipe and give presents. Elk Mountain chiefs met with Superintendent Head and the fighting seemed to be coming to a swift conclusion. In the minds of Mormon settlers and territorial officials the war was over.

FOLLOWING YEARS

CHAPTER 22

There were subsequent isolated incidents between settlers and Native peoples in central and southern Utah, though not directly connected to the Black Hawk War, until the forced relocation of all Utes to the Uintah Agency in eastern Utah in 1872.

As chief after chief gave up hostilities tensions slackened in 1869. There were reports of murdered Utes who happened to be in the wrong place when accosted by whites bent on vengeance. For example, an Ute girl raised in a Mormon family in Fairview was found with her throat cut. There were sporadic raids where a few horses were taken or a cow slaughtered by unknown parties. The Uintah Reservation was not a peaceful place, Ute from many bands were forced to live in close proximity which caused problems and the younger fighters wanted to be out raiding, but held in check by their leaders.

On 9 April 1868 we had a son, who we called George Robert – after George and my father, Robert. George adored him. He was his first son with me, and he was so proud. He made him a cot and rattles. He would pick him up and cuddle him at every opportunity. Of course, I would get annoyed, "George, I've only just got him off to sleep!" So, he would lay him down again, until little George fell back to sleep, then just look at him for ages, with a beaming smile on his face.

George's brother, Benjamin, at the time, had built his log hut and was well occupied digging the irrigation ditch from Red Butte Canyon through the city cemetery, along 7th Avenue and down 'J' Street to water the garden. They were raising fruit and vegetable and had a cow and a pig. They had to carry all the culinary water from a City Creek ditch, which ran along 4th Avenue. . The log hut had a mud roof. His wife was due to give birth and little John Francis was born on 19th September 1868. There was a heavy rain storm and water came through the mud roof. They had to put tin pans and umbrellas on the bed while little Benjamin was being born. Oh well, all part of life and at least little John Francis survived.

In 1869 George and I made a trip to Salt Lake City. On 5 October, we received our endowments and were sealed in the Endowment House.

The next two years were filled with heartache as I gave birth to two children but they both died in infancy. Lydia Ann was born on 1 March 1870 but died 5 months later and John was born on 24 January 1972 but died at the age of 7 months. There was nothing I could do to save them. To have one die, was enough, but to have the next child die too, was just something I could not bear and went into a fit of depression, just violent weeping. George tried his best to comfort me and I managed to see, through him, that it was not just me suffering, but he had lost two children as well. I was just, finally, bringing myself round to accepting what must be must be, when just 5 days later, on 14 August 1872, I got the news that my mother, Lydia M Munford, had passed away at her home, during the night. She was 71 years old. There was really no coming back from that, or that is how I felt at the time. Time heals, but slowly. My mum was my mum and always would be – a light had gone out in my world. She taught me so many things – all the beautiful sewing I could do was because mum taught me. It was mum who kept the family together, fed and clothed us, back in Norfolk, when we had no money or work. It was mum who went without. It was mum who had kept me going over the plains, when I had been so ill and almost died. It was mum who had walked with me when dad had driven off with the rest of the train, thinking we were in the waggon.

I remembered one time, mum had an Indian come to her door. He began to use abusive language, but being the strong-minded person that she was, my mum just picked up a hoe and chased him out. That memory made me smile. She was something, my mum.

We buried mum in Parowan cemetery.

But, at least the Black Hawk war was over and we could finally get back to some peace and normality.

I started a school, at first in our own house. I invited both boys and girls of all ages and taught them to read and write.

Emma Webb was one of my first pupils along with Nellie Marsden and Mary Ann Durham. Emma was quite an outgoing sort and was in one of the plays I allowed the children to perform. The children actually created these plays and performed them themselves. They bought clothes from home for costumes. Every so often we would have one of these plays enacted at the old fort wall, with parents as the audience. It was great fun and the children loved being part of these performances.

I also taught the girls sewing and embroidery and Libby Hoyle and Medora Halterman were amongst my best pupils. My embroidery work, though I say it myself, was much admired. I took some of my work to show off at local fairs and, more often than not, won first prize. I would come home with my ribbon and proudly show George.

It wasn't just my embroidery that I worked on but my daughter, Lucy, and I were asked to perform the onerous task of making clothes for the dead. I collected a little group together, which included Libby Hoyle and Medora Halterman and Mary Alice Benson to do this work and, even after they had left school, this group continued to make the burial clothes for the town's people for many years. This same group, plus other like-minded women, became part of my 'Relief Society Sewing Committee', and we had sewing bee competitions. As well as that, we would go into homes of women with large families or motherless families to lend a helping hand. Sometimes we would spend the whole day cutting out and sewing clothes for the family to get them ready for school.

On 9 October 1873, I gave birth to a boy, who we called Alfred James. My son, William, was now fifteen years old and working for some of the farmers in the valley.

Lucy was baptised in May 1874.

George had actually befriended some of our local Indians. He would do trades with them or even give them let-over bits of leather that he could spare, and food. They would have sit-down parleys, smoking pipes and George would make little toys for the Indian children.

Sometimes the Indians would come to the house begging for bread and other things. Sometimes they would offer to trade 'Hill Gum' (Pine Gum) for something they wanted. These little meetings were not always friendly though, and quarrels could develop, especially if there were no men around. One day, one of them came and began to quarrel with me, in a threatening manner. I just looked out of the door and said, "Oh, here comes my man." The Indian just turned tail as quickly as he could.

We were sitting at the supper table on day. George was there with the rest of the family. "George, can you pass the salt please." I said across the table. There was no answer, so I asked again. He seemed to be just staring at me, unmoving. The hair on the back of my neck stood up. "No, George... answer me." I got up and shook him lightly but there was no reaction. I took his hand, but it just fell limply down on the table. "Oh God", I screamed. " Lucy, run and get the doctor."

George had suffered a stroke. He could not move or speak. We put him to bed. The doctor could do nothing, we would just have to wait to see if he recovered. The doctor said he could well recover, given time, and that he was still young, so there was a good possibility. However, he added, "Mr Gunn, if he does recover will possibly not be able to walk for some time and one side will be frozen. That means he will not be able to lift one arm and one leg on the same side of his body. He also will not be able to smile on that same side and his eyesight will be affected. He will need exercise and massage to recover in any degree."

So, we had to wait. Lucy was crying, as we watched tears streaming down from George's eyes as he lay there, helpless.

One of the Indians, whom George had befriended, 'Pete Captain' visited and stood around with tears rolling down his face, watching while George lay in his bed.

He never recovered, and died a week later, on 31 May 1876. He was only 47 years old. We were all stricken by his death – he shouldn't have died so soon – we were all in shock.

Wearing our mourning clothes, we had a funeral. There were quite a few speeches about George being a good pioneering saint and about his works for the town. Others said he was a kind, good-natured man, greatly missed by his family and many friends. Pete Captain was there. "He was always so friendly to us, a jolly man. He had many friends in my tribe as he used to give us pieces of leather and such. He was a good man and will be sorely missed - we will always remember him."

I was too traumatised still to say anything apart from whisper to his coffin, "I love you, George, and always will."

It was the end of an era, an era of such strength, endurance and pioneering resourcefulness...... It was now over.

We buried George in Parowan Cemetery.

George Gunn

Son of John Gunn and
Ann Impey Brazier

* Born: July 18, 1828 in Bishop's Stortford, Eng
* Died: May 31, 1875 in Parowan, Utah
* Married **Ann Munford** March 1864 in
  Parowan, Utah

Children (5): **Lucy Albena**, George Robert, Lydia
Ann, John, & Alfred James Gunn

* His dad died when he was 12. He had to work
  hard to help his mother provide for the family,
  so he stopped attending school.

* George was part owner of the first tannery in
  Parowan which turned out some of the finest
  leather. Their home was filled with black &
  white sheep skinned rugs that he tanned.

* He had many friends among the Indians.

* He was a kind, good-natured,
  and jovial man who was greatly
  missed after his sudden death.

* After a stroke paralyzed George,
  an Indian chief came to say goodbye. His children remember tears
  rolling down the chief's face.

303

Parowan's first settlers were instructed to plant crops so that following immigrants could open up the coal and iron ore deposits, but local industries were also developed. Self-sufficiency was envisioned, and local industries included a tannery, sawmill, cotton mill, and factories for making saddles and harnesses, furniture and cabinets, shoes, and guns; there also were carpentry and blacksmith shops. George Gunn's tannery, saddles and harness business had been the first in Parowan.

After her husband, George, died, Ann's first son, William Stubbs Gunn, took over the farm. He had acquired some pasture land on the 'bottoms (land from the Parowan north fields to the little Salte Lake), where there was an abundance of salt grass, excellent for pasture for his cows. Eighteen days after his father's death, William married Isabell Gavin, a girl from St Louis, Missouri. He was 18, and Isabelle was 20. William continued to help support me and his brothers and sisters.

William built a nice home on the west side of Parowan, a farm with sheep and cattle. He and his wife, Isabelle, had ten children. Unfortunately, Isabelle died at the age of 43, leaving a young family. William did not marry again and raised the remaining nine children himself (one had died as an infant). He was a kind, good-natured man. He loved to tell Pioneer stories.

Lucy and her husband, Herbert, homesteaded a ranch on Parowan Bottoms and lived there 25 years. They then left the ranch and moved to their beautiful home across the hollow n Parowan. Herbert owned and operated the first shingle mill in Parowan. They had thirteen children; ten that grew to maturity.

Lucy's brother, George Robert, was a cattle man. He and his brother, Alfred, worked with men on the Arizona Strip, buying and settling cattle. George Robert's wife, Mary Ann, taught school at Pinto for a while and later she was a county recorder. She was instrumental in writing many of the important documents of the day. Their first home was a log cabin on the farm. They lived there several years then moved the cabin to town, adding more rooms onto it.

George Morphew and Harriet Munford

George Morphew was a son of Robert Munford and Lydia Murphy.

George and Harriet were sealed together in the St George Temple on 13 February 1878.

Both George and Harriet worked very hard. They moved back to Parowan, where their first son, Charles, was born, on 2 December 1866. In 1867 they moved to Beaver where they made their homes. Unfortunately, baby Charles died on 25 July 1868, aged just 19 months.

George was a brick-maker by trade. He made the brick for most of the early homes in Beaver. Harriet did her share of the work. She cooked for the men, who were hired to help make the brick. She also milked cows and made butter. George would butcher the pigs and Harriet would cure the meat. This meat was used to help pay the hired men for their work. Harriet worked early and late to help in every way she could. She was very hospitable and no-one was ever turned away from her door without a meal. George T, the third child was born in 1870. Harriet Alice came along in 1872. William James was

305

next to be born, in 1874. In 1876, another daughter, Lucy, graced their home, with Eliza Ann coming just two years later on Christmas Even 1878. George and Harriet were the parents of 8 children, 5 girls and 3 boys.

In the 1880s George attempted to develop irrigation. He built a reservoir, located in the Tushar Mountains east of Beaver at the head of the north fork of South Creek. Because of the size of the dam, he must have had a team of horses and probably a scraper and plough. The last three quarters of a mile to a mile of this area is very steep and thick with timber. How he got the equipment up to the reservoir is not known. It was an early attempt to build an irrigation system. The reservoir was filled by clear, clean spring water. It had beavers living in it for many years. The water level was high and fishing was very good (four and five pound native fish have been caught out of this body of water). Ducks nest there every year. Tall green water grass existed half way around the edge of the reservoir.

Munford Reservoir was named after him. The Lake is located up the Canyon from Beaver City, Utah.

Stopping at Greenwood Wildlife Management Area while visiting Kerr Lake it is possible to hike Robert Munford Trail. There's a small parking area at the end of gravel Greenwood Road. The trail runs about 7 miles to the other trailhead at Taylor's Ferry Road, but we didn't hike the entire trail. The main trail is blazed purple and follows old roads. In about a mile, a blue-blazed trail leads to the cemetery where Robert Munford is buried. Munford was a prominent citizen of early Mecklenburg County who served under George Washington in the American Revolution. There are a couple of other old home sites and other points of interest along the trail along with some nice views of the lake. The trail is pretty remote with not many visitors.

George was ordained an Elder in 1865 by William P Hobbs; a Seventy, on 22 May 1885, by Johnathan Crosby. His daughter, Lucy, died that same year on 3 January at the age of 8. On 22 July 1888 he was set apart as President of the Second Ward Sunday School by John R Murdock. On 24 March 1890, he was ordained to the office of High Priests and set apart as Bishop of the Second Ward of Beaver City, by President George Q. Cannon. Just 13 days earlier, his young daughter off 11 years, Elize Ann, died.

At the consolidation of the two wards in June 1891, at the Quarterly Conference of the Beaver State of Zion, George was set apart as Bishop of Beaver West Ward by Apostle Francis M Lyman. Altogether, he served 12 years in the Bishopric. On January 11, 1903, he was honourably released and ordained a Patriarch by Apostle George Teasdale.

In the year 1902, he paid a visit to his native land and gathered much valuable information regarding his ancestry.

Harriet was very ill when Mary Ann Waight came to live with them. Mary Ann, or 'Aunt Polly' as she was lovingly called, took care of Harriet Paice Munford until she died, on 5 December 1920, in Beaver, Utah, at the age of 74 years.

On 7 March 1911, George was married in the St George Temple to Mary Ann Waight. She had been born on 4 August 1860 in West Ham, Essex (now London). It was a happy marriage.

George Munford was a faithful Latter-Day-Saint and, during the time he was Bishop he was very faithful in caring for the widows and the poor and needy in the ward. In his later years, George and Mary Ann, had charge of the sacrament meetings held each Sunday morning at the homes of the aged people and those that were unable to get out to meetings.

For about two weeks, George had been suffering excruciating pain from a carbuncle on the back of his head. He felt that this was to be his final illness, and did not seem to rally very much at the time. Just as the clock was striking the midnight hour, on Monday, 13 June, Patriarch Munford passed from this life to the great beyond. His death was recorded as 14 June 1921. He was 80 years old.

William Gunn

In later years their log house was vacated for a home built nearer to the highway. This was a brick home of two large rooms with high ceilings, with a hall running between the kitchen and bedroom. The family was small now and that was ample room. The old log home now served as a store house and granary for wheat and oats, where the grandchildren used to play. The old cupboards and shelves, the bed with the great high posts and ropes stretch across to hold the straw ticks, remained there for many years.

His grandchildren remembered him as a very fine specimen of manhood with a splendid physique, kindly blue eyes and hair streaked with solver. He loved children and many time would have his grandchildren sat on his knee, laughing with delight as he pretended to be very fierce. He was a singer, with a very fine voice and loved social activities and dancing. He gave a large piece of land to the community upon which to build a Church house. This place is still being used today. The Relief Society, for many years had their place of meeting in a little frame building on the northeast corner of his farm. An addition was built onto the chapel and the Relief Society moved their new quarters there.

He was not a trained singer but had a very fine voice. He loved social activities and was especially fond of dancing. Generous almost to a fault, no stranger was ever turned from his door. He gave a large piece of land to the community upon which to build a Church house. The Relief Society, for many years, had their place of meeting in a little frame building on the northeast corner of his farm. This building was used until an addition was built on the chapel and the Relief Society moved their new quarters there and the old building was used until it was torn down.

In his declining years, William enjoyed visiting with his old friends. He was the father of 11 children, four by his first wife, Emma Baker, (William, Fannie, Betsy and Lois, and 6 by Elizabeth Judd – Susan (mother of Lucy), John, Emma, Emily, Heber and Sophia.

His death was caused by bladder and kidney trouble, at the age of 68 years, on 14 June 1890. He was buried in the family plot on the hillside overlooking his farm. The farm is still owned by his family.

William Gunn had been a faithful Latter-Day Saint. He held the Priesthood of a Seventy to which he was ordained on 16 February 1861 by J Clearsy.

His wife, Elizabeth, lived 17 years after his death. He was much loved by his family.

Benjamin Gunn 1841-1899

Benjamin and Alice Bowdidge Gunn had two children, Alice and Benjamin, born in the 12th Ward.

Benjamin worked part time in the paint shop of Naylor Brothers carriage and waggon shop. President Brigham Young had his work done at this shop and, as a boy, John Francis Gunn, Benjamin's son, remembers seeing President Brigham's carriage in the shop and seeing him riding in it afterwards.

Next, Benjamin worked for the Utah central and Utah Southern railroad, which later became part of the Oregon Short Line and part of the Union Pacific Railroad system. Later he opened a meat market at 231 'J' Street, a seacoast city. It was damp and cold and foggy at Brighton and, as he was suffering from diabetes, after eighteen months, he was released to return home. Then Benjamin devoted his time to Temple work. Sometimes he could hardly walk, as he was so ill. After completing all the work for the names he had, he passed away on 12 March 1899.

Benjamin Gunn was baptised in 1854 by S Homes; Ordained a Seventy by Mark Lindsey. He was also a faithful Later-day Saint.

William Holyoak, George Gunn's partner in his tannery business, became Mayor of Parowan twice

MAYORS of Parowan

Wm. H. Holyoak	1887-1889
Wm. C. Mitchell	1889-1891
Wm. H. Holyoak	1891-1896
Wm. H. Lyman	1896-1900
Alvin Benson	1900-1902
Thomas Durham	1902-1904
L. Marsden	1904-1906
Wm. H. Holyoak	1906-1908

Wm H Holyoak

Ann Munford Gunn

As Ann approached 90, people remembered her as 'the little lady with the black bonnet and cape'.

The following article appeared in a Beaver, Utah newspaper 5 May 1922:

"The death of Mrs Ann Gunn, sister of the late Bishop George Munford, occurred in Parowan Sunday evening about 6pm. Mrs Munford, who has spent considerable time with Mrs Gunn during the past winter, was with her, as was her son, Alfred Gunn. Relatives who went to attend the funeral were, Mrs Hattie Ashworth, Mr and Mrs F T Gunn, and daughters Grace Larson and Mrs John F Joseph."

Early Settler of Parowan Is Laid at Final Rest

(Special to The News.)

PAYSON. May 4 —Funeral services for Mrs Ann Mumford Gunn, 90, widow of George Gunn who died at her home Sunday, of ailments incident to old age, were held in the stake tabernacle Tuesday afternoon The music was furnished by the ward choir, with a solo by Fred C Graham of Salt Lake. The speakers included John Stephens and M M Decker. There was a profusion of flowers. Interment was in the Parowan cemetery, where Thomas Gunn dedicated the grave.

Mrs. Gunn was born in England April 24, 1832, and was one of the early settlers of Parowan. She was a sister of the late George Munford, of Beaver.

With Faith In Every Footstep,

Ann Munford Gunn

Ann began her journey to Zion when she was 31 years old.

Sailed on the ship Amazon
Departed London, England
4 June 1863
Arrived in New York, New York
18 July 1863

Traveled overland in the
Samuel D. White Wagon Company
Departed Florence, Nebraska
15 August 1863
Arrived in Salt Lake City, Utah
15 October 1863

Born
24 April 1832
Costessy, England

Died
30 April 1922
Parowan, Utah

The Amazon immigrants' achievements as individuals were notable.

Lavinia Triplett became Utah's leading female vocalist in her day.

Edward L Sloan was an outstanding writer and newspaper editor.

The Castleton family became prominent merchants,

The Larkins respected morticians.

William McLachland became the first president of the Pioneer Stake in Salt Lake City.

George Sutherland, an infant when the Amazon sailed, became a US Senator and a justice of the United States Supreme Court.

Others were bishops, patriarchs, state legislators, and fine parents – people who contributed in many ways to the building of their communities.

To use Charles Dickens' phrase, they became the "pick and flower" of western America.

John Smith Company (1860)

The following are the names of persons in Capt. John Smith's company of immigrant saints, as per his report forwarded to President Brigham Young from Laramie on the 27th of July:

John Smith; Lorin, Lovina, Hyrum S. [Smith], Jerusha C. [Celesta], Edwina M. [Mariah], Emma T. [Irene], William A. [Arthur] and Sarah E. [Ellen] Walker; Minor J. [Jewett], Lucy M. [A.], Sarah [Adelia], Eliza [Alida], and Francis Prisbrey; Mary Ann [Marianne] Pearson; Minor G. [Grant], Mary Ann [Hershey], Joseph [Smith] and Lucy Ann Prisbrey; Nathan [Cutler], Isabella [Wells], Wingaliea [Wingallea], Carey F. [Cora Isabelle] and Lydia B. [Lydia Rebecca] Davis; Alfred Holmes; William [B.], Ann [Annie Hayes], Thomas Stennett], Sarah Ann [Stennett], Martha [Stennett] and George [Joseph] Popfelton [Poppleton], Milam [Milan Lucian], Elizabeth [Sanborn], Edgar, Norman, James, Julia [Ann] and Alma [Milan] Fillmore; Daniel [Babcock], Thankful [Ann Grant], Martha [Minerva], [Daniel] Ranson, Marantha, Rosille [Thankful Rosella], Oscar

[Newman] and Antha [Elmira] Fillmore; Orin
Stoddard; Osmar, [Mary] Jane, Lucy Ann, Andrew
J. [Jackson], Clarence [Augustus], Eveline
[Augusta], Osmar G. and Charles [Merrit] Lamb;
James O. [Orrin], Mary

Jane [Fillmore], Jerome [Truman], Caliste [M.] and
Denver [Orrin] Lamb; William and Mariette Burbeck;
Karl G. [Gottfrid], Anna [Henrietta Meith], [Karl
Frederick] Reinhard and Ortille [Anna Ottillie]
Maeser; Camilla [Clara] Mieth; John [Jacob] Slaugh;
William [Wilkinson], Mary [Ellen Stones], Hannah
and Clementine Tuke; William and Jane Knapp
[Knopp]; John and Susan Reynolds; John, Anna
[Eva Dittmore], Henry, Mary [Elizabeth], and William
Herbert [Herbst], Henry Didmore [Dittmore]; Mary
and Henry S. Sheen [Sheets], William, Ann, Sarah,
Thomas H. and Albert H. Starkey; Elizabeth
Dunavan [Donovan]; William, Dinah [Ingham], John
and William [Ingham] Nutter; Nancy [Nutter] and
Elizabeth [Ann] Stemworth [Stanworth]; Henry,
[Agnes] Francis [Goble], Joseph, Henry S. [Sidney]
and Harriet J. [Jane] Howell; Eli, Martha and Ruth
[Alice] Whitely; Thomas and Sarah

Morgan; George and Eliza Gunn; William, Caroline [Hutchins] and Charles Brozier [Brazier]; Mary Ann [Gunn] Adey; Ann and Benjamin Gunn; John [C.], Caroline [Barham], John W. [William], Louisa B. [Barham] and Priscilla [Barham] Gunn; William, Emma [Baker], William [Baker], jr., Louisa, Fanny and Betsey Gunn; Betsey Judd; Cornelius, Frances [Hobbs], Jane [Caroline] and [Frances] Lucy Traveller; William [James], Jane [Gadsby] and Sarah J. [Jane] Panter; George Harrison; Nicholas, Julianna, Levi, Mary and Jane Lesater [Lasater]; John, Sarah [Blecher], Elizabeth, Louisa, Alice, Joseph, Hyrum and Esther Charrington [Cherrington]; John, Sarah and Ann Hughes; David, Ann, Sarah and John Evans; Philip [Phillip], Margaret [Davies], Elizabeth and Joseph [D.] Naughan [Vaughan]; John and Ann Beer [Beers]; James and Elizabeth Thompson; Henry, Caroline [Good], Malinda, Nancy A. [Ann] and Benjamin Hershey; Xavier F. and Mary Schlage; [James] Henry, Jane [Allen], John H. [Henry] and Mary J. [Jane] Blackner; Joshua, Elizabeth [Hoskins], Mary [Carter], Ellis [Davies], Benjamin [Hancock], William H. [Henry] and Caroline Salisbury; Mary [Whitehead], Mary A. [Ann] and Adam Chatwick [Chadwick]; James and Jane Sewell; Henry, Isabella [Elizabeth Archibald], Elizabeth and Henry [James] Anderson; Ellen [Easton] and George [Lawson] Scott; William, Eliza [Jane Broadbent], Frederic [William], Miranda [Jane], Mary [Elizabeth] and Sarah [Ann] Mullin; Mary E., Mary [E.] and Eliza Shawan [Shewan]; William and Ellen Young, Ann [Slater] Bunding [Bunting], Ann, John and Alfred Fenn; Stephen, Jane [Ellen Glover], James [William], Sarah, Margaret, Jane E. [Ellen] and Eliza [Elizabeth] Shelton [Skelton]; Benjamin, Phebe [Phoebe Davis], Margaret [Jane], Mary, Ann, Sarah, Emma and Thomas J. [John] Isaac; Daniel, Margaret [Evans], Ruth, Margaret, Samuel [H.] and Anna Williams; John O., Margaret [Jane John], Elizabeth, Emilie [Emily Caravena] and Chas. [Charles Cogan] Thomas; John E., Mary [Davies], Thomas, Evan [E.], Jane and Gorner [Gomer Isaac] Rees; Richard Williams; John [Haines], Sarah [Jane Davis], William [Davis], David [Davis], Thomas J. [John] and Ann L. [Anne Lianne] Williams; John Williams, sen.; William and Eva [Morgan] Bath; John Jenkins; Maria and Ann Bath; Hannah, Fanny and George Watson; Philip Bath; John, Hannah [Draycott], Mary A. [Ann] and Hyrum Bates; Joseph and Sarah Bradley; Evan and Margaret Thomas; John [Phillip] and Rachel [Williams] Isaac; Theophilus and Mary Williams; Thomas [Daniel] Stephens; Mary A. [Ann

Webb] Stephens; William D. Roberts; Rodney [Quinby] Shoemaker; William Willis and Herman Davis.

Translation from Norfolk Dialect

Page 152   "I want to call a family meeting."

Page 154   "I have some great news. As you know, from our many meetings and our discussions, as a family, on the possibility of emigrating to America, I have finally got backing and finance for us all to go."

"Dad, who's putting up the money for us to go?"

Page 155   "Well, I've managed to get assistance from the Parish – food, clothes and travel money – but it's the Mormons, their church, son – they've already set up in America and they are planning a big move to Utah. They want as many families as they can get, Mormon families, to set up new towns. They are doing all the arranging, transport and provisions from their base in Florence, Nebraska. We just need to get ourselves to Liverpool and on the ship. It's the right time to go."

Page 156   "There's a huge amount of things that have got to be done in preparation before we leave. There is a ship, "The Amazon" sailing from Liverpool to New York in June and I suggest we aim to be on it. Between me and the gatepost, it's going to be a long, old journey – taking weeks to get from Liverpool to New York, and months before we get to our final destination. We're going to Utah. We don't know what we'll come up against, there are mountains, hundreds of miles of vast plains to cross, as well as dangerous countryside. That's only just the beginning – we've got to take possession of the land we're allotted and work and toil until we can make a going of the land. However, I have to say, and I know you don't want to hear this, but we may never make it. Think about what I've said and let me know if you are coming with me and your mother."

Page 157   "Hold on a minute, everyone". This was my brother, George, speaking, "I know the situation we are facing in Norfolk, is desperate, and getting worse, but I haven't been able to persuade my Harriet to leave. She's worried about our little one, Louisa. She's only 4 years old, and she's delicate. I think we will have to put this on hold, at this time. I'll keep begging and pleading with her, but I think the only way to persuade Harriet to take the journey is if we get news from you that you have all arrived safely. I am sure you can understand our worries."

Page 158   "Sorry.....I think I've changed my mind." This was Lucy. "Yes, I want to go, but I think I want to know you're all safe first."

"That's alright, dear," maw replied, "I am sure we all understand. It's scary. We're all scared. We don't know what to expect and what dangers we will come across. Your paw and me, well, we're getting on, so that' won' be all that bad if we don't make it'. But you're young and you have your whole life ahead of you. We are putting our lives in God's hands."

Page 158   "Tell you what, Lucy," I piped up, "If we make it, and I know it's a big if, take the next ship with George and Harriet and Louisa. I am sure Harriet would appreciate the company and have someone to help her with Louisa."

"Yes, that sounds a good plan."

Page 161   "Yes, things never picked up, as you know. Pay was cut all over. We just never had the money to buy anything. Food was scarce and the Pore Relief was not enough to

324

sustain a family. The rich folk, those landed gentry and business owners, didn't want to put their hands in their pockets to increase the Pore Relief. If people didn't move out, they were dying of starvation or put in the dreaded workhouse, never to return. So, the government explored the possibilities of assisted emigration."

Page 162   "you know, those land-owners made things worse for us farm-hands."

"We were at the beck and call of the land-owners. Those land-owners just employed casual landlords to look after their lands. We have no truck with the landlords and neither them with us, which made matters worse for us farm-hands. They didn't know what to do for the best – if they laid off the workers to reduce their losses, that would incur more debt as they were required to pay the parish towards the Poor Relief, which they weren't inclined to do, so what did we end up with - mass unemployment and depression. Nothing's changed."

"I've got a letter here from Lord Sidmouth".

Page 163   Our wages dropped from 10s a week to 8s 5d by 1823. I am sorry, lass, but can you recall the last time we had meat? Must have been Christmas last, when your mother and I did without, just to give you children a good meal, along with bread and potato, washed down with a cup of water. We've survived, but that's all. I feel so sorry for you children, but I cannot do more. I've been in touch with your brother, John, telling him our plans. He's got some savings and is going to help us out for our move to America. We'll need food on the journey."

Page 164   "What's changed for the worse, more recently, is that dreadful threshing machine. Oh, if there's not enough

325

unemployment as it is, why not bring in a machine that can do the work of 20 men? Machines everywhere, putting good, hard-working, men out of work."

Page 170   "These are old, dad, dating from the 1830s. Why didn't we all take off then? Why have you waited so long?

"Well, I'll tell you, girl. If you read a bit further, you'll find that the first emigrants went to the eastern coastal cities, where they often found themselves worse off, amongst the bad conditions, high living costs, disease, epidemics and employment was scarce. Here, look, that's what you need to read."

Page 171   Oh, some managed alright, indeed but I wasn't taking my young family over to have them catch diseases and die on me. No, and you were only 3-years-old in 1835. No, girl, I waited. Many returned. I heard that unemployed emigrants were being paid in store goods that they couldn't sell on for a good price. That's the same system the north is up in arms about here – truck shops. Then I heard the west was opening up. A lot further to go, indeed, but there's more chance if we just pass quickly through New York.

Page 183   "Stop crying, or you'll start me off as well."

Page 185   "I cannot believe the foolhardiness of some people on board. Don't they realise that they will need money just to get from New York to Florence, let alone the journey on from there. They will have to find provisions or starve, or be dependent on others for food."

Page 187   "I don't feel at all well today."

"It's just that you're not feeling well, my love, and we do not know what the future holds, but we'll get there, together, don't you worry, we'll get to our Zion. Hold on to the dream of the future, not your dream of the past."

Page 203   "Leave poor John alone, you're just being a bully. You should be kind to everyone. If I see you being unkind again, I will tell your father."

Page 205   "Do you think they can turn them?"

Page 206   "It looks like a storm brewing, looking at the clouds."

Page 209   I am shivering.

Page 210   There, William, that will keep you a bit warmer.

Where's the waggon train, mum.

Well, that's something.

"Look, Ann, you can see its trail. It's left a small cloud of dust. We'll have to run to catch up with them."

"Oh, how could they go without us, surely dad would have known we weren't on board?"

Page 210   "You stupid, scatter-brained sod. If you were a child, you'd get a right clip round your ear.

"For God's sake, give your tongue a rest an stop going on – there's no stopping your moaning, and that's a fact."

Page 211   "You're not too big a man that I couldn't put your over my knee and give you a good hiding"

"But, mum, I didn't know you weren't in the waggon. I didn't see you go off. I thought you had fallen back with the following waggons and were talking to friends you'd made."

"Mum didn't half give me a cuff round my ear!"

That will teach you to be more observant."

"Hitch up man, then there'll be room for me as well on the seat. My stomach's aching."

Page 217   "So, this promised-land we are making our way to, has been stolen from the Native Americans."

Page 220   "Oh mum, I really feel unwell."

Page 223   "I'll have a sleep while you cook the dinner, mum. I'll help with the washing-up afterwards."

Page 223   "Bless me, that's a right old hoar frost this morning."

Page 225   "We went all over it, and in the southern portion of it we found a cave formed by the rocks, and the walls and roof were covered with names of different persons who had been there. And there was a note painted on with tar. One name had been there 18 years! We didn't have any tar with us so we took pieces of wood and bones, which we found in the cave and wrote our names and dates on them and stuck them in chinks of the rocks. There were a huge number of other names elsewhere on the hill, cut with a chisel."

Page 226   "It snowed and snowed all day!" young William commented.

"Don't you throw a snowball at me, young sir?"

Page 229   "Let the younger men do that. No, I daren't do that. If I do, I might tumble down."

"It's slanting" and "The wheel is spinning."

"Well, yes Ann" and he laughed. "Somewhat, I suppose, but the coal dust would be black – you'd be covered over with black soot. And that would be a sight, that's a fact!"

Page 229   "I wonder what the family at home will be doing now, mum. I know George and his family are coming over but will we ever see the rest of the family?"

Page 230   "Oh, Ann, Margaret, Mary and John have made their own lives, gone their own way, so we never saw much of them anyway. You can always write. Hush now and cheer up, we have a new life to create now."

Page 234   That was a strange encounter, William... but he seemed extremely nice. I think I would like to encounter him again."

"Why did you speak so strangely, mum?

"Oh, so people not from where we were born can understand us. You'll learn it by and by."

Page 241   "Then, by all means, if Ann is happy, I give my agreement."

Page 256   "Oh what are we going to do, mum? I do so want to get married."

Page 256   "I'll tell you what, sweetness. We will have your wedding, say your goodbyes, then you and George, dad and Thomas can make their way to the site. I will stay behind to see to the guests and keep the place here."

Page 264   "Ah but there were beautiful sunsets when the sea was calm and glossy."

"It was pouring down with rain most of the way. A thunderstorm."

Page 265   "The same thing happened to Ann and me. Your father had gone on without us and we had such a trek, with little William with us too, trailing after them in the blazing sun with no water. We were so ill afterwards, Ann especially so. We thought she was going to die at one point.

ACKNOWLEDGEMENTS

Carol Brown Cooper – Faith in Every Footstep – 1997

From the Life of John Clark Dowdle, 1866 -Humour on the Plains
From the Life of Zebulon Jacobs, 24 August 1861 - Humour on the Plains
From the Life of Henry William Nichols, 1861 - Humour on the Plains

The Mormon Pioneer Trail – Douglas-Sarpy Counties (NE) Mormon Trails Association.

Pony Express National Historic Trail Topographical Map

GIS Interactive Map – The National Park Service Geographical Resourses Program

Ann Munford (Excerpt from "From the Waves of the Past: The Munford Story")

The Munford Book Committee:
Research of Kathy Hadlock
Ramona Munford – story co-ordinator
David L Munford – Graphics and Art
Geraldine Munford – Computer Graphics
Helen Bauer – typist
James C Hadlock – Editor
Barbara Benson - Editor

George Gunn
From the Waves of the Past – The Munford History for
George Gunn
History of Iron County Mission by Louella A Dayton
Our Pioneer Heritage – Recollection of 1860
Utah Pioneer Biographies – vol 18, pg 54-56
John Johnson's Reminiscences, page 7
John Peter Johnson's Rasmus. Diary
Emigrant Ships – 'George Washington' page 86
Film #1259746, JH 31 Dec 1860 Supplement
Research of Kathy Hadlock

Ann Munford Gunn
From the Waves of the Past – The Munford History for Ann
Munford
Sources:
Research in England and Emigration Records by Kathy M
Hadlock
History of Iron County Mission by Louela R Adams
"Some Incidents of the Life of Lucy Albena Gunn Hyat" by
Lucy Hyatt
Memories of Anna Bell Stubbs Heyborne
Help from Mary Abbott, Klea Knight, Chester Benson and
Mina Orton, Chester Stubbs
Our Pioneer Heritage, Vol 13, pg 438
Photographs from Ila Mae B Borup
....
Reminiscences and Diary of Robert Stoney
Diary of Elijah Larkin
Excerpt from the Journal of Elder George Q. Cannon - June
4, 1863
William Henry Perkes journals
Letter of William Bramall - June 8, 1863
Letter of William Bramall - July 19, 1863
Reminiscences and Journals of William McLachlan

Reminiscences of Charles Henry John West
Hayes, John Henry, Reminiscences,
Henry Stokes Reminiscences
Adam Williams, autobiography
The Voyage of the Amazon: A Close View of One Immigrant
Company by Richard L Jensen and Gordon Irving
John Watts Barrett's diary – The Amazon
BIB: Dickens, Charles, The Uncommercial Traveller and
Reprint Pieces etc.(Oxford: Oxford University Press, 1987)
[pp. 220-32]. (CHL)

History of William Gunn – compiled by Lois Astin, a
granddaughter

Biography of Benjamin Gunn 1841-1899 with additional
biography of his mother Ann Brazier Gunn - by John Francis
Gunn 1868-1943

Robert Munford
From the Waves of the Past – the Munford history for George
Munford
Researcher: Kathy Hadlock
Story Co-ordinator   Ramona Munford
Graphics and Art   David L Munford
Computer Graphics   Geraldine Munford
Typist   Helen Bauer
Editors   James C Hadlock and Barbara Benson

Munford History for George Munford:
From the Waves of the Past
Researcher: Kathy Hadlock
Story Co-ordinator   Ramona Munford
Graphics and Art   David L Munford
Computer Graphics   Geraldine Munford
Typist   Helen Bauer
Editors   James C Hadlock and Barbara Benson

Resources:
Harriet Munford Ashworth
Marsha Dalton
Kathy Hadlock
Alice A Harris
Faye Patterson Hollingshead
Eliza R Stevens
National Archives Microfilm Publications
"Our Pioneer Heritage"
Diaries from the ship 'Hudson'

Biography of Benjamin Gunn – 1841-1899 with additional biography of his mother Ann Brazier Gunn – 1793-1878 – by John F Gunn – 1868-1943
Https://en.m.wikipedia.org/wiki/Black_Hawk_War

Other historical novels by the author:

Series:

Footsteps in the Past- ISBN 978-0-244-25919-8

This is history turned into a gripping novel. All historical facts are true.

Jane finds herself whisked back in time to 1842, after seeing a ghostly figure running away from the Ash Hall nursing home where she works.

She finds herself working for Job Meigh, the entrepreneur pottery master who built Ash Hall. He was a violent Victorian, but a great philanthropist and a magistrate. He, and industrialist pottery and mine owners had grown rich from the labours of their workers, who were driven to starvation when their pay was repeatedly cut. The Chartists wanted to get the People's Charter approved by Parliament to offer the people representation in Parliament and the vote. This was rejected, resulting in the violent Pottery Riots.

Jane has to discover why she has been sent back into the past and how to get back, and gets involved with the riots – which lead her into life-threatening danger. She also has to find out who the ghostly figure was.

Footsteps in the Past – The Secret – ISBN 978-0-355-63374-2

The Secret takes the main characters 39 years on from the Pottery Riots of 1842. There is a mining disaster in Bucknall, Stoke, in which Jane and John's son is involved. While nursing John back to health, after his attempt to rescue their son, Jane reminisces what has happened since they met.

Her stories unravel while desperately awaiting news if their son is still alive or not. All historical facts are true.

Footsteps in the Past – John's Story –

ISBN 978-1-716-16818-127

This tells John's story from his youth in the countryside village of Hanley in the 1820s through its industrialisation.

It tells John's poignant story of his life, loves and losses in the background of the traumatic times and struggles of people fighting for their rights, representation in Parliament and the vote, leading to the Pottery Riots of 1842. The book takes you through the Cholera Pandemic of 1832 (similar to Covid today) and his time in the workhouse.

Printed in Great Britain
by Amazon

12402843R00210